THE FUTURE OF EXTENDED DETERRENCE

THE FUTURE OF EXTENDED DETERRENCE

The United States, NATO, and Beyond

STÉFANIE VON HLATKY
and
ANDREAS WENGER
Editors

Georgetown University Press
Washington, DC

Library of Congress Cataloging-in-Publication Data

The future of extended deterrence: the United States, NATO, and beyond / Stéfanie von Hlatky and Andreas Wenger, editors.
pages cm
Includes bibliographical references and index.
ISBN 978-1-62616-264-8 (hc : alk. paper) — ISBN 978-1-62616-265-5 (pb : alk. paper) — ISBN 978-1-62616-266-2 (eb)
1. Deterrence (Strategy) 2. North Atlantic Treaty Organization. 3. Nuclear weapons. 4. Ballistic missile defenses. 5. Security, International. I. Von Hlatky, Stéfanie, 1982– editor. II. Wenger, Andreas, editor.
U162.6.F86 2015
355.02'17—dc23
2015007457

∞ This book is printed on acid-free paper meeting the requirements of the American National Standard for Permanence in Paper for Printed Library Materials.

16 15 9 8 7 6 5 4 3 2 First printing

Printed in the United States of America

Cover design by Beth Schlenoff

To our families and friends

CONTENTS

ILLUSTRATIONS

Tables

Figure

ACKNOWLEDGMENTS

For scholars of transatlantic relations, two themes tend to recur: the demise of NATO and the return of the Cold War. We now live in an era where the two themes seem to coexist. The long war in Afghanistan, combined with the 2008 global economic crisis, sapped the will of NATO countries to wage war and eroded their tolerance for high levels of defense spending. Simultaneously, Russia reacted imperialistically following the 2014 Euromaidan revolution in Ukraine. It seems that, despite protections offered by the United States and its NATO allies, European countries with Russian minorities might be the targets of Russia's nostalgia for its former foreign policy. Friction points are also being felt in other regions such as East Asia, where China is attempting to uphold its interpretation of maritime boundaries in the East and South China Seas. It seems sometimes that the only factor upholding the regional status quo is the promise of US protection offered by long-standing alliance commitments.

In light of recent changes in the contemporary security environment, both of us were inspired to gather the viewpoints of colleagues who have done research on deterrence and on the military capabilities that support it. We were fortunate to organize a workshop at the Center for Security Studies (CSS) at ETH Zurich to debate the merits of the US alliance systems, the role of NATO in upholding European security and deterring adversaries, and the controversial role of nuclear weapons and missile defense in contributing to the extended deterrence arrangements of this alliance system. The workshop made clear to us that these issues were complex and deserving of further investigation. We are indebted to each author for answering the call and writing original and thoroughly researched chapters for this volume.

Special thanks also go to Raphael Zaffran, as well as Aaron Ettinger, Jeffrey Rice, and Lauren Cardinal from Queen's University for their research assistance. Finally, we would like to thank our families and friends for their love and support. We do this because we care but mostly to make you proud.

Stéfanie von Hlatky
Kingston, Canada

Andreas Wenger
Zurich, Switzerland

ABBREVIATIONS

ABM	Anti-Ballistic Missile Treaty
ACA	Arms Control Association
ADN	arms control, disarmament, and non-proliferation
AEW	airborne early warning
ALTBMD	Active Layered Theater Ballistic Missile Defense
AN/TPY-2	Army/Navy Transportable Radar Surveillance
AWACS	Airborne Warning and Control System
BASIC	British American Security Information Council
BMD	ballistic missile defense
BMDR	Ballistic Missile Defense Review
CAS	close air support
CSBM	confidence- and security-building measures
CDU	Christian Democratic Union of Germany
CEA	*Commissariat à l'énergie atomique et aux énergies alternatives*
CES	Central European States
CPI	counterproliferation initiative
CRS	Congressional Research Service
CSIS	Center for Strategic and International Studies
CSU	Christian Social Union of Bavaria
C2BMC	command and control, battle management, and communications
DCA	dual-capable aircraft
DDPR	Deterrence and Defense Policy Review
DOD	US Department of Defense
EPAA	European Phased Adaptive Approach
EU	European Union
EUCOM	US European Command
FDP	Free Democratic Party (Germany)
FRG	Federal Republic of Germany
GBIs	ground-based interceptors

GPALS	Global Protection Against Limited Strikes
HLG	High Level Group
IAEA	International Atomic Energy Agency
ICBM	intercontinental ballistic missile
IFSH	Institute for Peace Research and Security Policy
IISS	International Institute for Strategic Studies
INF	intermediate-range nuclear forces
IR	international relations
JDEC	Joint Data Exchange Center
JSF	joint strike fighter
LEP	life-extension program
LRS&T	long-range surveillance and track
MAD	mutually assured destruction
MAS	mutually assured security
MBRM	medium-range ballistic missile
MLF	Multilateral Force
MUNSS	Munitions Support Squadrons
NAC	North Atlantic Council
NATO	North Atlantic Treaty Organization
NOFUN	no first use of nuclear weapons
NPG	Nuclear Planning Group
NPR	Nuclear Posture Review
NPT	Nuclear Non-Proliferation Treaty
NSNW	nonstrategic nuclear weapons
NWFZ	nuclear-weapons-free zone
OTAN	*Organisation du Traité de l'Atlantique Nord*
PAC-3	Patriot Advanced Capability-3
PGS	prompt global strike
PLYWD	Precision Low-Yield Weapon Design
PNI	Presidential Nuclear Initiative
QDR	Quadrennial Defense Review
RAMOS	Russian-American Observation Satellites
RMA	Revolution in Military Affairs
RUSI	Royal United Services Institute
SAMP/T	Surface-to-Air Missile Platform/Terrain
SBRM	short-range ballistic missile
SBX	sea-based X-band radar
SC	Strategic Concept
SDI	Strategic Defense Initiative
SDP	Social Democratic Party

SHAPE	Supreme Headquarters Allied Powers Europe
SIOP	Single Integrated Operational Plan
SLBM	submarine-launched ballistic missile
SLV	space launch vehicle
SM-3	Standard Missile-3
SNOWCAT	Support of Nuclear Operations with Conventional Air Tactics
SRBM	short-range ballistic missile
START	Strategic Arms Reduction Treaty
STRATCOM	US Strategic Command
TLAM-N	Nuclear Tomahawk Land-Attack Missile
UK	United Kingdom
UN	United Nations
UNSC	United Nations Security Council
US	United States
WMD	weapons of mass destruction

INTRODUCTION

American Alliances and Extended Deterrence

Stéfanie von Hlatky

The American alliance system is in flux. Since the end of the Cold War, the United States has adjusted and adapted its alliance commitments in different regions of the world, especially in Europe and Asia, where it has invested intensely since the end of the Second World War. Constantly adapting to perceived threats, the United States has deployed military assets to protect its closest allies. These assets, both nuclear and conventional, support American extended deterrence commitments. US extended deterrence in the NATO context should be understood as a package of security assurances that has been pledged by the United States to its European allies with the goal of deterring potential threats and adversaries. American extended deterrence arrangements have proven remarkably durable not only in Europe but also in Asia where the United States has extended security assurances to Japan, South Korea, Australia, the Philippines, and Taiwan. NATO has developed into a deeply institutionalized, collective defense system; in Asia, states like Japan and South Korea manage their alliance ties with the United States bilaterally.

Since 2011, however, the United States has announced a rebalance toward Asia, given the anticipated strategic challenges represented by China's rise, maritime disputes in the South and East China Seas, and the ongoing nuclear crisis involving North Korea.[1] Concerns were heard in Europe regarding this Asia pivot or rebalance in American foreign policy, which were compounded by disparaging statements made by American officials about the state of European defense. Former secretary of defense Robert Gates offered some scathing views about how lopsided burden sharing within NATO continues to be, calling European allies to do more to help themselves:

> In the past, I've worried openly about NATO turning into a two-tiered alliance: Between members who specialize in "soft" humanitarian, development and peacekeeping, and talking tasks, and those conducting the "hard" combat missions. Between those willing and able to pay the price and bear the burdens of alliance commitments, and those who enjoy the benefits of NATO membership—be they security guarantees or headquarters billets—but don't want to share the risks and the costs. This is no longer a hypothetical worry. We are there today. And it is unacceptable.[2]

The onset of the Ukrainian crisis in 2014 is forcing US attention back to the European continent. The resurgence of Russia's aggressive foreign and defense policy behavior is urgently challenging European allies to bolster alliance capabilities and reaffirm American security commitments on NATO's eastern flank. Is US extended deterrence robust enough? Will Russia push NATO to invoke Article V, the pledge of collective self-defense enshrined in the Washington Treaty? The current security environment is seriously testing US commitments to its allies. In addition to the situation in Eastern Europe, regional instability in East Asia, South Asia, and the Middle East, as well as nonconventional threats like terrorism and nuclear proliferation, are putting even greater pressure on the US web of alliances worldwide.

On the economic front, the enduring effects of the 2008 global financial crisis are having a profound impact on the defense budgets of the United States and its allies. In this context, how will American extended deterrence arrangements be affected and according to which strategic priorities? In Europe, NATO's membership has grown dramatically since the end of the Cold War and now includes twenty-eight member states. Was expansion a wise policy? This expanded membership means that achieving a consensus on which threats should dominate the agenda is more difficult than ever. In Asia, the escalation of aggressive rhetoric between China and its neighbors is putting pressure on the United States to strengthen its security commitments to the region. With finite resources, a greater American presence in Asia can unintentionally affect the credibility of its commitment to Europe. While Russia is certainly testing the strength of American commitments in Eastern Europe, an overt provocation targeting a NATO country would mean the failure of US extended deterrence.

The purpose of this book is to revisit extended deterrence arrangements in light of a fluctuating security environment at the international level, as well as significant political and economic constraints at the domestic level. Alliance negotiation and cooperation attempt to reconcile both levels of analysis.[3] The book engages in a cross-sector intellectual exercise, bringing together experts from academia, think tanks, and the policy world to assess the future of deterrence for the United States and its allies. The volume also pays special attention to alliance debates about the role of nuclear weapons and missile defense as backbone capabilities in support of extended deterrence. The common research questions addressed by the contributors are both theoretically important and relevant for policy about alliance management and extended deterrence:[4]

- Are extended deterrence arrangements still robust and sustainable in the current international security context?
- What role should nuclear weapons and missile defense play in supporting extended deterrence?
- What are the alternatives to the status quo when considering changes to extended deterrence arrangements?
- How is regional instability, especially in Eastern Europe, challenging our current understanding of extended deterrence in theory and in practice?

This introduction provides theoretical background on extended deterrence and extended nuclear deterrence. It then examines how deterrence arrangements are carried out in practice in Europe, drawing some parallels with US allies in Asia. Finally, the case of NATO is discussed in greater depth. The alliance is an ideal testing ground to assess how new or resurgent threats affect extended deterrence.

Transatlantic deterrence arrangements are complex. They include forward deployed troops, collective missile defense, and nuclear sharing. Furthermore, the maintenance of these capabilities is subject to consensus-based, decision-making dynamics; enduring defense budget cuts; and periodic reassessments of NATO's security priorities, which are affected by regional instability in Eastern Europe, East Asia, and the Middle East, in addition to a growing list of global threats.

Extended Deterrence in Theory and in Practice

In the deterrence literature, some scholars have acknowledged the increasing complexity of deterrence relationships in the twenty-first century with the rise of China and a resurgent Russia, asymmetric adversaries in unstable regions, so-called rogue states, and new nuclear states in dangerous standoffs like India and Pakistan.[5] Others emphasize the role of military and technological changes to illustrate how new threats affect deterrence equations and alliance relationships.[6] As Patrick Morgan alludes to in his reexamination of the deterrence literature, the threats faced by the international community are significantly different from the Cold War days, which brings into question the relevance of deterrence theory.[7] The concept of deterrence must address competing goals held by allies: credibly address (and potentially respond to) a growing list of security threats, and preserve alliance cohesion and share the burden in a way that is politically feasible for its members. Which capabilities are best suited to uphold deterrence and satisfy the security needs of allies in a credible manner?[8] Does the United States, for instance, still need nuclear weapons to protect its allies?

America's deterrence posture has evolved from its Cold War version, which was based on existential nuclear threats, to one that relies on a more balanced portfolio of capabilities. The United States continues to play a central role as a security provider and determines the appropriate mix of conventional (including missile defense) and nuclear assets to back up its alliance commitments. While upholding the credibility of extended deterrence protection remains a priority, US officials are also sensitive to the moral hazard that accompanies security guarantees. The American view is that allies should not relinquish their burden-sharing responsibilities because they trust that the United States will compensate accordingly.[9]

Deterrence can be summarized as a state attempting to convince an adversary not to use military force, either by threatening retaliation (deterrence by punishment) or by thwarting the adversary's operational plans (deterrence by denial).[10] Extended deterrence thus involves a commitment to intervene offensively or defensively on an ally's behalf. It is a state's attempt to convince an adversary not to use military force against one of its allies by resorting to both defensive and offensive strategies. Assurances to allies with regard to the credibility of the commitment are key for extended deterrence to work as intended. The guarantor state must be able to convince its allies that the capabilities are sufficient to deter potential threats (general extended deterrence) and that it will act to protect them in case of crisis (immediate extended deterrence).[11]

The burden of deterrence can also be collective, as is the case for NATO. As Morgan notes, collective-actor deterrence means that a group of actors or a multinational organization act either "as deterrers or targets of deterrence efforts."[12] The mechanisms of deterrence are thus inherently more complex given that multiple actors must agree on threats, capabilities, and responses in order to support a credible deterrence posture. In theory, collective-actor deterrence is extended to individual members of the group,

Table I.1. US Nuclear Guarantees to Allies

Nuclear Guarantees	*Allies*	*Threats*
BILATERAL: Protection from nuclear capabilities of one state	Guarantor: United States Recipients: Japan, South Korea, Australia (Ambiguous: Israel, Philippines, Taiwan)	• Regional instability in Asia • Rise of China • Maritime disputes in the South and East China Seas • Nuclear North Korea
MULTILATERAL: Protection from nuclear capabilities of two or more states	Guarantors: United States, France, and United Kingdom Recipients: NATO members	• Regional instability in or near transatlantic region • Nuclear or missile attack from Iran • Diffusion of current conflicts (ex.: Ukraine)
COLLECTIVE: Arrangements where both nuclear and non-nuclear allies participate in nuclear burden sharing	Guarantors: NATO members except France Recipients: NATO members	• Existential threat posed by a nuclear adversary • Attack on their territory

but in practice, alliance politics play a big part in how credible deterrence commitments appear.

A number of factors can motivate a state to extend security guarantees to protect its allies: the safeguarding of valuable resources held by allied states, arms sales, prevention of nuclear proliferation, power projection, prestige, cultural and historical legacies, and domestic and sometimes diaspora politics.[13] Indeed, different motivating factors and threats are at play in each region where the United States has extended security guarantees to its allies. The ultimate guarantee includes the American nuclear umbrella: extended *nuclear* deterrence means that nuclear threats are made or implied to uphold an allied commitment. As many of the chapters in this book illustrate, the nuclear dimension of extended deterrence can be quite problematic and controversial from an alliance standpoint.

Approximately thirty allies benefit from the US nuclear umbrella (see table I.1): NATO states; Japan; South Korea; Australia; and, though debatable, we could also include Thailand, the Philippines, Israel, and Taiwan.

Bilateral, multilateral, and collective configurations of extended nuclear deterrence imply complex alliance politics about how nuclear weapons may address specific threats.

As table I.1 illustrates, deterrence can be configured in many different ways depending on which actors provide security guarantees, which actors benefit from protection, and which threats are prioritized. These guarantees are upheld through conventional forces, nuclear weapons, and/or missile defense systems, but political gestures can also increase the credibility of the commitment. For instance, NATO and Asian allies have a long-standing history of military cooperation and significant political and economic ties that may prove more convincing in communicating credibility when compared to allies of convenience.[14] The next section examines the various types of assurances implied in extended deterrence commitments.

Assurances and Alliance Commitments

The first step in assessing the strength of extended deterrence is to look at the alliance's collective capabilities in addition to American security guarantees. As already mentioned, whether extended deterrence commitments are backed by conventional forces or nuclear weapons, the effectiveness of deterrence is also about the strength of the underlying political commitment between the United States and its allies.[15] These political commitments are made explicit through institutional membership and official statements and policy, and they can be reinforced by a strong personal relationship between political leaders.[16] In addition, we can focus on more enduring features of the relationship between the United States and its allies, such as cultural and historical factors that provide important contextual information about the credibility of the commitment.[17] More routine economic and security arrangements can serve as additional proof of US commitment to its allies in different regions of the world. These range "from trade and diplomatic relations, to bilateral and multilateral institutions and consultations, to arms sales and training, to joint military exercises and basing arrangements."[18] In sum, the strongest commitments are multidimensional.

A further point of clarification relates to the difference between the European and Asian models of extended nuclear deterrence because of the aforementioned nuclear-sharing arrangements that include forward-deployed nuclear weapons, nuclear weapons–related exercises, both burden and risk sharing, as well as nuclear consultations and information sharing.[19] Allies disagree on what changes should be implemented based on a variety of reasons. Here are a few to consider:

(1) The external threat environment and regional security; that is, is there a growing sense of insecurity among allies?
(2) The normative environment whereby "shifting norms about the use of nuclear weapons would likely undermine the credibility and assurance roles of US nuclear guarantees."[20]
(3) The health of the bilateral relationship with the United States, including both public and elite attitudes toward the United States in allied countries.
(4) Shifts in American nuclear weapons policy as announced in its nuclear posture reviews.

In sum, to measure the credibility of US security guarantees to its allies, we should consider both sides of the equation: the resources deployed both by the United States and the alliance collectively to uphold extended deterrence against potential threats, as well as how these commitments are perceived by allies. Assurances are multidimensional in nature, including historical, political, economic, and military ties; thus several different factors can influence perceptions of commitment credibility. The rest of the section discusses extended nuclear deterrence in Europe and in Asia. A separate section takes a closer look at NATO's nuclear sharing arrangements.

Extended Deterrence in Europe

Extended deterrence in Europe has traditionally emphasized the role of American nuclear weapons, given the perceived conventional inferiority of NATO relative to the USSR during the Cold War. The end of the Cold War greatly reduced the salience of nuclear weapons in Europe as a military option under extended deterrence. Three factors contributed to this change. First, the likelihood of escalating nuclear threats decreased with the end of the bipolar confrontation, and strategic arsenals were correspondingly reduced. Dramatic reductions were implemented as a result of the 1991 Presidential Nuclear Initiative when the United States, under President George H. W. Bush, reduced the number of nonstrategic nuclear weapons assigned to allied commitments.[21] These numbers were further scaled down under the Clinton presidency, bringing the total number to about 500 by the beginning of the new decade. The United States is now estimated to have between 150 and 200 nonstrategic nuclear weapons (NSNW) deployed in Europe as part of NATO but none in Asia.[22]

The second reason relates to improvements in American conventional capabilities, starting with the revolution (or transformation) in military affairs (RMA) in the 1980s. While nuclear weapons were meant to compensate for American and European conventional inferiority during the Cold War, advances in US military technology secured a long-term advantage.[23] One could thus question the assumption that the removal of NSNW would undermine the credibility of US security guarantees given NATO's conventional predominance, which is apparent in both qualitative (weapons stocks) and quantitative (military expenditures) terms.

Third, different perceptions of threats undermine alliance cohesion, which leads to more conservative assessments related to the role of nuclear weapons in deterrence. In the NATO context, differences in threat perception are noticeable. For example, some allies, such as states on NATO's southern border, are preoccupied by Iran's program to develop nuclear weapons and long-range missiles. States on NATO's eastern border are more concerned about their contiguous border with Russia, especially in light of the Ukrainian crisis. For the Western European NATO members, the credibility of extended deterrence does not seem to be at stake.[24] Western NATO members seek general assurances about the American commitment in Europe while recognizing that this does not necessarily imply forward-deployed nuclear weapons. States such Germany, Belgium, the Netherlands, Luxembourg, and Norway have even called for a reduced American role with regard to NATO's nuclear posture. In essence, "NATO will have to bridge a spectrum of views that arguably runs from nuclear abolitionism to concrete fears of a resurgent Russia."[25] This is a growing concern for NATO, but this kind of ambivalence is also present in Asia.

Extended Deterrence in Asia

The NATO model of extended deterrence is often compared with American security assurances in Asia. Extended deterrence in Asia involves robust nuclear guarantees from the United States without having American nuclear weapons stationed on Asian territory. Rather, these assurances include forward-deployed American troops, a nuclear umbrella based on US strategic forces, missile defenses, treaty ties, and joint procurement. These assurances have proven sufficient because neither South Korea nor Japan is calling on the United States to significantly bolster its footprint in the region. In addition, the removal of NSNW from the Asian theater following the end of the Cold War has not resulted in nuclear proliferation by the United States' Asian allies.[26] Nevertheless, recent crises have tested American resolve when it comes to its alliance relationships in Asia.

To assess the importance of Asia in the American alliance network, one reliable measure is the significance of the US presence in the region. While the United States has institutionalized its security commitments by way of bilateral defense treaties, these treaties do not specify exactly how the pledges translate into concrete action and assurances. A number of historical and contextual variables influence the scope and depth of these security arrangements. The most recent change is the so-called Asia rebalance, which was announced in 2011. This rebalance is new, but it does not appear to be mere rhetoric. Several recent developments provide indications that the United States is indeed deepening its security commitments to the region to strengthen extended deterrence.

The first major event was the deployment of US marines in Darwin, Australia. In 2011, President Obama and Prime Minister Julia Gillard announced that US marines would be based in Darwin as part of six-month rotations to conduct exercises and training with the Australian Defence Force. The deployment has a target of 2,500 US marines. In addition, Obama's 2014 diplomatic tour in Asia reinforced the US commitment to the Philippines. On April 29, President Aquino III stated that he would expand access for American troops, ships, and planes in bases throughout the country. This commitment was made official by way of a defense agreement, which is valid for ten years. Perhaps the most significant move was Obama's assurances to Japan regarding its dispute with China in the East China Sea.

On April 24, 2014, Obama declared that the Treaty of Mutual Cooperation and Security between the United States and Japan meant an obligation on the part of the United States to protect Japan if a conflict erupts in the East China Sea. The timing is not accidental given that Japan's concerns increased after China declared an air defense identification zone over these waters in a move to bolster its sovereignty in the region and over the disputed islands (Senkaku/Diaoyu). President Obama stated: "Historically, they [the islands] have been administered by Japan, and we do not believe that they should be subject to change unilaterally. What is a consistent part of the alliance is that the treaty covers all territories administered by Japan."[27] This is undoubtedly an expanded definition of the United States' bilateral security arrangements with Japan and reinforces the statements previously made by Secretary of Defense Chuck Hagel and Secretary of State John Kerry.

It appears that the United States has indeed begun to implement the rebalance policy and has done so as the perception of threat has remained relatively constant in the region (disputes that are managed, with spikes in tensions not escalating to the crisis level or full-blown conflict).[28] Beyond these developments, the bilateral and ad hoc nature of extended deterrence arrangements in Asia translates into more idiosyncratic observations. NATO allies, by contrast, are challenged by complex multinational negotiations over collective defense capabilities, especially when it comes to reassessing the role of nuclear weapons in upholding extended deterrence.

Recent Developments in NATO's Deterrence Policy

At the heart of NATO's deterrence posture is the concept of nuclear sharing. Nuclear sharing involves consultations between NATO allies on nuclear weapons through the Nuclear Planning Group (NPG) and by active participation in the alliance's nuclear mission by hosting American NSNW on European territory for possible use in times of war.[29] As stated in the 2010 US Nuclear Posture Review, nuclear sharing entails "arrangements under which non-nuclear members participate in nuclear planning and possess specially configured aircraft capable of delivering nuclear weapons [which] contribute to Alliance cohesion and provide reassurance to allies and partners who feel exposed to regional threats."[30] Despite the acknowledgment that NSNW are of limited military utility, this capability is maintained in the name of alliance cohesion. The continued presence of these nuclear weapons in Europe has been controversial because domestic political audiences are generally hostile to these arrangements, especially in countries where these weapons are located (table I.2).[31]

These commitments are also being reevaluated in Washington because each base is estimated to cost $200 million per year for the United States.[32] These nuclear capabilities consist of B-61 gravity bombs and dual-capable aircraft (DCA). In addition, the United Kingdom's sea-launched ballistic missile (SLBM) warheads are assigned to NATO.[33] France also has strategic nuclear weapons; these are independent of NATO, although they serve the alliance's general deterrence posture.[34] The ultimate nuclear guarantee rests on the US strategic forces. In support of NATO's nuclear mission are the NPG, the High Level Group (HLG), the Support of Nuclear Operations with Conventional Air Tactics (SNOWCAT) procedure (which involves non-nuclear participants), and the Steadfast Noon exercises. These cooperative arrangements are meant to, as Tertrais mentions, favor nuclear socialization within the alliance.[35]

Table I.2. US Nuclear Weapons in Europe, 2011

Country	*Airbase*	*Dual-Capable Aircraft*	*Number of B-61s*
Belgium	Kleine Brogel	Belgian F-16	10–20
Germany	Büchel	German Tornado	10–20
Italy	Aviano	US F-16	50
	Ghedi Torre	US F-16	10–20
Netherlands	Volkel	Dutch F-16	10–20
Turkey	Incirlik	US fighter aircraft (rotating)	60–70
TOTAL			**150–200**

Data Source: Hans M. Kristensen and Robert S. Norris, "US Tactical Nuclear Weapons in Europe," *Bulletin of Atomic Scientists*, 67:1, 2011.

The latest update to NATO's nuclear posture occurred in 2012 with the Deterrence and Defense Policy Review (DDPR). The DDPR was meant to address the divisive issues that were left unaltered with the 2010 edition of the Strategic Concept (to say nothing of the 1991 and 1999 editions): "the role of nuclear weapons, including declaratory policy, in deterrence and defense; the role NATO intends to play in future arms control efforts—primarily with Russia; the willingness and ability of members to sustain the current nuclear mission, as well as alternatives to NATO's existing nuclear arrangements; and the future direction of relations with Russia."[36] NATO's post–Cold War policy changes have been driven by the end of the bipolar standoff but have left the basic architecture of extended nuclear deterrence unaltered: a model that relies on the strategic arsenals of the alliance's nuclear powers and forward-deployed nuclear weapons on European territory to symbolize nuclear sharing. The last three strategic concepts have acknowledged that nuclear weapons primarily serve a political function and have deemphasized their role accordingly, though not completely.[37] Russia's more aggressive foreign policy in its immediate region is further complicating any plan to change NATO's nuclear status quo.

Four main factors influenced the DDPR debates as Deputy NATO permanent representatives worked to build common ground on nuclear policy. First, there is the normative shift in favor of nuclear abolition introduced by four former US officials in a now famous *Wall Street Journal* op-ed and promoted by President Obama.[38] Second, there is Russia and how suspiciously it is perceived in the context of European security, especially since the onset of the Ukrainian crisis. The third factor is Iran and corresponding allied threat perceptions regarding its nuclear ambitions (of particular concern to Turkey and southern NATO states). Fourth, public attitudes regarding nuclear weapons remain a salient feature of alliance debates, especially in Germany, Belgium, Canada, and Luxembourg.

If the military utility of NATO's NSNW is questionable, what is the rationale for the alliance's current nuclear-sharing arrangements? The Pentagon's 2008 review of its nuclear mission outlines five points with regard to extended nuclear deterrence in Europe: (1) alliance cohesion and additional assurance about American commitments to NATO, (2) preventing the proliferation of nuclear weapons by allies, (3) preserving an important symbol of burden sharing by the alliance, (4) ensuring that the weapons are less vulnerable to attack given the multiple storage sites in Europe, and (5) enhancing the deterrence mission with NATO DCA.[39] As several chapters in this book point out, these arguments are debatable but continue to feature prominently in the public and official deliberations over the future of extended nuclear deterrence in Europe.

What about the arguments in favor of keeping NSNW in Europe? A recent Congressional Research Service report outlines the rationale for NSNW: "NATO policy still views nonstrategic nuclear weapons as a deterrent to any potential adversary, and they also serve as a link among the NATO nations, with bases in several nations and shared responsibility for nuclear policy planning and decision making. They also still serve as a visible reminder of the US extended deterrent and assurance of this commitment to the defense of its allies."[40] In the end, we can expect the status quo because it is unlikely that an agreement can be reached with Russia regarding its own nonstrategic nuclear weapons in light of the impasse over Ukraine.[41]

Conclusion

The preceding discussion has highlighted the importance of opting for a multidimensional understanding of security commitments between and among allies. This appears to be particularly important in the NATO context because allies must adopt a deterrence posture to accommodate different perceptions of threat. In Asia, allied interactions are more straightforward given the bilateral nature of US defense treaties in the region. However, America's Asian allies are increasingly vocal about their security concerns, namely, China's aggressive stance in the South and East China Seas.

Any deterrence posture "requires a fine balance between the preparations to use military force and demonstrations of resolve and the provocation of the potential attacker."[42] As the security environment shifts and new threats are prioritized, changing this fine balance demands careful design and implementation whereby the credibility of the commitment will not be weakened in the eyes of potential adversaries and, perhaps more importantly, in the eyes of allies depending on such commitments. It is therefore useful to take a broader view of deterrence, a multidimensional view, to highlight that commitment credibility is as much dependent on the provision of military capabilities as it is on the density and variety of assurances that exist between allies.

The following chapters are organized in three parts. In part I, extended deterrence is examined in different contexts to shed light on how threats, alliance politics, and regional configurations affect deterrence equations. In chapter 1, Joachim Krause addresses a range of global crisis management responsibilities held by the United States and its allies. He focuses on key international threats and regional focal points. In chapter 2, Jeffrey A. Larsen presents alternative models of extended nuclear deterrence, with an interesting discussion on the Asian model of extended deterrence.

Part II of the book provides an overview of the issues and debates on extended deterrence and nuclear weapons in the context of NATO. In chapter 3, Benoit Pelopidas offers an in-depth study of nuclear history in international relations to demonstrate how US thinking on nuclear weapons policy and security guarantees toward its allies failed to prevent proliferation. In chapter 4, Paul Schulte explains the intra-alliance disagreements over NATO's nuclear weapons and identifies both status quo forces and opposing strategic subcultures. In chapter 5, Hans Kristensen discusses the ongoing modernization of nuclear weapons in Europe and some contradictions in how nuclear weapons are discussed in the NATO-Russia context.

Part III addresses the politics of missile defenses by recounting the chronology of this technology as well as discussing the alliance politics surrounding the acquisition and deployment of this capability. In chapter 6, Oliver Thränert and Kerry Kartchner address the increased salience of missile defense as a core capability for the United States and its allies and what this means for extended deterrence dynamics. In chapter 7, Paul Bernstein discusses NATO's missile defense capabilities and explains why the US-Russian dialogue over missile defense is wrought with difficulties. In the conclusion, Andreas Wenger summarizes the contributions of the chapters and the general implications for the study of extended deterrence. He also puts the discussion in context by reviewing the historical legacy of NATO's nuclear-sharing arrangements and the deterrence challenges of increasing complexity, which continue to confront the United States and its allies worldwide.

Notes

1. Paul Eckert, "Obama's Asia 'pivot' Advances, but Obstacles Await," *Reuters*, June 15, 2012, http://www.reuters.com/article/2012/06/15/us-usa-pacific-pivot-idUSBRE85E1B420120615, (accessed May 3, 2013).

2. Robert M. Gates, "The Security and Defense Agenda (Future of NATO)," US Department of Defense, June 10, 2011, www.defense.gov (accessed August 1, 2013).

3. Stéfanie von Hlatky, *American Allies in Times of War: The Great Asymmetry* (Oxford: Oxford University Press, 2013).

4. *Nuclear umbrella* is a term commonly used to refer to American security guarantees to its allies that involve a nuclear component.

5. See authors in *Complex Deterrence: Strategy in the Global Age*, eds. T. V. Paul, Patrick Morgan, and James Wirtz (Chicago, IL: University of Chicago Press, 2009). See also M. Elaine Bunn, "Can Deterrence Be Tailored," *Strategic Forum* no. 225 (January 2007); David J. Trachtenberg and Herman Kahn, "US Extended Deterrence: How Much Strategic Force Is Too Little," *Strategic Studies Quarterly* 6 (2012): 62–92.

6. Patrick M. Morgan, "The State of Deterrence in International Politics Today," *Contemporary Security Policy* 33, no. 1 (2012): 85–107; Stephen J. Cimbala, "Chasing Its Tail: Nuclear Deterrence in the Information Age," *Strategic Studies* 19 (2012): 18–34.

7. Morgan, "The State of Deterrence in International Politics Today."

8. Robert Powell, *Nuclear Deterrence Theory: The Search for Credibility* (Cambridge: Cambridge University Press, 1990), 14.

9. This is a recurring concern within the NATO context. See Michael Howard, "Reassurance and Deterrence: Western Defense in the 1980s," *Foreign Affairs* 61 (1982–83): 311. See also George Perkovich, Malcolm Chalmers, Steven Pifer, Paul Schulte, and Jaclyn Tandler, *Looking beyond the Chicago Summit: Nuclear Weapons in Europe and the Future of NATO* (Washington, DC: The Carnegie Endowment for International Peace, April 2012), 11.

10. Alexander George and Richard Smoke, *Deterrence in American Foreign Policy: Theory and Practice* (New York: Columbia University Press, 1974); Michael Howard, "Reassurance and Deterrence: Western Defense in the 1980s," *Foreign Affairs* 61, no. 2 (1982–83): 315; Patrick M. Morgan, *Deterrence: A Conceptual Analysis* (Beverly Hills, CA: Sage Publications, 1977), 17–46; Paul K. Huth, *Extended Deterrence and the Prevention of War* (New Haven, CT: Yale University Press, 1988), 15.

11. Paul K. Huth, "The Extended Deterrent Value of Nuclear Weapons," *Journal of Conflict Resolution* 34, no. 2 (1990): 270–90.

12. Patrick M. Morgan, "Collective-Actor Deterrence," in *Complex Deterrence: Strategy in the Global Age*, ed. T. V. Paul, P. M. Morgan, and J. J. Wirtz (Chicago, IL: Chicago University Press, 2009), 259–76.

13. See, for example, Ariel E. Levite, "Reflections on Extended Deterrence in the Middle East," *Recherches et Documents* (IFRI) no. 3 (2010): 63–64.

14. Evan N. Resnick,"Strange Bedfellows: US Bargaining Behavior with Allies of Convenience," *International Security* 35, no. 3 (2010/11): 144–84.

15. Similarly, James Acton argues that large arsenals (versus small arsenals resulting from deep reductions) are not necessary for either general or extended deterrence because the most important factor is the strength of the political commitment. In

Acton, *Deterrence during Disarmament* (Washington, DC: International Institute for Strategic Studies, 2011), 93.

16. The point on leadership dynamics is in James A. Russell, "Extended Deterrence, Security Guarantees and Nuclear Weapons: US Strategic and Policy Conundrums in the Gulf," *Strategic Insights* 3, no. 5 (December 2009): 16–26.

17. For instance, it has been suggested that extended nuclear deterrence in the Middle East would lack credibility because the United States would not risk American lives to protect allied authoritarian regimes such as Saudi Arabia. See Eli Jacobs, "Extending our Umbrella to the Middle East," *CSIS*, 21 November 2011 (online). http://csis.org/blog/extending-our-umbrella-middle-east

18. Joshua Pollack, "Extended Deterrence and the Tactical Nuclear Mirage," *Bulletin of the Atomic Scientists*, March 12, 2010, www.thebulletin.org/node/8343.

19. Karl Heinz-Kamp and Robertus C. N. Remkes, "Options for NATO Nuclear Sharing Arrangements," in *Reducing Nuclear Risks in Europe: A Framework for Action*, ed. Steve Andreasen and Isabelle Williams (Washington, DC: Nuclear Threat Initiative, 2011), 89.

20. Matthew Hallex, "Extending Deterrence in the Gulf," in *Nuclear Scholars Initiative: Project on Nuclear Issues* (Washington, DC: Center for Strategic and International Studies, 2011), 86.

21. Daryl Kimball and Tom Collina, "The Presidential Nuclear Initiatives (PNIs) on Tactical Nuclear Weapons at a Glance," (Washington, DC: Arms Control Association), August 2012, www.armscontrol.org/factsheets/pniglance.

22. Steven Pifer, Richard C. Bush, Vanda Felbab-Brown, Martin S. Indyk, Michael O'Hanlon, and Kenneth M. Pollack, "US Nuclear and Extended Deterrence: Considerations and Challenges," *Brookings Arms Control Series* 3 (May 2010): 19.

23. Michel Fortmann and Stéfanie von Hlatky, "The Revolution in Military Affairs (RMA) and Deterrence Stability," in *Complex Deterrence: Strategy in the Global Age*, ed. T. V. Paul, Patrick Morgan, and James Wirtz (Chicago, IL: University of Chicago Press, 2009).

24. Michael Brzoska, Anne Finger, Oliver Meier, Götz Neuneck, and Wolfgang Zellneer, "Prospects for Arms Control in Europe." Study conducted for the Friedrich Ebert Stiftung and the Institute for Peace Research and Security Policy at the University of Hamburg (November 2011): 17.

25. Jean Bétermier, "How to Link Deterrence Theory to Strategic Planning," in *NATO and 21st Century Deterrence*, ed. Karl-Heinz Kamp and David S. Yost (Rome: NATO Defense College, Research Division, 2009), 189–190.

26. Pollack, "Extended Deterrence and the Tactical Nuclear Mirage."

27. Mark Landler, "Obama Says Pact Obliges US to Protect Japan in Islands Fight," *New York Times*, April 24, 2014.

28. Based on the International Crisis Behaviour Project definition: "foreign policy crisis as a situation in which three conditions, deriving from a change in a state's external or internal environment, are perceived by the highest-level decision-makers of the state: (a) a threat to basic values, (b) an awareness of finite time for response to the external threat to basic values, and (c) a high probability of involvement in military hostilities."

29. The term *nonstrategic nuclear weapons* will be used throughout (instead of *tactical nuclear weapons*) to reflect the terminology used in NATO's 2012 Deterrence and

Defense Posture Review, released during the Chicago Summit and the 2010 US Nuclear Posture Review.

30. U.S. Department of Defense. 2010. *Nuclear Posture Review*, www.defense.gov/npr/docs/2010%20Nuclear%20Posture%20Review%20Report.pdf, xii (accessed September 25, 2013).

31. M. Chalmers and S. Lunn. 2010. NATO's Tactical Nuclear Dilemma. *RUSI Occasional Paper*, http://www.nonukes.nl/media/files/2010-03-rusi-natos-tactical-nuclear-dilemma_0.pdf, 14–15 (accessed September 25, 2013); Tom Nichols, Douglas Stuart, and Jeffrey D. McCausland, *Tactical Nuclear Weapons and NATO* (Carlisle, PA: Strategic Studies Institute, 2012).

32. Quoted in Tom Sauer and Bob van der Zwaan, "US Tactical Nuclear Weapons in Europe after NATO's Lisbon Summit: Why Their Withdrawal Is Desirable and Feasible," Belfer Center Discussion Paper, no. 2911-05, Harvard Kennedy School, (May 2011): 24.

33. Malcolm Chalmers, "Words That Matter? NATO Declaratory Policy and the DDPR," in *Reducing Nuclear Risks in Europe: A Framework for Action*, ed. Steve Andreasen and Isabelle Williams (Washington, DC: Nuclear Threat Initiative, 2011), 56.

34. Ibid.

35. Bruno Tertrais, "Defining the Right Mix of Capabilities: The Irreplaceable Role of NATO Nuclear Arrangements," in *Managing Change: NATO's Partnerships and Deterrence in a Globalised World*, Report from NATO conference in Bologna, June 21–22, 2011, 1–7.

36. Joan Rohlfing, Isabelle Williams, and Steve Andreasen, "Reassembling a More Credible NATO Nuclear Policy and Posture," in *Reducing Nuclear Risks in Europe: A Framework for Action*, ed. Steve Andreasen and Isabelle Williams (Washington, DC: Nuclear Threat Initiative, 2011), 3.

37. See archives on NATO website. http://www.nato.int/cps/en/natohq/topics_56626.htm

38. George P. Shultz, William J. Perry, Henry A. Kissinger, and Sam Nunn, "A World Free of Nuclear Weapons," *Wall Street Journal*, January 4, 2007, A15.

39. Cited in Robertus C. N. Remkes, "The Security of NATO Nuclear Weapons: Issues and Implications," in *Reducing Nuclear Risks in Europe: A Framework for Action*, ed. Steve Andreasen and Isabelle Williams (Washington, DC: Nuclear Threat Initiative, 2011), 69. See *Report of the Secretary of Defense Task Force on DoD Nuclear Weapons Management—Phase II: Review of the DoD Nuclear Mission* (December 2008): 14, www.defense.gov/pubs/pdfs/PhaseIIReportFinal.pdf.

40. Amy F. Woolf, "Nonstrategic Nuclear Weapons," *CRS Report for Congress* (February 14, 2012): 25.

41. Simon Lunn and Ian Kearns, "NATO's Deterrence and Defence Posture Review: A Status Report," (London: European Leadership Network for Multilateral Nuclear Disarmament and Nonproliferation, February 2011).

42. Huth, *Extended Deterrence and the Prevention of War*, 200.

PART I

NEW THINKING ON DETERRENCE

CHAPTER 1

Threat Scenarios, Risk Assessments, and the Future of Nuclear Deterrence

Joachim Krause

NATO APPEARS TO BE in a perpetual state of crisis, a crisis that has two origins. First, there are deep-seated (one might call them fundamental) differences as to the role of military means in comparison to diplomatic instruments and multilateralism—not only between the United States and Europe but also within Europe and within the United States.[1] The clearest indicator for this inability to agree on the Alliance's necessary military capabilities was the outcome of NATO's 2012 Deterrence and Defense Posture Review (DDPR). This document was full of generic language that did not pay tribute to real security challenges and basically papered over fundamental differences between allies. The muted responses by NATO to the Russian aggression against Ukraine and to the unveiled threats against the Baltic States in 2014 also serve to demonstrate just how far the Alliance is from having a unified position in this area. Second, defense spending in most NATO states is declining due to the post-2008 economic crises facing all Western democracies. These developments are sure to undermine NATO's ability to respond collectively to a broad range of contingencies. The Alliance is already losing critical capabilities, and the United States and Europe armed forces will be less and less able to work together (a problem that also exists within the European Union).[2]

This crisis is definitely not the first for NATO, and the Alliance has proven historically to be outstandingly resilient. NATO was able to overcome these crises and was subsequently hailed by many as the most successful military alliance in history.[3] What made it easier to overcome those crises in the past was either the presence of a clear military threat (the former Soviet Union) or the necessity to respond to a specific international crisis (such as the war in Bosnia-Herzegovina). In dealing with threats and crises, political leaders and international officials, time and again, have tapped into the knowledge of the international strategic community to resolve key issues plaguing the Alliance. The international strategic community consists of academics, active and retired politicians, diplomats, generals, journalists, and entrepreneurs who attend conferences, write books and papers, and try to combine the wisdom and insights of many without having to represent governments or political parties.

This chapter focuses on the potential of the international strategic community as a source of solutions to the current NATO crisis over the Alliance's core military capabilities and its deterrence posture. The starting point of this chapter is a critical review of NATO's DDPR. It then proceeds to analyze the academic debates on deterrence from the 1990s to today. In doing so, it also draws on the academic debate about escalation control as a central element of deterrence strategy. The chapter concludes with some policy recommendations for NATO about deterrence issues. Deterrence will most likely become a salient subject for NATO because Russia is not the only one seeking a strategic competition with the West: Iran is following suit. The Alliance will also have to address the role that nuclear weapons should play in the twenty-first-century security environment if the vision of Global Zero is not realized. This analysis draws on different threat scenarios, which are helpful as heuristic models to better understand future deterrence challenges.

Deterrence Theory Since the End of the Cold War

One can draw several lessons from the academic and policy debates on deterrence since the end of the Cold War. *The first lesson is that the very notion of deterrence has become much broader than before.* Dissuading the Soviet leadership from initiating a major war is no longer the overarching goal for NATO. As Lawrence Freedman put it, "deterrence can be a technique, a doctrine and a state of mind. In all cases, it is about setting boundaries for actions and establishing the risks associated with the crossing of these boundaries."[4] Despite what is commonly assumed, the applicability of deterrence has grown during the past two decades in response to new and complex security problems.

Three dimensions of deterrence need to be addressed in this regard, and all three entail a careful evaluation of the role of nuclear weapons.[5] The first dimension comprises efforts to deter state and nonstate actors from challenging the existing international order. There is, for instance, a liberal international order that is built on the nonuse of violence in interstate interactions and the promotion of free trade and cooperation. Yet some actors challenge this order more or less openly, and some of them are resorting to violence as a means to achieve their policy goals, all the while seeking nuclear weapons, with the aim of protecting themselves from international interventions.

The second dimension involves the role of nuclear weapons in the relationship among the major established nuclear powers, that is, the United States, Russia, China, and to a certain degree France and the United Kingdom. Here the issue is the possibility of arriving at a common understanding among them over the abolition of nuclear weapons or, alternatively, how to promote strategic stability to prevent nuclear wars and to ensure that nuclear states will not engage in any new strategic armament competitions.

The third dimension relates to the reemergence of traditional Article 5 threats to NATO that might, under certain circumstances, involve nuclear weapons. Such threats could come from Russia or from new nuclear states, that is, states that have challenged the international nuclear order and whose challenges have not been dissuaded by the diplomatic efforts of the international community. Devising deterrence concepts against such threats seems to be imperative because a coordinated response by NATO is required for deterrence threats to be credible. The recent crisis between Russia and NATO over Ukraine, for example, has amply demonstrated that this security challenge is no longer merely a hypothetical one.

The second lesson is that the relevance of nuclear weapons has been downgraded. During the past twenty-five years, most scholarly writings on deterrence were focused on the necessity to rely less (if at all) on nuclear means, including nonmilitary instruments such as sanctions and political isolation.[6] Deterrence today means deterrence by denial rather than deterrence through punishment. As a consequence, nuclear weapons might become weapons of last resort, to be used only in cases where there is a clear existential threat, with non-nuclear weapons instead becoming more relevant for deterrence purposes.

This trend reflects the evolving nature of security challenges in the post–Cold War world but also the availability of new, non-nuclear military capabilities. Especially relevant is the modernization of the US armed forces since the 1990s, the so-called revolution in military affairs (RMA), or transformation, which made more and more non-nuclear military options feasible.[7] In looking at the results of the various nuclear posture reviews that were undertaken under the Clinton, George W. Bush, and Obama administrations, there is a clear tendency toward a reduced role of nuclear weapons.[8] President Obama even made it clear in his Prague Speech in April 2009 that the United States was ready to address in a serious way the abolition of nuclear weapons because the US armed forces could make do without nuclear weapons if others reciprocated. What further contributed to the reduced salience of nuclear deterrence was the fact that, after the attacks of September 11, 2001, Salafist jihadism (resorting to terrorism and insurgency) became the new strategic challenge. As is now painfully clear, Salafist jihadism is a threat that does not conform to many of the assumptions underlying nuclear deterrence.[9]

The third lesson one can draw from the literature on deterrence is that the United States and its allies have to be prepared for asymmetric nuclear threats. According to the US military, asymmetric approaches are attempts by adversaries to circumvent or undermine US strengths while exploiting their weaknesses.[10] Asymmetric nuclear threats have been discussed in the literature since the 1990s. Most writings dealt with regional crisis situations in which US adversaries might consider threatening the use of nuclear weapons or even using them from a weak position.[11] As one author put it in 2000, "it is difficult to conceive of a rational actor electing to employ nuclear weapons against the United States in a direct strategic attack. To do so would invite annihilation."[12] After September 11, however, more authors began to consider the use of nuclear weapons by terrorists or by state adversaries and referred to a different, non-Western understanding of rationality.[13] The intention of these adversaries, some authors argue, is to protect themselves from US intervention in their region.[14] This might involve strategies of asymmetric nuclear brinkmanship.

President Obama's Global Zero agenda has not assuaged these concerns. More than five years after the Prague Speech, the nuclear missile programs of North Korea and Iran have continued to grow, with North Korea in March 2013 openly announcing that it was considering a preemptive nuclear precision strike against the United States.[15] Pakistan is producing more and more plutonium for weapons purposes and is thought to be sharing sensitive technologies—and possibly sensitive materials, too—with others. For its part, Russia continues to cling to its special status as a global strategic nuclear power, and it has made nuclear weapons threats against European states since late 2014, in particular in the Baltic area. The emerging competition between the United States and China has a nuclear strategic component, too. With the exception of the US-Russian strategic balance, these are all asymmetric nuclear relationships. It is certain that NATO will become involved the very moment one of these regional adversaries feels tempted to threaten international forces with nuclear weapons.

The fourth lesson that can be drawn from the academic literature is that any deterrence strategy has to be fine-tuned to the respective threat scenario. Most authors have used the concept of tailored deterrence to describe this new understanding of deterrence, with the Quadrennial Defense Review of the US Department of Defense making specific mention of it in 2006.[16] This concept simply expresses the wish to understand deterrence not in the sense of massive nuclear retaliation but to give it a new and more differentiated meaning in a world with threats that are hardly comparable to those of the Cold War era. The idea of tailored deterrence in a certain sense rejects the notion of a one-size-fits-all model of deterrence.[17] Basic ideas were devised in 2001 by Keith Payne, who stressed the need to look at the decision-making processes of challengers, go after their strengths and weaknesses, and look for the various factors "that may be critical to the functioning of deterrence and coercive threats in a specific case." He argued in favor of US deterrence policies that were specific to challengers and the respective context.[18] Similarly, Elaine Bunne stressed that deterrence had to be tailored to specific actors in particular situations and that it was necessary to devise adequate means of communicating with a challenger.[19]

As with the debate on deterrence in the 1990s, the increased relevance of conventional weapons as well as nonmilitary means was emphasized, in particular because new technologies of the RMA would allow force to be used with much greater precision.[20] However, very few excluded the use of nuclear weapons. Nuclear weapons were given a central role in strategic deterrence, that is, in deterring the use of or the threat of using nuclear weapons by adversaries that either already possess them or are on the verge of acquiring them.

The debate on tailored deterrence was focused in part on rogue states and other states that might challenge the international order. But it was also referring to the reemergence of traditional strategic challenges. Another central element of this debate was that the concept of nuclear deterrence might also be relevant in analyzing the behavior of states or actors challenging the international status quo by engaging in strategies of counterdeterrence or deterrence evasion or of asymmetric forms of warfare to exploit the perceived weaknesses of Western democracies.[21]

The fifth lesson, which is closely related to the preceding one, is that escalation dominance is an indispensable requisite for any successful deterrence strategy under conditions of regional or strategic conflict. A RAND study from 1994 already concluded that escalation dominance must credibly deter nuclear threats against the US homeland or US forces overseas when the adversary's objective was to prevent US intervention. A US strategy of extended deterrence based on escalation dominance, backed by theater defenses, should prevent US regional allies from being intimidated by an adversary's nuclear threats. It concluded by arguing that US strategy should shift away from retaliatory deterrence to highly effective damage limitation, such as counterforce capabilities backed by effective defenses.[22]

The next section offers some general lessons about deterrence and extended deterrence based on the preceding discussion regarding the state of the literature on strategic issues.

Deterrence in Support of International Order

The international system of the past decades has been characterized by a remarkable absence of major war. The absence of major war has been paired with paradigmatic efforts by the international community to prevent wars and to intervene when necessary for the sake of regional stability. Today's international order can be understood as the result of US efforts after World War II aimed at establishing a functioning international system based on free trade; adherence to the rule of the nonuse of violence; and the institutionalization of cooperation on a global, regional, and transregional level.[23] At the same time, deterrence strategies were also involved, such as strategic coercion or in some cases military interventions (as in the case of the former Yugoslavia) or even preemption (as in the case of Iraq in 2003).[24]

Conceiving of deterrence as a means to support the international order, however, is a politically sensitive topic in Europe. The term *international order* is mainly associated with upholding principles and international law, and the prevailing opinion is that (economic and diplomatic) sanctions as well as military operations should take place only if approved by the United Nations Security Council. Although NATO states have more or less violated this rule in two cases (with the bombing of Serbia in 1995 and 1999), there is a strong commitment on behalf of member states to adhere to the rules of the UN Charter and the procedures of the UN Security Council. The aim is to operate as much as possible within the framework of Chapter VII of the charter, which has its own specific logic—as well as many shortcomings. From this perspective, the concept of deterrence is only seldom, if ever, used. This is deplorable because there is a definite number of problematic state actors (some call them rogue states) for whom the reaction of the international community (which is mainly tantamount to the United States and its allies) is a crucial factor in deterring them from further action or encouraging them to proceed further.

A critical issue in this respect has always been how far deterrence should play a role in restraining states such as Iraq under Saddam Hussein, Iran, or North Korea from acquiring nuclear weapons, that is, from breaking the rules of the international nuclear order. A bone of contention was always whether the Western Alliance should react by diplomatic means only or whether military means (mainly surgical strikes, regime change, but also even the threat of nuclear retaliation) should play a role. The transatlantic strife over the forceful regime change in Baghdad in 2003 demonstrated how delicate this issue was and how small the room for unanimous agreement is within the Western Alliance when it comes to military intervention.

Nevertheless, the idea of using military deterrence instruments in cases where diplomacy fails is still relevant.[25] This option has to be considered in the context of pivotal states, such as Iran and North Korea, succeeding in developing their nuclear and missile programs. There are analyses on non-nuclear options to destroy Iranian nuclear and missile installations.[26] Others even suggest that "U.S. policymakers and military planners must be prepared to confront nuclear-armed rogue states, even contemplating the role of U.S. nuclear deterrence."[27] Here the element of escalation dominance under asymmetric conditions is at hand. It is difficult to define how to establish escalation dominance against these types of adversaries and how deterrence can apply to them. Keith Payne has argued that the nature of the adversaries was quite different in comparison to the Kremlin leadership of the Cold War era and that this might spell problems for states that want to enforce the international order:

> Effective deterrence threats must be credible to the opponents. Unfortunately, leaders of terrorist states and tyrants who recognize the appropriate priority we place on avoiding civilian casualties may not believe U.S. deterrent threats that would produce the high yields and moderate accuracies of the remaining Cold War arsenal.[28]

According to this logic, the United States should have a broad set of military alternatives, including weapons that would allow counterstrike options in a conventional and non-nuclear way.[29] Authors such as Keith Payne have pointed to the necessity for the United States not to lose escalation control in a regional crisis, and they stress that tactical nuclear weapons could contribute to that goal. Critics argue that in view of the current target precision of non-nuclear US weapons the resort to new nuclear arms was not needed.[30] Whether nuclear counterforce options can be limited to non-nuclear means alone is a debate that is active in the United States when considering different regional crisis scenarios, in particular Iran and North Korea. In Europe, with the exception of France and Great Britain, there is no such debate.

Mutual Nuclear Deterrence

Another area, at least within NATO, where the deterrence issue is more or less neglected is the existing strategic nuclear balance between the United States and Russia. This issue also resonates in the emerging nuclear strategic balance between the United States and China. For the time being, the strategic nuclear balance between the United States and Russia is the most relevant issue. In the long run, however, the strategic relationship between Washington and Beijing is more important. Here the question is: Will nuclear deterrence (one-sided or mutual) play a major and possibly decisive role in shaping security interactions between Washington and Beijing?

Regarding the US-Russian strategic competition, it is a strange thing that twenty-five years after the end of the Cold War, Russia and the United States are still trapped in a nuclear strategic standoff. Despite a remarkable reduction of more than 70 percent in their total strategic nuclear arsenals since 1990, the nuclear strategic standoff is ever present: More than two thousand nuclear weapons remain pointed at each other. The 2010 New START treaty, which has been hailed as a huge step toward Global Zero, is unlikely to alter this situation. Its agreed ceilings are slightly below existing stocks (as in the case of strategic offensive arms carrier systems) and even allow some more flexibility.[31]

It is astonishing that very little attention is given to the strategic nuclear duel that still persists to this day, as well as the risks associated with it. During the past twenty-five years, Russia and the United States have not become friends, but their relationship has not been so fundamentally hostile that they have to threaten each other with nuclear devastation. Unlike the dynamics of Cold War confrontations, where a Soviet invasion army stood in the center of Europe and the United States was prepared to deter an attack eventually with nuclear weapons, there is no strategic logic for either side to maintain a Cold War nuclear posture toward one another. This political anomaly has been rightly identified as being one of the major obstacles for any progress toward the abolition of nuclear weapons. As the International Commission on Nuclear Non-Proliferation and Disarmament put it in 2009, "Maintaining thousands of nuclear warheads on dangerously high launch-on-warning alert is the ultimate absurdity of nuclear deterrence twenty years after the end of the Cold War."[32]

One reason for the persistence of the strategic nuclear duel might be that the established mode of strategic stability—mutually assured destruction (MAD)—actually inhibits further reductions of strategic offensive weapons. The MAD concept was devised in the 1960s as a means to avoid instabilities resulting from emerging first-strike incentives. Under the concept of mutually assured destruction, strategic stability is higher when there are a lot of nuclear weapons on each side and when these weapons are in locations that are not vulnerable to nuclear strikes. The large Cold War strategic arsenals hence ensured stability in the sense that during a crisis neither side would be tempted to resort to nuclear weapons with the intention of disarming the other side. Also today, strategic stability between the United States and Russia is still based on the notion that neither side should be able to launch a disarming first strike against the other's nuclear arsenal and command and control facilities. So long as strategic stability is perceived in this way, further reductions in quantities and quality of strategic nuclear weapons will be limited on both sides. But the following question remains: Does it still make sense to base strategic stability on MAD scenarios when mutually assured destruction works *against* further radical reductions in quantities and quality of strategic nuclear weapons on both sides?

The futility of devising workable alternative modes of strategic stability under conditions of strategic nuclear competition might explain why there has been no more progress in reducing the strategic standoff. In the academic world, alternative concepts of strategic stability have been discussed, in particular de-alerting, virtual nuclear arsenals, and the integration of ballistic missile defense capabilities.[33] While these concepts found their way into policy, action has also followed. In 2000, former US president George W. Bush called for abandoning MAD and moving toward something he termed mutually assured security (MAS).[34] Obviously, during his tenure this shift in stability doctrine had turned out to be much more difficult to achieve than originally envisaged. While consensus about the principal utility of de-alerting might be easy to find, in reality, concrete proposals have been met with skepticism.

During the Bush administration, de-alerting proposals were rejected because of the perceived risks. One author who was involved in the work of the administration argued that de-alerting could potentially undermine the strategic balance.[35] As the 2010 Nuclear Posture Review reveals, the Obama administration seems to have similar problems with this concept, and the

Congressional Commission on the Strategic Posture of the United States did not support it.[36] Similar problems have been raised with regard to virtual nuclear arsenals. Again, this is primarily an American debate, not a European one.

The academic literature proposes several alternative paths for thinking about these issues. Two American authors hold that the logic of MAD has already become outdated and that the US-Russian nuclear standoff is no longer symmetrical. They argue that, in view of massive improvements in the field of missile targeting accuracy, conventional precision strike, antisubmarine warfare, ballistic missile and air defense, intelligence and reconnaissance, as well as cyberwarfare, the United States might already be in a position of strategic superiority (or primacy) vis-à-vis Russia. In theory, the United States could destroy the nuclear arsenals of Russia, China, and others. Hence the traditional equation of MAD might no longer be applicable.[37] If this is true, how will the strategic relationship between the United States and Russia evolve? What about the relationship with China? One possible answer is that this situation itself presents some incentives for the other nuclear weapons states to abide by the vision of Global Zero. In a certain sense, there must be a major interest by Chinese and Russian leadership to avoid both a continued strategic inferiority and a costly and dangerous arms race with the United States. However, neither Russia nor China has shown any interest so far in discussing Global Zero with the United States—a fact that militates against the hypothesis presented by Lieber and Press.

Another interpretation comes from Stephen J. Cimbala, who seems not to be alarmed by the continuing nuclear standoff. So long as no such fundamental political differences and strategic interests remain between Russia and the United States—as there were during the Cold War era—he argues, neither side has any political motive to initiate a nuclear war or to pursue a risk-prone crisis strategy.[38] This might be the predominant view in both Moscow and Washington; otherwise there would be much more political debate about this issue. One might add that the US-China relationship so far has not been affected by the reality of US strategic nuclear superiority. In the long run, this could mean that the nuclear strategic relationship between the United States on the one side and Russia and China on the other side might more and more resemble the relationship among Washington, Paris, and London, provided that the diplomatic relations do not sour. That would mean a slow shift toward a benign US nuclear primacy that could translate into more leverage to push nuclear abolition. What militates against this hypothesis is that Russia is modernizing its strategic nuclear arsenal, which reflects the idea that Russia will not accept any kind of benign US hegemony.

An alternative scenario, of course, is that the political situation might deteriorate further still. As the recent crisis between Russia and the West over Ukraine has amply demonstrated, a situation of strategic competition is already there. The Russian leadership increasingly depicts the United States and the West as fundamentally hostile to Russia and its interests while preparing its population for a lengthy period of conflict. The Russian military has upgraded the role of nuclear weapons in its national defense strategy, and it seems to cling to the strategic nuclear standoff because it offers Moscow a claim as a great power equal only to the United States. What also militates against the optimism voiced by Stephen Cimbala is the fact that China is increasingly converting its economic power into military power. Many authors already argue that a strategic competition is emerging between China and the United States in East Asia. While the United States seeks to support regional powers that look for deterrence against a growingly assertive China, the leadership in Beijing is trying to prevent the United States from building regional alliances and to put US military forces in the region under a threat.[39] It is foreseeable that the already complicated nature of the strategic competition between Russia and the United States might deteriorate and will become more complicated with the People's Republic of China entering the scene as a peer competitor for both.[40]

The potential for a trilateral nuclear strategic competition has not been discussed very intensively within NATO. While it is understandable that the US-China relationship has not entered the NATO agenda, the nature of the deterrence balance between the United States and Russia has been at the center of the debate on regional ballistic missile defense (BMD) in Europe.[41] The extremely negative and uncompromising Russian attitude toward BMD might be an indicator that Moscow shares the view that the nuclear strategic balance—even under conditions of negotiated parity—is slowly shifting toward the United States and that missile defense was just one more step toward US nuclear strategic primacy. Thus Russian policy could be understood as an attempt to use the Europeans as a lever by which Russia could influence US decisions on the future direction of their nuclear strategic policy.

So long as the United States continues its benign nuclear supremacy and so long as neither Russia nor China is determined to challenge the United States head on, this will be rather unproblematic. However, US nuclear strategic policy might become a controversial issue the moment the United States reconsiders its strategic interests in a world that is characterized by a growing number of nuclear weapons states, states whose leaders are less moderate than those in Moscow or Beijing and who are aiming their nuclear arsenals on targets in the United States or on the territories of its allies.

Deterrence against Old and New Threats

The third dimension of the deterrence debate is the possibility of threats to the territorial integrity of NATO by states that possess or are seeking nuclear weapons. First and foremost, these are *classical Article 5 threats* precisely because they involve threats to the territorial integrity of NATO member states. These threats should be discussed not only in a generic way but also with a view to those countries that are most exposed to them, namely, Estonia, Latvia, Lithuania, Poland, Romania, Slovakia, and Turkey. In any of these cases, various scenarios can be devised that encompass likely and possible contingencies involving nuclear weapons. Besides threats coming from Russia, new strategic threats to the security of NATO members by states in the Middle East, in particular by Iran, will have to be addressed. Analyzing these scenarios teaches us that they are less generic than usually thought and that they are very context-dependent. To engage in this type of analysis, several assumptions are warranted.

First, in terms of traditional Article 5 threats (where the territorial integrity of NATO member states are concerned), one has to look first at small member states bordering Russia, Belarus, or Ukraine. Here the danger is less a repetition of the traditional "Soviet" threat (i.e., a large invasion conquering major parts of Europe) but rather the emergence of unconventional (hybrid) warfare on a limited scale. Here, not losing escalation control is of utmost importance for Western deterrence strategy.

Second, Turkey is the NATO member state most likely to be confronted with serious threats, either from Iran, Syria (whatever the results of the civil war), or other sources (Caucasus, northern Iraq). One has to analyze whether any of these scenarios might entail the necessity to consider seriously extended nuclear deterrence threats as an instrument to redress the situation.

Third, we have to think about possible scenarios in which Iran might consider the use of nuclear weapons against targets in Europe. Which role can ballistic missile defense realistically play? At which point do we need a credible nuclear deterrence posture? Who has to provide for it? What are the best weapons systems for such a purpose?

Russia and NATO

In the twenty-first century, Russia does not present the same strategic threat as did the Soviet Union. Its military options are limited and its strategic goals are principally defensive in nature; however, the meaning of the term *defensive* in Russian thinking involves the self-assumed right to determine the foreign policy and domestic orientation of neighboring states, which is understood by the latter as a flagrant incursion into their sovereign rights. As a consequence, one cannot exclude the possibility that the Russian government is using (or is considering the use of) military force on a limited scale in order to pursue national interests in areas adjacent to Russia (in particular if the status of Russians in the Baltic States are at risk or if the principally pro-Russian orientation of Ukraine or Belarus is in danger). The political logic behind Russian moves might be defensive in nature, but the readiness to use military force against neighbors cannot be excluded, as has been vividly demonstrated since spring 2014 in Ukraine. The fact that Russia still possesses more than two thousand strategic nuclear weapons directed against the United States, in addition to roughly four thousand nonstrategic warheads in Europe, adds a somewhat dramatic dimension to this matter.

In light of Russia's behavior during the Georgia war in 2008 or in Ukraine in 2014, one should proceed from the assumption that in a similar regional or local crisis, it might resort to the use of military power at a relative early point in time, in particular if the resolve of the Russian government to protect the interests of Russians or Russian-speaking citizens is in question. In most cases, this would turn into a strategic threat to any of the three Baltic States (Estonia, Latvia, and Lithuania). The danger is not only the premeditated military offensive against all of them but also a crisis during which Russia is intervening on behalf of allegedly suppressed Russian minorities. Currently any such move by Russia would put NATO in a situation where it does not have at hand instruments to control escalation. The decisions taken at the NATO summit in September 2014 are a first step to create such a capability. However, the measures envisaged at the Wales Summit remain very limited.

Unlike the Cold War period, NATO so far does not have any concept of how to control escalation during such a crisis. Escalation control was one of the prime purposes of deterrence strategy during the Cold War, and it provided a level of strategic stability that was important for periods of crisis.[42] Under the scenarios outlined above, the lack of a strategy aimed at escalation control might have disastrous consequences. Given the still limited conventional military options available to Russia, it cannot be excluded that Russia, during such a crisis, might try to control escalation by resorting to the threat of using tactical nuclear weapons early on. One need only imagine a major crisis over the treatment of Russians in Estonia or Latvia during which an armed militia of Russian citizens in Estonia or Latvia takes control of strategic buildings and institutions (something we have seen in Ukraine), and where Estonian or Latvian regular forces prepare to fight the militias. Both sides would ask for outside help, with Russian forces already standing close to the border in a high state of readiness. To prevent NATO from sending troops to the Baltic States, Russia might move theater nuclear weapons into the area and threaten to use them if allied troops enter the region.

A similar situation could arise if Russian troops were to occupy all three Baltic States in a surprise attack—something Russian armed forces have simulated during a major military exercise in fall 2013. Any such situation would overburden NATO. The Alliance would have to choose between the option of either losing the Baltic States or risking escalation that it could not control. Hence, it would be appropriate to discuss in peacetime how to react in such a crisis. Which nuclear weapons would serve appropriately as credible counterweight to Russia threatening the initial use of tactical nuclear weapons? Would it be better to resort to nuclear weapons already stationed in Europe? Or would NATO be better off with theater nuclear weapons that have to be moved in from the United States?

The main purpose of raising the specter of these crises is that crisis stability is an extremely important aspect when dealing with a neighbor like Russia. Russia is both a possible partner as well as a potential foe and possesses a substantial arsenal of nuclear weapons (both strategic and nonstrategic). Its leadership feels—mainly for domestic reasons—deeply insecure and acts increasingly in an assertive and aggressive way. NATO member states will have to address these strategic and political realities in the coming years with as much candor as possible, in particular after the events surrounding Ukraine in 2014. The goal is not to depict a grim Russian threat but to be wary of escalating situations that may be exacerbated by Russia's peculiar domestic situation, which involves many incentives for the Kremlin leadership to seek the escalation of external conflicts in order to keep domestic political support high. So far, there is no indication that NATO governments (except the US administration) are even prepared to broach this issue within the Alliance or at home. Nonstrategic nuclear forces are being discussed only as an arms control issue; however, Russia has not demonstrated the slightest interest in dealing away its (estimated) four thousand theater nuclear forces (TNF) for the withdrawal of about two hundred US B61 bombs from Europe.

Turkey's Security Problems Are NATO's Problems

Although the Turkish government tends to avoid these debates, it is important to discuss threats facing Turkey in its region. Some of them can be solved by Turkey alone, like the challenge of Kurdish separatism, while others might need indirect support from NATO members. Turkey is subject to an emerging strategic Iranian threat, even if the Turkish government so far refuses to accept this notion openly. This threat could translate into a nuclear one if, or when, Iran acquires nuclear weapon capabilities. This should be of concern to NATO for two reasons: (1) Inaction might push Turkey to reconsider its non-nuclear weapons status, and (2) NATO should prepare for the potential of a crisis escalating in the region. Again an important question is will BMD be sufficient to cope with the Iranian nuclear threat? If not, is the threat of US strategic weapons (strategic bombers, ICBMs, SLBMs) the best way to respond to the Iranian threat? These scenarios also present challenges for NATO's relationship with Russia. Would Russia be able to discern between preparations on the US side that are limited in scale and directed against Iran, or would such preparations cause major concerns in Russia? Given the complexity of these scenarios and the severe implications of a crisis in Turkey's vicinity, it is surprising that there has been no thorough debate within NATO on the subject.

Iran as a Possible Strategic Threat to Europe

The Iranian nuclear program is a nuclear weapons program in disguise. If international diplomatic measures fail under President Rouhani or if neither the United States nor Israel succeed in destroying their program with surgical strikes, we can expect that Europe will be within reach of nuclear-tipped missiles from Iran in the not-so-distant future.[43] NATO's phased theater ballistic missile defense system aims to make European NATO states (and US forces in Europe) less vulnerable against these weapons (with the eventual goal of full-scale protection). Should the threat posed by Iran persist in addition to Russian obstructionist strategies vis-à-vis NATO's BMD plans, which in turn might slow down the political momentum in many European capitals, the Alliance will have to rely on extended nuclear deterrence against Iranian nuclear threats. In this context, which weapon systems should NATO rely on? Strategic nuclear bombers, ICBMs, or strategic submarines are difficult because these might alarm Russia. Would naval systems be better? Or would nuclear weapons based in Europe be an appropriate solution? NATO should also start planning for these crisis scenarios to prevent the weaker side from gaining the advantage of escalation control.

Conclusion

This chapter has shown that when considering deterrence challenges (in particular those dealing with extended deterrence) there is a marked difference between what is being discussed within NATO (and how it is being discussed) and the international academic debates, which, perhaps surprisingly, appear more invested in the analysis of crisis scenarios in the context of extended deterrence. The political debate, in contrast, has been characterized by attempts to eschew vexing questions and has become quite philosophical and focused on generic principles and rules. In the NATO context, the DDPR as well as the Strategic Concept from 2010 are written using vague language and broad terms, making no mention of real crisis situations. While it is understandable given the multiplicity of political opinions among twenty-eight member governments that the Atlantic Alliance needs to be somewhat vague in an era of uncertain risks and challenges, it is imperative, at least for the leading states, to think through future crises and emergencies with greater scrutiny. Otherwise, the Atlantic Alliance might be caught by total surprise during a real international crisis.

Discussing deterrence has become politically incorrect in many countries. This is a problematic development because deterrence is, to a certain degree, the most appropriate way liberal democracies can approach defense and security issues. Through a strategy of deterrence Western liberal democracies can demonstrate, on the one hand, that they no longer consider military violence as a legitimate instrument of foreign policy while, on the other hand, still credibly demonstrate their commitment to defend themselves and the liberal international order they are standing for. Deterrence though, is no alternative to diplomacy. Rather, it should be considered as an instrument of diplomacy that seeks to envisage the use of violence in international affairs only when other options have failed. A policy of deterrence involves the use of threats by one party to convince another party to refrain from initiating violence or aggression—a kind of coercive diplomacy aimed at dissuading others from the use of violence.[44] During the Cold War, deterrence policy was directed against the threat of a Soviet invasion, and it was heavily focused on the deterring role of nuclear weapons. The deterrence policy of the Western Alliance was not only directed toward dissuading the Soviet leadership from initiating a war, it was also thought as signalling that the overarching aim was to prevent war in the first place. As Bernard Brodie put it, the main utility of nuclear weapons would be their nonuse.[45]

If the Western Alliance wants to stick with the very notion that deterrence policy is part and parcel of a broader policy that intends to prevent wars or other forms of organized violence to shape international relations, then deterrence has to be adapted to the new international context. This context not only changed after 1989 but is currently undergoing new changes that are, in the long run, much more profound than changes almost twenty-five years ago.

Deterrence is no longer tantamount to nuclear deterrence. Today the practitioners of coercive diplomacy have a much broader range of options at their disposal. As long as these options exist, however, nuclear weapons should not be ignored and deterrence policy has to account for their continued, if diminished, relevance. On the one hand, they are an important element of existential deterrence and the backbone of Western (i.e., United States) military superiority. On the other hand, nuclear weapons in the hands of adversaries are a continuing source of irritation and friction. NATO states would do well to consider the challenges posed by asymmetric forms of nuclear counterdeterrence. This chapter showed that the Alliance should also work to defuse the existing strategic nuclear standoff between the United States and Russia and the emerging strategic nuclear competition with China.

This chapter's main purpose was to highlight the necessity of thinking through the evolving global nuclear strategic balance and, in particular, to consider future risks and threats associated with deterrence that the United States and its allies might face. To summarize, three dimensions of a deterrence posture will need to be addressed because in each of them nuclear weapons might play a significant role. The most preferable approaches to solving these problems are diplomatic and political initiatives. And nuclear disarmament might be a solution for all these problems in the end. Yet before this can be achieved (if ever), allied states should assess the strategic contingencies in terms of crisis escalation. The policy implication for NATO and other alliances is that gaining escalation control is key in any scenario where nuclear threats are envisaged by belligerent states or even nonstate actors.

Notes

1. Joachim Krause, "Multilateralism—Behind European Views," *The Washington Quarterly* 27, no. 2 (Spring 2004): 43–59.

2. F. Stephen Larrabee, "NATO Forces Approach Financial Day of Reckoning," *RAND-Review* 36, no. 3 (Winter 2012/2013): 17–19; see also F. Stephen Larrabee, Stuart E. Johnson, John Gordon IV, Peter A. Wilson, Caroline Baxter, Deborah Lai, and Calin Trenkov-Wermuth, *NATO and the Challenges of Austerity* (Santa Monica, CA: RAND, 2012).

3. This phrase was used, for instance, by US President Bill Clinton in his welcome letter to the participants of the fiftieth anniversary summit meeting of NATO in 1999, http://clinton2.nara.gov/WH/New/NATO/welcome.html.

4. Lawrence Freedman, *Deterrence* (Cambridge, UK: Polity Press, 2004), 116. See also Gary Schaub Jr., "When Is Deterrence Necessary? Gauging Adversary Intent," *Strategic Studies Quarterly* 3, no. 4 (Winter 2009): 49–74.

5. See Joachim Krause, "Emerging Concepts of Deterrence in the 21st Century," in *NATO and 21st Century Deterrence*, ed. Karl-Heinz Kamp and David S. Yost (Rome: NATO Defense College, 2009), 143–52.

6. Gary L. Guertner, Robert Haffa, Jr., and George Quester (eds.), *Conventional Forces and the Future of Deterrence* (Carlisle Barrack, PA: US Army War College, 1992); Charles T. Allan, "Extended Conventional Deterrence: In From the Cold and Out of the Nuclear Fire?" *The Washington Quarterly* 17, no. 3 (Summer 1994): 203–23; Stephen Cimbala, *Strategy after Deterrence* (New York: Praeger, 1991); Stephen J. Cimbala, *Military Persuasion: Deterrence and Provocation in Crisis and War* (University Park, PA: Pennsylvania State University Press, 1994); Keith Payne, *The Fallacies of Cold War Deterrence and a New Direction* (Lexington: University of Kentucky Press, 2001). See also David S. Yost, "Nuclear Debates in France," *Survival* 36, no. 4 (Winter 1994): 113–39.

7. Michel Fortmann and Stéfanie von Hlatky, "The Revolution in Military Affairs: Impact of Emerging Technology on Deterrence," in *Complex Deterrence: Strategy in the Global Age*, ed. T.V. Paul, Patrick M. Morgan, and James J. Wirtz (Chicago, IL: University of Chicago Press, 2009).

8. Joachim Krause and Benjamin Schreer, "Salvaging Global Zero: Diplomacy in the Second Nuclear Age," *RUSI Journal* 155, no. 3 (June/July 2010): 48–52.

9. David Kilcullen, "New Paradigms for 21st Century Conflict: The Need for a Grand Strategy for Combating Terrorism," *E-Journal USA* 12, no. 5 (May 2007): 40–45. For the limited role of deterrence as a means to fight terrorism, see Andreas Wenger and Alex Wilner (eds.), *Deterring Terrorism: Theory and Practice* (Stanford, CA: Stanford University Press, 2012). For an Israeli perspective, see Shmuel Bar, "Deterring Non-State Terrorist Groups: The Case of Hizballah," *Comparative Strategy* 26, no. 5 (2007): 469–93.

10. For a discussion of this and other definitions, see David L. Buffaloe, *Defining Asymmetric Warfare* (Arlington, VA: The Institute of Land Warfare, 2006), http://www.ausa.org/SiteCollectionDocuments/ILW%20Web-ExclusivePubs/Land%20Warfare%20Papers/LWP_58.pdf.

11. Dean Wilkening and Kenneth Watman, *Nuclear Deterrence in a Regional Context* (Santa Monica, CA: RAND 1994); Kenneth McKenzie, Jr., *The Revenge of the Melians: Asymmetric Threats and the Next QDR*, McNair Paper 62 (Washington, DC: National Defense University, 2000); Vincent Lanata, "Faire face: l'ere des nouveaux defies," *Défense nationale* 49 (August/September 1993): 12–13; Henry de Roquefeuil, "Les composantes air de la dissuasion nucléaire aujord'hui et demain," *Défense nationale* 49 (August/September 1993): 41; Yves Cuau, "Les forts, les faibles et les fous," *L'Express* (November 11, 1993): 46.

12. McKenzie, *The Revenge of the Melians*, 24.

13. Anthony Cordesman, *Defending America: Asymmetric and Terrorist Attacks with Radiological and Nuclear Weapons* (Washington, DC: CSIS, 2001). See also Josiane Gabel, "The Role of U.S. Nuclear Weapons after September 11," *The Washington Quarterly* 28, no. 1 (2004): 179–95. For a more recent discussion, see Red Thornton, *Asymmetric Warfare. Threat and Response in the 21st Century* (Cambridge, UK: Polity Press, 2007), 15–16.

14. Patrick M. Morgan, "Evaluating Tailored Deterrence," in *NATO and 21st Century Deterrence*, ed. Karl-Heinz Kamp and David S. Yost (Rome: NATO Defense College, 2009), 32–49.

15. Choe Sang-Hun, "Two Koreas in Doomsday Threats after Vote at U.N." *New York Times*, March 9, 2013.

16. US Department of Defense, *Quadrennial Defense Review Report* (Washington, DC: US Government Printing Office, 2006), vi, 4.

17. David S. Yost, "NATO and Tailored Deterrence: Surveying the Challenges," in *NATO and 21st Century Deterrence*, ed. Karl-Heinz Kamp and David S. Yost (Rome: NATO Defense College, 2009), 11–31.

18. Payne, *The Fallacies of Cold War Deterrence*, 103.

19. Elain Bunn, "Can Deterrence Be Tailored?" *Strategic Forum, Institute for National Strategic Studies* 1, no. 225 (Washington, DC: National Defense University, 2007), 1–8, http://permanent.access.gpo.gov/lps496/Strforum /sf225/SF225+new.pdf.

20. Morgan, "Evaluating Tailored Deterrence," 37.

21. Ibid.

22. Wilkening and Watman, *Nuclear Deterrence in a Regional Context.*

23. G. John Ikenberry, *After Victory: Institutions, Strategic Restraint, and the Rebuilding of International Order* (Princeton, NJ: Princeton University Press, 2001), 163–272; G. John Ikenberry, *Liberal Leviathan: The Origins, Crisis and Transformation of the American World Order* (Princeton, NJ: Princeton University Press, 2011). See also Philip Bobbitt, *The Shield of Achilles: War, Peace, and the Course of History* (New York: Anchor Books, 2002).

24. Freedman, *Deterrence*, 119.

25. Robert S. Joseph and John E. Reichart, "Deterrence and Defense in a Nuclear, Biological and Chemical Environment," *Comparative Strategy* 15, no. 1 (Spring 1996): 59–80; Philip L. Richardson, "Proliferation and the Challenge to Deterrence," *Strategic Review* 23 (Spring 1995): 38–48; Lewis A. Dunn, "Rethinking the Nuclear Equation: The United States and New Nuclear Powers," *The Washington Quarterly* 17, no. 1 (Winter 1994): 5–25; Marc Dean Millot, "Facing the Emerging Reality of Regional Nuclear Adversaries," *The Washington Quarterly* 17, no. 3 (Summer 1994): 41–71; Thomas Dowler and Joseph S. Howard II, "Stability in a Proliferated World," *Strategic Review* 23, no. 2 (Spring 1995): 26–37; George H. Quester and Victor A. Utgoff, "No-First-Use and Nonproliferation: Redefining Extended Deterrence," *The Washington Quarterly* 17, no. 2 (Spring 1994): 103–14.

26. Richard L. Russell, "Military Options for Preventing a Nuclear-Armed Iran," in *Iran's Nuclear Programme: Strategic Implications*, ed. Joachim Krause (London: Routledge, 2012), 137–58.

27. Jason Zaborski, "Deterring a Nuclear Iran," *The Washington Quarterly* 28, no. 3 (Summer 2005): 153–67; Payne, *The Fallacies of Cold War Deterrence;* Keir A. Lieber and Daryl G. Press, "The New Era of Nuclear Weapons, Deterrence, and Conflict," *Strategic Studies Quarterly* 7, no. 1 (Spring 2013): 3–14.

28. Quoted in Mark B. Schneider, "Prevention through Strength: Is Nuclear Superiority Enough?" *Comparative Strategy* 28, no. 2 (2009): 121.

29. See Keith B. Payne, *The Great American Gamble: Deterrence Theory and Practice from the Cold War to the Twenty-First Century* (Fairfax, VA: National Institute Press, 2008); Lieber and Press, "The New Era of Nuclear Weapons;" Schneider, "Prevention through Strength;" Mark B. Schneider, "The Future of the U.S. Nuclear Deterrent," *Comparative Strategy* 27, no. 4 (2008): 345–60.

30. George P. Shultz, William J. Perry, Henry A. Kissinger, and Sam Nunn, "A World Free of Nuclear Weapons," *Wall Street Journal*, January 4, 2007, 15.

31. Krause and Schreer, "Salvaging Global Zero."

32. International Commission on Nuclear Non-Proliferation and Disarmament, *Eliminating Nuclear Threats: A Practical Agenda for Global Policymakers* (Canberra: ICNND, 2009), 27.

33. Michael J. Mazarr (ed.), *Nuclear Weapons in a Transformed World: The Challenge of Virtual Nuclear Arsenals* (New York: St. Martin's Press, 1997); *Reframing Nuclear De-Alert: Decreasing the Operational Readiness of U.S. and Russian Arsenals* (New York: The East-West Institute, 2009).

34. "Presidential Election Forum: The Candidates on Arms Control," in *Arms Control Today*, September 2000, https://www.armscontrol.org/act/2000_09/pressept00.

35. For instance, Christopher A. Ford, *Playing for Time on the Edge of the Apocalypse: Maximizing Decision Time for Nuclear Leaders* (Washington, DC: Hudson Institute, 2010).

36. US Department of Defense, *Nuclear Posture Review* (Washington, DC: April 2010); William J. Perry and James R. Schlesinger, *America's Strategic Posture: The Final Report of the Congressional Commission on the Strategic Posture of the United States* (Washington, DC: United States Institute of Peace, 2008). For a Japanese perspective, see Sukeyuki Ichimasa, "The Concept of Virtual Nuclear Arsenals and a World without Nuclear Weapons," *NIDS Journal of Defense and Security* 13, no. 3 (December 2012): 23–37.

37. Lieber and Press, "The New Era of Nuclear Weapons," 4; Keir A. Lieber and Daryl G. Press, "The Rise of U.S. Nuclear Primacy," *Foreign Affairs* 85, no. 2 (March/April 2006): 42–54; Keir A. Lieber and Daryl G. Press, "The End of MAD? The Nuclear Dimension of U.S. Primacy," *International Security* 30, no. 4 (Spring 2006): 7–44; Keir A. Lieber and Daryl G. Press, "Superiority Complex: Why America's Growing Nuclear Supremacy May Make War with China More Likely," *Atlantic Monthly* 300, no. 1 (July/August 2007): 86–92.

38. Stephen J. Cimbala, "Russia's Strategic Nuclear Deterrent: Realistic or Uncertain?," *Comparative Strategy* 26, no. 3 (2007): 185–203.

39. Geoffrey Till, *Asia's Naval Expansion: An Arms Race in the Making?* (Abingdon: Routledge for IISS, 2012); Aaron L. Friedberg, *Beyond Air–Sea Battle: The Debate over US Military Strategy in Asia* (Abingdon: Routledge for IISS, 2014); Evan Braden Montgomery, "Contested Primacy in the Western Pacific: China's Rise and the Future of US Power Projection," *International Security* 38, no. 4 (Spring 2014): 115–49; Christian Le Mière, "The Spectre of an Asian Arms Race," *Survival* 56, no. 1 (February–March 2014): 139–56; David C. Gompert and Martin Libicki, "Cyber Warfare and Sino-American Instability," *Survival* 56, no. 4 (August–September 2014): 7–21; Stephen J. Cimbala, "Anticipatory Attacks: Nuclear Crisis Stability in Future Asia," *Comparative Strategy* 27, no. 1 (2008): 113–32; Roger Cliff, Mark Burles, Michael S. Chase, Derek Eaton, and Kevin L. Pollpeter, *Entering the Dragon's Lair: The Implications of Chinese Antiaccess Strategies* (Santa Monica, CA: RAND, 2007); David Shambaugh, *Modernizing China's Military: Progress, Problems and Prospects* (Berkeley, CA: University of California Press, 2002).

40. Jeffrey G. Lewis, *The Minimum Means of Reprisal: China's Search for Security in the Nuclear Age* (Cambridge, MA: MIT Press, 2007); Brad Roberts, "Great Power Deterrence and Relationships in the Early 21st Century," in *NATO and 21st Century Deterrence*, ed. Karl-Heinz Kamp and David S. Yost (Rome: NATO Defense College,

2009), 100–110; Brad Roberts, *China-U.S. Nuclear Relations: What Relationship Best Serves U.S. Interests?* (Alexandria, VA: Institute for Defense Analyses, 2001).

41. Roberts, "Great Power Deterrence and Relationships in the Early 21st Century," 109.

42. Albert Wohlstetter and Richard Brody, "Continuing Control as a Requirement for Deterring," in *Managing Nuclear Operations*, ed. Ashton B. Carter, John D. Steinbruner, and Charles A. Zraker (Washington, DC: Brookings Institute, 1987), 142–96. For the nuclear planning within NATO at that time, see Catherine M. Kelleher, "NATO Nuclear Operations," in *Managing Nuclear Operations*, ed. Ashton B. Carter, John D. Steinbruner, and Charles A. Zraker (Washington, DC: Brookings Institute, 1987), 445–69; Paul Bracken, *The Command and Control of Nuclear Forces* (New Haven, CT: Yale University Press, 1983). For a critical review of NATO's approaches during that period, see Daniel Charles, *Nuclear Planning in NATO: Pitfalls of First Use* (Cambridge, MA: Ballinger, 1987).

43. For an assessment of the strategic implications of the Iranian nuclear program, see Joachim Krause and Charles King Mallory IV, "Strategic Implications of the Iranian Nuclear Programme," in *Iran's Nuclear Programme: Strategic Implications*, ed. Joachim Krause (London: Routledge, 2012), 11–33.

44. Alexander George, *Forceful Persuasion: Coercive Diplomacy as an Alternative to War* (Washington, DC: United States Institute of Peace Press, 1991), 3–14.

45. Bernard Brodie, *War and Politics* (London: Cassell, 1973).

CHAPTER 2

US Extended Deterrence and Europe

TIME TO CONSIDER ALTERNATIVE STRUCTURES?

Jeffrey A. Larsen

THE STATEMENTS IN NATO'S Deterrence and Defense Posture Review (DDPR), released at the Chicago Summit in May 2012, committed the United States and the North Atlantic Treaty Organization (NATO) to retain US nonstrategic nuclear weapons (NSNW) stationed in Europe indefinitely. As the DDPR stated, "Nuclear weapons are a core component of NATO's overall capabilities for deterrence and defense alongside conventional and missile defense forces. The review has shown that the Alliance's nuclear force posture currently meets the criteria for an effective deterrence and defense posture."[1] This agreement on the status quo was hailed by many in the Alliance as a show of continuing commitment to the underlying deterrent foundations that buttress NATO's ultimate security guarantee to its members, as stated in Article 5 of the Washington Treaty. Yet others have argued that this was simply a way station, a temporary halt, to the vector on which Alliance nuclear policy is headed.

In other words, the consensus found in the DDPR stating that the current mission and nuclear-sharing arrangements are sufficient can be seen in either of two ways: The allies have committed to an open-ended, indefinite period of the current arrangement, or this was a politically expedient and temporary agreement that will buy the Alliance time to come up with a better and more permanent solution. In fact, goes the second argument, within a short time, NATO is likely to resume moving incrementally toward the end of its reliance on nonstrategic nuclear weapons in Europe—meaning the eventual withdrawal of the few remaining US weapons. This would not imply the end of the nuclear deterrent mission for the Alliance, however. Nor would it mean the end of the provision of extended deterrence by the United States to its European allies. But it does imply that the means for doing so may change over the coming ten to fifteen years.

This issue has returned to center stage in NATO debates for the first time in over twenty years as the result of several high-level events: the April 2010 NATO foreign ministers meeting in Tallinn, where then secretary of state Hillary Clinton provided a framework for discussions over nuclear policy with her Five Principles for a nuclear alliance; the release of the US Nuclear Posture Review (NPR) in April 2010; the US Senate's demand upon ratification of the New START treaty that negotiations over future reductions with Russia should include tactical nuclear weapons; NATO's 2010 Lisbon Summit, which resulted in a New Strategic Concept and associated documents; the Lisbon-mandated 2012 Deterrence and Defense Posture Review; and the rise of a more aggressive Russia on the Alliance's eastern border, including a new Russian military doctrine and use of military force against Ukraine in 2014.

These factors make it less likely that the Alliance will take any drastic action regarding its nuclear policy in the short term. But anti-nuclear feelings still resonate among some members of the Alliance. Therefore, this chapter discusses the possibility of applying a new model of extended deterrence to NATO should the current trend continue and the remaining US nonstrategic nuclear weapons be withdrawn from Europe. One option would be to apply the so-called Asia model of deterrence to Europe. In this model, the United States provides extended deterrence guarantees to its allies in the region using an alternative to forward-deployed weapons and delivery systems, with the ultimate deterrent being provided by the strategic forces of the nuclear members of the Alliance—principally the United States. The wording in the latest NATO Strategic Concept and DDPR sets the stage for possible changes from the current model to one more akin to that in place in Asia-Pacific, albeit with three nuclear member states that could provide protection for Europe.

While the Chicago Summit and the DDPR put a positive spin on current NATO nuclear policy, the Alliance may actually be moving toward disarmament by default, a withering away of its nuclear capabilities, on a glide path that neither the organization nor its members seem to have the motivation to correct. All recent key documents by the United States and the Alliance point in that direction, regardless of the spin put on them. Even the Chicago communiqué has been read by multiple analysts as a default nondecision favoring a continuation of the status quo. If that is the case, the Alliance needs to begin considering its options for providing Article 5 guarantees when the day arrives that there are no longer any US nuclear weapons in Europe.

Background: Nuclear Weapons in US Strategy

The ultimate purpose of US nuclear weapons today remains the same as it has been since the late 1940s: to deter an armed attack against the US homeland, its forces and interests abroad, and its friends and allies. For more than sixty years this mission has been associated in the public mind with the deterrence of an adversary's use of its own atomic weapons and, more recently, of any weapon of mass destruction (WMD). Nuclear weapons have been thought of primarily as a tool—one of many available to a nation-state, including diplomatic and economic efforts, conventional forces, arms control, and active and passive defenses—to prevent aggression of any kind against America's vital national interests.

The United States has global interests, and its military has global responsibilities. Nuclear weapons—*all* US nuclear weapons—will continue to play a vital role as the ultimate guarantor of the nation's security for the foreseeable future. The category of US nuclear weapons known as nonstrategic weapons, however, may not exist much longer. The small number of weapons of this type will remain in the US inventory, but the name of the category may soon be eliminated as a relic of the Cold War. Instead, today's nonstrategic nuclear weapons may be absorbed into the manned bomber leg of the triad in what are now referred to as strategic weapons. This reflects a growing recognition that any nuclear use would have strategic consequences and that these weapons still have a role to play in assuring allies through extended deterrence guarantees. The 2001 NPR created a new triad that included all nuclear and non-nuclear strike capabilities in one category, so in essence dual-capable aircraft (DCA)—fighter-bombers that can deliver either conventional or nonstrategic nuclear weapons—and B61 tactical nuclear bombs have already been part of the larger matrix of nuclear forces for more than a decade.[2] What this implies is that in the future, rather than just NSNW stationed on European soil, the entire US nuclear arsenal will serve the needs of extended deterrence in Europe through offshore guarantees, as it already does for America's allies in East Asia.

America's perspective on nonstrategic nuclear weapons has historically been to view them as valuable political tools for reassuring allies and also at times as having operational value as war-fighting tools against the threat of attack by a neighbor. But their current value appears to be diminishing—indeed, some analysts and politicians even see them as impediments on the road to Global Zero. Yet the United States is caught in the challenging position of having to continue guaranteeing security to other states while facing uncertainty over the future of weapons that have traditionally served to show that commitment to its friends and partners. In short, NSNW may be on the road to obsolescence, but they still serve some modest purposes that preclude their elimination in the short term. In fact, as consensus builds that any nuclear use would have strategic significance, thus eliminating the need for, and terminology of, nonstrategic nuclear weapons, these weapons and their delivery systems may be seen in the future as simply a part of the strategic forces available for a president's use in crises or conflicts.

Extended Deterrence

As a sovereign, independent nation-state, the United States' primary national security goal must be the protection of its own people, territory, and interests. This is considered a core security requirement, and the deterrent value of America's nuclear arsenal is unquestioned in this realm. But as the president stated in his 2009 Prague Speech, the United States has also promised to protect many of its friends and allies around the world.[3] It does this by extending its nuclear and conventional umbrella over more than thirty states.[4] The concept of extended deterrence simply means that one state will provide security for another state through the threat of punishment against a third party that may wish to attack or coerce the second state. It is a logical extrapolation of deterrence theory and is a commitment that is not made lightly, nor is it offered to everyone. Extended deterrence commits the United States to the possibility of going to war with another great power in order to protect a more vulnerable allied state.[5] It is a policy that extends the protection of America's military, and typically its nuclear umbrella, over friends and allies far from North America and the US homeland. The traditional US rationale for extended deterrence has been to attempt to address the danger as far as possible from its shores, fighting, if necessary, an away game. Extended deterrence does not have to be accomplished with nuclear weapons. During the Cold War, however, the two concepts were nearly always synonymous, and many of today's analyses still conflate the two ideas. In any case, when the United States chooses to give formal extended deterrence guarantees to another state, that commitment includes all measures of defense, up to and including nuclear weapons as the ultimate deterrent.[6]

The purpose of extended deterrence during the Cold War was to provide security for America's allies. This required the United States to convince potential adversaries—meaning primarily the Soviet Union—that US security commitments were genuine and that they would be carried out if necessary. In addition, extended deterrence served a number of additional purposes. It created caution among the nuclear players on the world stage; it reduced adventurism, not only by the nuclear states but by those protected by the guarantee; and it may have helped to prevent nuclear proliferation by the allies. This latter point was part of the grand bargain that the United States struck with its European allies: In return for a US security guarantee, they agreed not to pursue their own nuclear capabilities.[7] This same bargain was in place in Northeast Asia for the purpose of keeping allies such as Japan and South Korea nuclear-free.

The US umbrella also extends to other regions of the world. In Asia, the United States has long-standing security commitments to Japan through the US-Japan Security Pact.[8] Both sides have always assumed that this meant the possible use of US nuclear weapons to protect Japanese territorial sovereignty against potential aggression, Japan's antinuclear stance in its constitution notwithstanding. In 2009, the US secretary of state made a trip to Japan to proclaim publicly that this solemn commitment by the United States to defend Japan was intact in the face of North Korean military threats, and it did include the ultimate weapon.[9] The White House reiterated this commitment to extended nuclear deterrence on behalf of Japan in early 2013.[10] South Korea is also the recipient of the US nuclear security guarantee. US nuclear weapons were stationed in South Korea until 1992, when they were removed and returned to storage in North America.[11] And Australia assumes that the US nuclear umbrella extends over its territory as well, as it has declared in a succession of defense white papers (most recently in May 2013).[12]

Multiple studies have come to the conclusion that nuclear weapons are here to stay. Regardless of national objectives calling for a nuclear-free world, such weapons are likely to remain part of the global security environment for the foreseeable future and will continue to play a central role in US security policy. Because the United States has determined that continuing to provide a security guarantee for its allies remains in its vital interests, it needs to ask whether extended deterrence requires forward-based nuclear systems. This was believed to be the case during the Cold War, but today there is another model that may prove instructive. Unlike the situation in Europe,

Northeast Asia and some states in the Middle East benefit from American security guarantees without having any US nuclear weapons on their soil. Nor would such a guarantee necessarily require nuclear weapons—perhaps conventional forces or, some argue, robust multinational missile defenses could fill that requirement. Deterrence, after all, is essentially psychological, working on the perceptions of the potential adversary. Deployed weapons may not be required to assure one's allies or deter one's adversaries. If the United States were to move toward an Asian model for Europe, however, it would certainly require greater nurturing and assurances to its allies that America would be there when and if needed.

The 2010 Nuclear Posture Review

The 2010 NPR may not have gone as far toward radical reductions or policy changes as some had hoped following President Obama's Prague Speech, but it did serve as an important document that laid out the administration's goals and made some modest moves in the direction of reduced reliance on nuclear weapons.[13] It emphasized the foundational concept that "the fundamental role of US nuclear weapons, which will continue as long as nuclear weapons exist, is to deter nuclear attack on the United States, our allies, and partners."[14] It stated that the United States will continue to strengthen conventional capabilities and reduce the role of nuclear weapons in deterring non-nuclear attacks, with the objective of "making deterrence of nuclear attack on the United States or our allies and partners the sole purpose of US nuclear weapons." In the new global security environment, the United States will only consider the use of nuclear weapons "in extreme circumstances to defend the vital interests of the United States or its allies and partners."[15]

The NPR focused on five key objectives of US nuclear weapons policies and posture: (1) preventing nuclear proliferation and nuclear terrorism; (2) reducing the role of US nuclear weapons in US national security strategy; (3) maintaining strategic deterrence and stability at reduced nuclear force levels; (4) strengthening regional deterrence and reassuring US allies and partners; and (5) sustaining a safe, secure, and effective nuclear arsenal.[16] The fourth objective on this list is the one that we normally think of when we consider the role of non-strategic nuclear weapons. The NPR stated that the United States is "fully committed to strengthening bilateral and regional security ties and working with allies and partners to adapt these relationships to 21st century challenges. Such security relationships are critical in deterring potential threats, and can also serve our nonproliferation goals."[17]

Nonproliferation is served by dissuasion—"demonstrating to neighboring states that their pursuit of nuclear weapons will only undermine their goal of achieving military or political advantages"—and by reassurance to America's non-nuclear allies and partners, assuring them "that their security interests can be protected without their own nuclear deterrent capabilities."[18]

For more than sixty years the United States has provided a nuclear umbrella over its allies through a combination of means—the strategic forces of the US nuclear triad, nonstrategic nuclear weapons deployed forward in key regions, and US-based nuclear weapons that could be quickly deployed forward to meet regional contingencies. As the NPR made clear, the mix of deterrence means has varied over time and from region to region. The long-standing tangible commitment to US allies in Europe, however, has been somewhat amended since the end of the Cold War by the reduction in the number, location, and visibility of forward-deployed US nuclear weapons. Still, a small number of US nuclear weapons remain in Europe. The NPR reiterates the standard Alliance claim that "[a]lthough the risk of nuclear attack against NATO members is at an historic low, the presence of US nuclear weapons—combined with NATO's unique nuclear sharing arrangements under which non-nuclear members participate in nuclear planning and possess specially configured aircraft capable of delivering nuclear weapons—contribute to Alliance cohesion and provide reassurance to allies and partners who feel exposed to regional threats."[19] In this sense the Obama administration was paying homage to the status quo in Europe, despite the president's visionary Prague Speech. The United States also keeps "a small number of nuclear weapons stored in the United States for possible overseas deployment in support of extended deterrence to allies and partners worldwide."[20]

The United States has also relied on non-nuclear elements to strengthen regional security architectures, including a forward-based US conventional presence and effective theater ballistic missile defenses. The role of those elements of extended deterrence, according to the NPR, will increase. "As the role of nuclear weapons is reduced in US national security strategy, these non-nuclear elements will take on a greater share of the deterrence burden. Moreover, an indispensable ingredient of effective regional deterrence is not only non-nuclear but also non-military—strong, trusting political relationships between the United States and its allies and partners" as well as "enhancing regional security architectures." Strengthened regional security architectures include, according to the NPR, "effective missile defense, counter-WMD capabilities, conventional power-projection capabilities, and integrated command and control—all underwritten by strong political commitments."[21]

The US Rebalance toward Asia

In January 2012, the Obama administration released new strategic guidelines that modified the 2010 US National Security Strategy. The key concept was that the United States would rebalance its forces and its security interests away from Europe and toward regions of increasing importance and potential instability, primarily East Asia and the Middle East. As the guidelines stated:

> Europe is our principal partner in seeking global and economic security, and will remain so for the foreseeable future. At the same time, security challenges and unresolved conflicts persist in parts of Europe and Eurasia, where the United States must continue to promote regional security and Euro-Atlantic integration. The United States has enduring interests in supporting peace and prosperity in Europe as well as bolstering the strength and vitality of NATO, which is critical to the security of Europe and beyond. Most European countries are now producers of security rather than consumers of it. Combined with the drawdown in Iraq and Afghanistan, this has created a strategic opportunity to rebalance the U.S. military investment in Europe, moving from a focus on current conflicts toward a focus on future capabilities. In keeping with this evolving strategic landscape, our posture in Europe must also evolve.[22]

With reference to deterrence and the role of nuclear weapons, the guidelines stated, "It is possible that our deterrence goals can be achieved with a smaller nuclear force, which would reduce the number of nuclear weapons in our inventory as well as their role in U.S. national security strategy."[23] This shift to Asia and the Middle East comes at a time of European fatigue from years of out-of-area military operations, as well as a growing sense of security complacency in the public, during a period of economic crisis and global recession. None of these trends bode well for the European member states of the Alliance to increase their commitment to defense spending, including nuclear-sharing arrangements, even in the face of a resurgent and aggressive Russia.[24]

Keeping US Options Open

Specifically addressing the continuing importance of extended nuclear deterrence, the NPR made clear that the United States will retain the capability to forward-deploy nuclear weapons on tactical fighter-bombers and heavy bombers. In addition, the Obama administration decided to proceed with a full-scope life-extension program for the remaining B61 bombs, including safety, security, and surety enhancements. The B61-12 will be able to be carried by the F-35 Joint Strike Fighter and the B-2 bomber.[25]

Moving beyond Europe, the NPR stated that "in Asia and the Middle East—where there are no multilateral alliance structures analogous to NATO—the United States has maintained extended deterrence through bilateral alliances and security relationships and through its forward military presence and security guarantees."[26] The United States withdrew its forward-deployed nuclear weapons from the Pacific region at the end of the Cold War. This included removing nuclear weapons from naval surface vessels and general-purpose submarines, as well as from bases in South Korea. Since then, the United States has relied on "its central strategic forces and the capacity to redeploy non-strategic nuclear systems in East Asia, if needed, in times of crisis."[27] The Obama administration is "pursuing strategic dialogues with its allies and partners in East Asia and the Middle East to determine how best to cooperatively strengthen regional security architectures to enhance peace and security, and reassure them that US extended deterrence is credible and effective."[28]

Despite twenty years of US and NATO documents stating that US non-strategic nuclear weapons would be kept up to date as necessary and deployed in Europe, and that these weapons provided an essential military and political link between Europe and North America, the 2010 NPR dropped this critical phrasing.[29] So did NATO's new Strategic Concept, which was approved during the Lisbon Summit in November 2010, and the 2012 NATO Deterrence and Defense Posture Review.[30] This change in verbiage, while not highlighted by US or Alliance leaders, is nevertheless a significant departure from the standard post–Cold War deterrence phraseology and may open the door to a future Alliance decision to remove the remaining US warheads located in the European theater. In fact, the DDPR explicitly recognized this possibility, stating that the allies needed to prepare "in case NATO were to decide to reduce its reliance on non-strategic nuclear weapons based in Europe."[31]

The Role of Nonstrategic Nuclear Weapons in NATO Policy and Alliance Strategy

The level of commitment and credibility required for extended deterrence to work has less to do with how the United States feels about that commitment than it does the perceptions of the other players in the relationship. It is the mind of the protected partner that must be assured of America's commitment, and the mind of the potential adversary that must be similarly convinced of America's capabilities as well as its will to carry out its threatened response.

Some analysts have questioned whether the United States needs to continue to deploy nuclear weapons in Europe. After all, they say, it has been nearly twenty five years since the collapse of the Warsaw Pact and demise of the Soviet Union; surely these weapons are no longer needed to ensure peace in Europe. Others have raised questions about whether the United States and NATO might benefit from the removal of these weapons from bases in Europe for reasons of safety and security, as well as for cost savings. Some analysts have suggested that, in response to these concerns, the United States might consolidate its nuclear weapons at a smaller number of bases in Europe. According to another study, officials at US European Command have argued that weapons deployed outside Europe could be just as credible as forward-deployed weapons to deter an attack on NATO.[32] In fact, some observers now argue that reducing or eliminating US nuclear weapons in Europe would not only address the US Air Force's operational and security costs associated with their deployment but also could serve as a signal to Russia of NATO's intentions to address Russia's perception of the threat from NATO.[33]

Yet official NATO policy still views nonstrategic nuclear weapons as a deterrent to any potential adversary, and they also serve as a link among the NATO nations, with shared responsibility for nuclear policy planning and decision making. They also still serve as a visible reminder of the US extended deterrent and assurance of its commitment to the defense of its allies. But as a Congressional Research Service report stated, if the United States and its allies agree that this assurance can be provided with either conventional capabilities or strategic nuclear weapons, the need for forward basing in Europe may diminish. Some argue that, because these weapons play no military or political role in Europe, they no longer serve as a symbol of Alliance solidarity and cooperation. Others, however, including some officials in newer NATO member states, have argued that US nonstrategic nuclear weapons in Europe not only remain relevant militarily, in some circumstances, but that they are an essential indicator of the US commitment to NATO security and solidarity.[34]

Political trends in Europe may accelerate these changes to US forward deployment of nonstrategic nuclear weapons. A number of factors appear to be driving the Alliance toward ending the nuclear mission—or at least removing the remaining US warheads.[35] Russia has had a strategy for years that uses diplomatic and political pressure against the United States and its allies in Europe to remove the remaining US warheads. The European allies are suffering from two generations of military and particularly nuclear malaise, and some seem unwilling to continue this effort given the political and economic costs of buying a next generation of nuclear-capable aircraft. In addition, the European states are tired after nearly twenty years of out-of-area military operations in the Balkans, Southwest Asia, and North Africa. This fatigue may carry over to planning for future DCA requirements and responsibilities. In addition, the pending technical expiration of the service life of both the warheads and their delivery systems means that a decision has to be made to continue the NATO nuclear deterrence mission. The United States has instituted a life-extension program for the B61 bomb and is purchasing nuclear-capable variants of the F-35 Joint Strike Fighter, but it is enjoying little support for either of these programs from its European allies.

Organizational changes in recent years within NATO's Nuclear Policy Directorate and the Supreme Headquarters Allied Powers Europe (SHAPE) Nuclear Planning office have marginalized the nuclear mission to a considerable extent.[36] For example, until recently the Nuclear Planning Directorate at NATO headquarters was headed by a deputy assistant secretary general with direct access to defense and foreign ministers and who directly advised the secretary general on issues regarding NATO's nuclear deterrence posture. That position has been downgraded to a staff officer position who must report through three levels of bureaucracy and who no longer has direct access to the secretary general. The directorate was moved from the policy and plans division to a new Emerging Security Challenges Division, which is focused as much on cyber- and energy security threats as it is on nuclear policy. Further, in the past four years the directorate has had its staff reduced by more than 25 percent, and its budget has been cut to the point where it is increasingly difficult to meet all its staffing obligations and policy requirements. The Nuclear Planning Group (NPG), which used to meet at least once and sometimes twice per week, now meets at most only biweekly, and staff members have difficulty fulfilling requests from Allies to meet and discuss issues related to NATO's deterrence posture. Of equal concern is the fact that the ability of SHAPE's Nuclear Planning staff members to meet their responsibilities has suffered due to significant reductions in manning. Those officers who remain have been moved into smaller offices with much-reduced visibility and responsibilities. Many positions throughout the Supreme Allied Commander-Europe (SACEUR) staff have been left unfilled or have been filled by those not trained in the nuclear mission, or who were given additional duties that left little time for fulfilling the nuclear mission.

Within the Office of the Secretary of Defense, the civilian side of the US Department of Defense, similar if less public changes have reduced the importance of the nuclear mission. It is no secret that the US Air Force has never liked this mission and has little in the way of US-based DCA capabilities to back up existing mission requirements in Europe or Asia. As one reflection of these changes, more than a decade ago NATO increased its response time for alert aircraft from *minutes*, as it was during the Cold War, to *weeks*—the result of the Alliance's recognition of a changed international security environment, as well as these organizational and operational changes.[37]

Various schools of thought exist within elite US circles about the value, role, and future of NSNW in Europe. These perspectives range from traditional supporters to believers in selective engagement, to proponents of arms control, to disarmament advocates.[38] In fact, there are forcefully expressed arguments on both sides of the debate over whether to maintain or eliminate the remaining US nuclear weapons in Europe. On the one hand, all parties agree that these weapons have provided a means of ensuring coupling, transatlantic linkages, military capabilities against an uncertain future, and risk and burden sharing. On the other hand, some allies see benefits to further reductions in the remaining arsenal in the cause of global disarmament—and they point to President Barack Obama's 2009 Prague Agenda as justification for some of those views. Coupling may be strong enough, they argue, through conventional burden sharing or a new emphasis on cooperative missile defense. The long history of Alliance cooperation may preclude the necessity for continued deployment of nuclear weapons for that purpose. The contribution of a few hundred invisible weapons to coupling, according to this argument, is minimal, so the benefits of removing US nuclear weapons may exceed those of retaining them.

Any of the factors pushing for the elimination of the remaining US weapons in Europe could be accelerated by more dramatic and immediate events, such as a nuclear accident or incident in Europe involving US weapons, a decision to end the US mission arbitrarily (by either the United States, NATO, or one or more of the host nation allies), or a decision to use the remaining NSNW as bargaining chips in arms control negotiations with Russia. Any of these events would precipitate a much more drastic end to the US forward-deployed mission. Kicking the can down the road, as the DDPR did, would allow the Alliance to maintain the status quo for a few more years, but the ultimate long-term result will be the withering away of the mission. One analyst has called this possibility "disarmament by default."[39]

At their meeting in Tallinn, Estonia, in April 2010, NATO's foreign ministers sought to balance the views of those nations who sought the removal of the weapons with those who argued that these weapons were still relevant to their security and to NATO's solidarity. At the conclusion of the meeting, then Secretary of State Clinton said that the United States was not opposed to reductions in the number of US nuclear weapons in Europe but that the removal of these weapons should be linked to a parallel reduction in the number of Russian nonstrategic nuclear weapons. The foreign ministers also agreed that no nuclear weapons would be removed from Europe unless all twenty-eight member states of NATO agreed.[40]

For a time in recent years, some allied nations were pushing the idea that, in the near term, missile defenses could supplant the function performed by US nuclear weapons in Europe either in terms of providing deterrence or in serving as a military or political replacement for the existing Alliance nuclear-sharing function. Yet that seems to be unrealistic for multiple reasons. Missile defenses are unlikely to be able to achieve one or both of these goals until the arrival of a technology and weapons regime in which the defense is superior to offense. The transition to such a defense-dominant world, one in which, as President Ronald Reagan envisioned, nuclear weapons would have become "impotent and obsolete," does not appear to be likely anytime soon, despite President Obama's call for a nuclear-free world.[41] The Alliance, while supporting the development and deployment of missile defenses to protect Europe, now officially recognizes the limitations inherent in trying to replace nuclear weapons with missile defenses as the glue holding the Alliance together in NATO risk and burden sharing. The 2014 Wales Summit declaration expressed it clearly: "missile defense can complement the role of nuclear weapons; it cannot substitute for them."[42]

NATO's Nuclear Alternatives

The interaction among the factors already described may lead the Alliance to adopt one of at least thirteen identifiable options for its nuclear future.[43] As shown in figure 2.1, these range from modernization of the force to a continuation of the status quo, to withdrawal of remaining American weapons, to the abdication of a nuclear role for the Alliance.

The more intriguing insights come from an examination of the eleven options that fall between the two extremes, particularly the multitude of possibilities for replacing US weapons if they were withdrawn, but the Alliance wanted to continue to have a nuclear deterrent of some type. In that case, one can envision a number of potential alternatives to the current nuclear deployment pattern and operational planning assumptions that would still

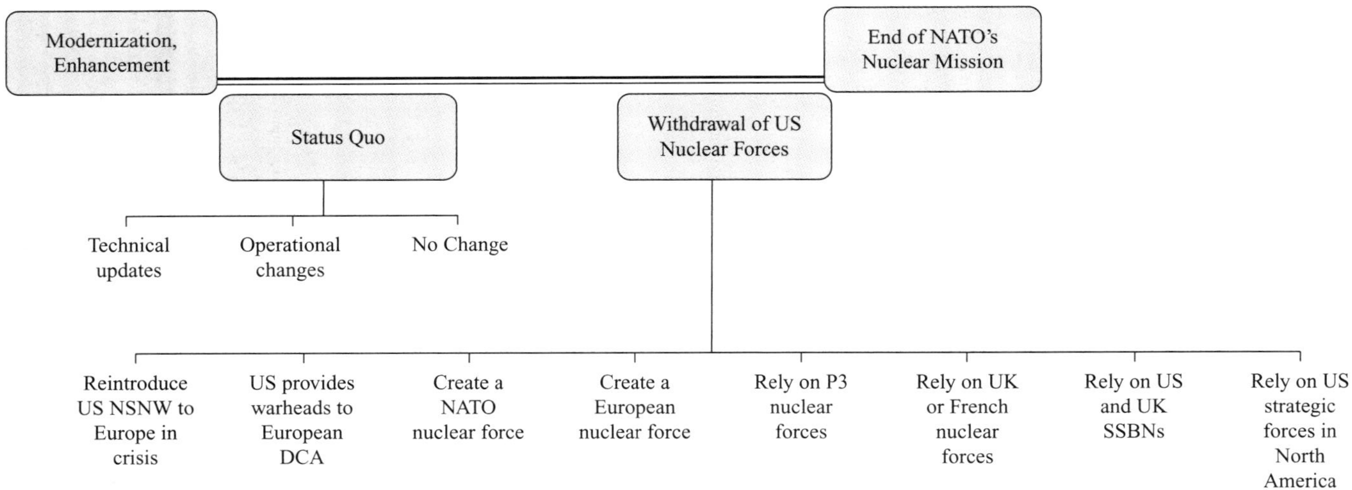

Figure 2.1. NATO's Nuclear Alternatives Spectrum of Options

provide a nuclear deterrent umbrella for the Alliance.[44] For the moment, of course, NATO has chosen to stick with the status quo, as explained in the 2012 DDPR. But that consensus may not last.

Modernization and Enhancement

Modernization and enhancement of NATO's nuclear forces constitute the current preferred option. In addition to US life-extension programs, security upgrades, and new dual-capable aircraft, the allies concerned could decide to replace their current Tornado, F-15, and F-16 fleets with a new type of aircraft, such as the nuclear-certified F-35 Joint Strike Fighter. This would maintain the DCA role into the next generation. As the 2010 NPR stated, the United States is already pursuing this F-35 capability in order to provide the Alliance with the option of retaining a DCA mission. Similarly, the United States has decided to pursue a service life-extension program for its arsenal of B61 bombs—the type currently stored in Europe for use by NATO DCA. One can call these steps modernization or simply technical updates to maintain the status quo. Either way, the fact that the United States took such steps under a president who has expressed a vision of nuclear disarmament showed a significant commitment to assuring its allies and maintaining this element of the Alliance's deterrence posture.

Status Quo

Some variant of the status quo is officially preferred by every member state and was the choice of the Alliance in its consensus agreement in the DDPR released at the Chicago Summit in May 2012. New rationales that could justify keeping or enhancing NATO's nuclear weapons may include deterring chemical or biological weapons threats from the Middle East and North Africa, deterring a nuclear-armed Iran, providing protection for deployed NATO forces by offering mobile deterrent capabilities, or enhancing deterrence of Russia on behalf of the Alliance's Central European members. Variants of the status quo include technical updates, operational changes, and no change at all.

TECHNICAL UPDATES

This first category involves continued maintenance, upkeep, and modest technological improvements that could lead to improved capabilities. Even without a commitment to that level of investment, however, any decision to continue relying on NATO's long-standing deterrent forces as provided by the United States will require a renewed commitment to investment in modernized weapons, training, delivery systems, maintenance, and security issues given the age of the existing systems in place. The life-extension program for the B61 bomb is one step in this direction. The European DCA states could decide to replace their aging F-15 and F-16 fleets with nuclear-capable F-35s, with or without Germany as a partner in that mission. Germany could decide to pay for the necessary hardware and software upgrades to make its new Eurofighter fleet nuclear-capable.

OPERATIONAL CHANGES

A second broad category under the status quo would include operational changes to the way NATO thinks about its nuclear strategy and how best to achieve its twin goals of effective deterrence and assurance. For example, the Allies could decide to move all the US nuclear weapons to storage sites in Southern Europe. Or one or more of the current DCA states may decide that it no longer wishes to participate in the Alliance's nuclear mission, focusing instead on so-called role-specific tasking contributions to Alliance security—much as the new East European member states must do now and as some non-DCA member states have always done. This could precipitate changes to force deployments, DCA responsibilities, or even the inclusion of new states as members of the DCA club as long as NATO abides by its three no's commitment to Russia not to deploy nuclear weapons on the soil of new member states.[45] One day, for example, we might see Polish F-16s on alert at a Belgian base prepared to carry American bombs. Short of such a major step, new member states may undertake roles in nuclear crisis management operations such as air refueling, combat air support, intelligence, surveillance, and reconnaissance or any of the myriad functions that would make up a combined strike package. Alternatively, the United States could continue to perform its historical role of nuclear delivery in Europe while all the European DCA states give up that mission.

NO CHANGE

The third option, and the preferred choice over the past two decades among most member states, is to do nothing to change the status quo. "Let sleeping dogs lie" is not a policy, but it seems to be the preferred approach by member state governments that believe the current posture is the best available choice. The Alliance has a long history of muddling through and eventually reaching agreement on divisive issues. A significant number of Allies and staff members in NATO headquarters believe that dual-capable aircraft and their associated systems for nuclear sharing provide the best means of ensuring the widest possible risk and responsibility sharing within the Alliance. With some modest commitments to modernization, they argue, DCA can continue to do so indefinitely. As such, the status quo should be maintained.

One could argue, however, that no decision to select a replacement dual-capable aircraft in the near term would count as a decision, too. Nothing would change in the short term, but that would then leave the Alliance at the whim of procurement decisions, with ambivalence, neglect, and obsolescence determining the future without a conscious decision by the allies. This is, in fact, the alternative preferred by some allies. They would rather not talk about it and not change the direction of current procurement plans, with the result that eventually the DCA mission would simply wither away. Alternatively, without European support for this mission, the United States might decide that there is no longer a need for its forces in Europe and could choose to withdraw its weapons unilaterally. Secretary of Defense Robert Gates warned of the possibility that America will tire of its open-ended, expensive commitment to European security in his farewell speech at NATO headquarters in June 2011.[46]

End of NATO's Nuclear Mission

The US withdrawal of its nuclear weapons and a NATO renunciation of its reliance on a nuclear deterrent would be the most extreme alternative, and one that is particularly unlikely. One of the Clinton principles from Tallinn states that "as long as nuclear weapons exist, NATO will remain a nuclear alliance." The same wording appeared in the new Strategic Concept. This option also has the greatest potential for causing irrevocable rifts in the Alliance. On the other hand, should the Alliance survive such a change, many of the current coupling functions could be retained. The NPG, for example, could be kept as a consultative body, perhaps with a new name to reflect its non-nuclear purpose. It is important to remember, of course, that as long as NATO survives as a political institution, it will remain a de facto nuclear alliance because three of its members have independent atomic arsenals.

Many in NATO fear any alternative that involves the removal of US nuclear weapons. Doing so in hopes that Russia would follow suit is dangerous, they argue. Several new member states from Central and Eastern Europe in particular see American extended deterrence guarantees as the bedrock foundation of the Article 5 commitments of the Washington Treaty for which they signed up. One senior NATO official has made the claim that the removal of U.S weapons from Europe "would be the beginning of the end of the Alliance."[47] On the other hand, others advocate the immediate and complete withdrawal of US weapons for the simple reason that the Alliance can no longer answer the foundational question of the purpose of those weapons in Europe. Removal would eliminate the last NATO tactical nuclear weapons on European soil, save money, and appease those in Russia who point to NATO's nuclear forces as proof of its aggressive nature.[48]

US Withdrawal but Continued NATO Reliance on Some Form of Nuclear Deterrent

This alternative carries the most possibilities for future nuclear options. Some are obviously less likely than others, but all are possible and therefore worthy of consideration. Some of these options were apparently considered by the High Level Group and the Group of Experts in the studies that led up to the Lisbon Summit, as well as in DDPR discussions. Under this scenario, the United States withdraws its weapons but keeps the infrastructure in place in order to reintroduce weapons in a crisis. One way to reduce public criticism of the current situation would be to remove all remaining US warheads from Europe and announce the move for public relations purposes. But the Alliance would keep the technical and physical infrastructure associated with nuclear sharing—including the storage sites and associated security forces—in place so that the warheads could be reintroduced to the theater and mated with their DCA delivery vehicles quickly in a crisis. Given the Alliance's current nuclear response time using NATO DCA (measured in weeks or months), and the ability to use realistic weapons trainers (practice bombs) to exercise the flight and maintenance crews, this type of virtual nuclear sharing could technically work. But it would be politically challenging and nearly as expensive as if the weapons were still in place. Would allied governments maintain the investments for weapon site security, aircraft certification, training, personnel reliability programs, and so forth if the weapons were not in Europe?

The fact that the Alliance has not yet taken this step reflects concerns that political pressures might be too great ever to allow the United States to reintroduce such weapons in Europe, particularly in a crisis when fears of taking steps that escalate tensions would abound. There is also some concern that, without the actual weapons on their soil, the European members of the Alliance may lose their interest in the weapons. Some proponents of the status quo fear that NATO's nuclear policy may fade into irrelevance if the real weapons are withdrawn.

THE UNITED STATES CONTINUES TO SUPPLY WARHEADS FOR EUROPEAN DCA

In this alternative, the United States would withdraw its nuclear-capable aircraft from the European theater or at least end the US DCA role in a NATO nuclear delivery mission. The other NATO states with a DCA responsibility would continue to carry out that mission, however, under dual-key arrangements with the United States for US warheads stored either in Europe or in the United States. This would resolve many of the US Air Force's concerns about the costs of continuing to support the European DCA mission and possibly its security concerns about weapons storage areas were the weapons stored outside Europe. This option might also prove valuable to American arguments to the world community about its commitment to the Nuclear Nonproliferation Treaty and its Article VI disarmament measures while still providing a nuclear guarantee to NATO. It would show a level of Alliance cohesion and commitment to nuclear deterrence, and maintain the linkage between Europe and North America. However, while NATO has always planned any nuclear strike mission to include several member states' aircraft to avoid singularity by any one nation, it was understood that any mission would most likely include one or more American jets in the package. The absence of US DCA might make such an option difficult to carry out politically, particularly given recent calls by several European states for the end of their nuclear-sharing commitments.

CREATE A NATO NUCLEAR FORCE

This option could be accomplished with the development of a NATO combined air wing with DCA responsibilities, modeled along the lines of NATO's Airborne Warning and Control System (AWACS) operation. Another possibility would be an internationally manned vessel, either a strategic nuclear submarine (SSBN) with submarine-launched ballistic missiles (SLBMs), perhaps a retired British Trident boat or a new submarine, or some other option, such as was considered in the Multilateral Force (MLF) concept of the 1960s. The MLF, for example, envisioned intermediate-range ballistic missiles on a vessel, such as a barge or surface combatant, manned by a multinational crew with representation from at least three European nations at all times. This would avoid concerns over singularity and would ensure a multinational decision to carry out an order to launch, with three hands on the trigger (or on the lock).[49] But this alternative is also unlikely given the historical memory of the MLF concept and the likely unwillingness of member states to rely on a committee decision regarding nuclear strike systems.

CREATE A EUROPEAN NUCLEAR FORCE

A European nuclear force could be provided by Britain, France, a joint commitment by those two nations, or some type of new collective European nuclear force, possibly under the auspices of the European Union (EU). France has in the past implied its openness to discuss such an arrangement. Of course, this alternative raises a lot of questions, not least of which is the appropriate organizational venue for debating the issue. Some non-NATO EU members (such as Ireland or Sweden) object to nuclear deterrence in principle. The new nuclear force would need a body equivalent to NATO's Nuclear Planning Group as its organizational and consultative heart.

RELY ON THE NUCLEAR FORCES OF THE NATO P3

Nuclear deterrence and assurance could be provided for NATO without the requirement for US weapons based in Europe by simply declaring that the three allies with nuclear weapons would extend their security guarantees over their neighbors and allies. The United States, Great Britain, and France (the P3) could rely on their strategic weapons and delivery systems to extend a deterrence umbrella over the Alliance without the nuclear-sharing arrangements currently found in NATO. The NPG might become simply a vehicle for the P3 states to announce their (possibly coordinated) national decisions regarding nuclear weapons and strategy. Of course, even under these circumstances France may not wish to participate in such an organization given its refusal since 1967 to join the NPG.

RELY ON BRITISH OR FRENCH NUCLEAR FORCES

The United Kingdom has committed its nuclear forces to NATO, subject to supreme national interest clauses, since 1962. Since 1972, France has declared that its deterrent offers de facto protection to its neighbors and allies. The allies recognized the contributions of France and the United Kingdom to NATO's overall deterrent posture in the 1974 Ottawa Declaration and in the

1991, 1999, and 2010 Strategic Concepts. In 2006, President Jacques Chirac said, "The development of the European Security and Defense Policy, the growing interweaving of the interests of the European Union countries, and the solidarity that now exists between [sic] them, make French nuclear deterrence, by its very existence, a core element in the security of the European continent."[50] These commitments could be made more explicit following removal of the remaining US tactical weapons. But it is not clear whether all European allies would regard British or French protection as an adequate substitute for US nuclear forces in Europe.

RELY ON US AND UK SSBN FORCES

Throughout the Cold War the United States supposedly dedicated a certain number of SLBMs in its Atlantic fleet to the Supreme Allied Commander-Europe in time of war as part of the single integrated operational plan. That commitment may still be in place today, as is the continuing commitment of Britain's Trident fleet to NATO assignments. It would be fairly simple to make those commitments more public and to codify them in NATO documents as necessary to enhance their deterrent value. France might be persuaded to commit some portion of its SSBN forces to a naval deterrent for NATO as well.

RELY ON US STRATEGIC FORCES BASED IN NORTH AMERICA

This is a concept utilized in other parts of the world—including the so-called East Asia model—and one that would seem to provide a simple solution to Europe's conundrum. But what effect would such a dramatic shift in the Alliance correlation of forces have on deterrence credibility in the eyes of NATO's adversaries? One of the rationales for NSNW based in Europe during the Cold War, after all, was to ensure coupling and a seamless web of deterrence based on the deliberate escalation from conventional forces to tactical nuclear weapons to US strategic forces based at sea and in North America. This alternative would require a new level of assurance to allies that have grown to expect that middle rung of the escalatory ladder to remain in place in Europe. The experience of America's allies in Northeast Asia may be instructive in this regard. South Korea and Japan, both beneficiaries of the Asia model of extended deterrence, are today apparently less assured of US deterrence guarantees than they were when US weapons were physically located in the Pacific theater.

The East Asia Model

Many Europeans seem to be suggesting the more relaxed East Asia model may be appropriate for future extended deterrence guarantees to Europe, and some of the NATO members would prefer less American leadership. At the same time, some Asian allies would prefer a version of the more formalized NATO model. But can or will the United States swap its thinking on the two regional approaches? The United States has spent nearly forty years reducing its presence in Asia, including ending all nuclear stationing in the region. It is now doing much the same in Europe. Does it want to return to deeper involvement in the Asia-Pacific region? The NPR's call for dual-capable F-35s that can be globally deployed, with upgraded B61 bombs, seems to imply that is the case. So does President Obama's January 2012 pivot toward Asia in his revised defense priorities.[51]

When considering the application of the two models to different regions of the world, difficulties and obstacles become immediately apparent.[52] These challenges are more onerous when trying to create a NATO-type nuclear-sharing arrangement with America's allies in East Asia than they would be to do the converse: changing European extended deterrence into a variant of the Asia model. For the most part, applying the East Asia model to Europe would simply require the deconstruction of many Cold War organizational and operational arrangements. For example, the Alliance would no longer rely on forward-deployed US nuclear warheads based in Europe but instead would count on the strategic forces of the United States (and the other nuclear member states of NATO, France and the United Kingdom) to provide extended deterrence from over the horizon. As a result, the Nuclear Planning Group may or may not remain as a consulting and coordinating body because there would be little in the way of coordination left to be discussed. Those states with nuclear-capable aircraft and dual-key arrangements would ostensibly end their responsibilities. The remaining US warheads in Europe would be returned to the continental United States. The munitions storage sites may be closed or may be put in a cold storage status for the unlikely but possible return of US warheads to the theater in a crisis. Theater nuclear planning, already emasculated from its Cold War era size and level of importance at SHAPE, may be eliminated completely, or it could be retained as a possible adaptive planning cell at US European Command or US Strategic Command. Other changes would naturally follow. In short, the Alliance would be more or less out of the nuclear business, relying on the three nuclear allies to provide for its protection without the assurance provided by in-theater forces. Some allies will not like that arrangement; others may find it a relief to be

Table 2.1. Comparing the NATO and East Asia Models of Extended Deterrence

	NATO Model	*East Asia Model*
Threat	Cold War: USSR Today: existential (but really Iran and a resurgent Russia)	North Korea, potentially China
Commitment	Multilateral collective defense organization; Washington Treaty, Article 5; high visibility, nuclear sharing, strong cultural and historical ties	Bilateral with Japan and South Korea; Australia-New Zealand-US Treaty for Australia; all low profile
Types of Systems Deployed	Everything; focus today on DCA with B61 bomb, backed by strategic forces; also large conventional forces and theater missile defenses	No nuclear systems, modest conventional forces, growing theater missile defenses
Consultative Arrangements	Formalized and cooperative: Nuclear Planning Group, High Level Group, Defense Committee, NATO summits	Modest bilateral consulting, increasingly institutionalized
Location of Systems	In theater and offshore	Over the horizon (the United States calls this continuous presence through regional deployments)
Regional Factors	Allies are geographically contiguous; most are members of the European Union, similar cultures	Diverse states, each facing a distinct threat

rid of the burdens associated with DCA missions. Table 2.1 compares some of the features of the two models of US extended deterrence.

Conclusion

As President Obama observed in his strategic guidance to the US military, announced on January 5, 2012, "our nation is at a moment of transition."[53] He was referring to the end of the Iraq War and increasing fiscal constraints, but this was equally true for the coming decisions the United States would have to make regarding its remaining nonstrategic nuclear forces. The primary missions of the US armed forces will continue to include deterring and defeating aggression, and they must therefore be "capable of denying the objectives of—or imposing unacceptable costs on—an opportunistic aggressor."[54] While this mission can be conducted using various types of military force, for three generations, such language has served as code for nuclear weapons. So one of the military's continuing missions will be to maintain a safe, secure, and effective nuclear deterrent. As the 2010 NPR and 2012 US revised strategic policy guidance have stated, "As long as nuclear weapons remain in existence, the United States will maintain a safe, secure, and effective arsenal . . . that can under any circumstances confront an adversary with the prospect of unacceptable damage, both to deter potential adversaries and to assure US allies and other security partners that they can count on America's security commitments."[55] These views have been echoed by NATO in similar language found in the 2010 Strategic Concept, 2012 DDPR, and 2014 Wales Summit declaration.

While these weapons may one day disappear from Europe, NATO will remain at the core of US national security strategy and its international commitments. As the 2010 US National Security Strategy stated,

> Our relationship with our European allies remains the cornerstone for US engagement with the world, and a catalyst for international action. We will engage with our allies bilaterally, and pursue close consultation on a broad range of security and economic issues. The North Atlantic Treaty Organization is the pre-eminent security alliance in the world today. We are committed to ensuring that NATO is able to address the full range of 21st century challenges, while serving as a foundation of European security.[56]

America has enduring national security interests, and nuclear weapons remain a vital part of ensuring that security. As the emphasis for US security shifts from Europe to the Middle East and the Pacific Rim over the coming decades, the country may find that today's nonstrategic nuclear weapons will continue to play a similar role in assuring allies in those regions as they did for generations of Europeans. They may no longer be called nonstrategic, and they may find themselves lumped together with other nuclear warheads, bombs, and strategic delivery systems that have deterrence and extended deterrence responsibilities. But even if no longer a discrete category of weapons, the political and military need for such weapons will continue to exist for the foreseeable future. This does not imply, however, that they will necessarily continue to be deployed in Europe.

The United States today maintains its smallest arsenal of nuclear weapons since the 1950s, and the numbers continue to decrease. There is less concern over central nuclear war with a major global adversary. Yet as the president said in Prague, and the NPR reiterated, "The threat of global nuclear war has become remote, but the risk of nuclear attack has increased."[57] Therefore we can expect the United States, as well as the other nuclear powers of the world, to maintain at least a small but robust inventory of nuclear weapons for years to come. They will continue to serve as they always have: as the ultimate guarantor of US resolve, power, and national security, with valuable spin-off benefits for those states over whom the United States provides an extended deterrence umbrella.

Notes

1. *Deterrence and Defense Posture Review*, NATO Press Release (2012) 063, Chicago, May 20, 2012, para. 8, http://www.nato.int/cps/en/natolive/official_texts_87597.htm?mode=pressrelease.

2. J. D. Crouch, "Special Briefing on the Nuclear Posture Review," January 9, 2002, http://www.defenselink.mil/news/Jan2002/t01092002_t0109npr.html.

3. Barack Obama, "Remarks by President Barack Obama," Hradcany Square, Prague, Czech Republic, April 5, 2009, www.whitehouse.gov/the_press_office/Remarks-By-President-Barack-Obama_In-Prague.

4. The exact number of states under America's security umbrella remains vague. A recently retired senior Department of Defense (DoD) official often referred to the number of states covered by US nuclear deterrence guarantees as "up to 40."

5. An excellent overview of deterrence can be found in Austin Long, *Deterrence from Cold War to Long War: Lessons from Six Decades of RAND Research* (Santa Monica, CA: The RAND Corporation, 2008). See also Amy F. Woolf, "Nuclear Weapons in US National Security Policy: Past, Present, and Prospects," *CRS Report for Congress*, RL34226 (Washington, DC: Congressional Research Service, 2011); *US Nuclear Deterrence in the 21st Century: Getting It Right* (Washington, DC: The New Deterrent Working Group, July 2009); and Amy F. Woolf, "US Nuclear Weapons:

Changes in Policy and Force Structure," *CRS Report for Congress*, RL31623 (Washington, DC: Congressional Research Service, 2012, updated less regularly). For more on extended deterrence, see Long, *Deterrence from Cold War to Long War;* Thomas Scheber, "Contemporary Challenges for Extended Deterrence," unpublished paper for National Institute of Public Policy, Washington, DC, 2009; Clark Murdock and Jessica Yeats, "Summary of Findings and Recommendations from June 3, 2009, Workshop on Extended Deterrence," unpublished PPT presentation, Center for Strategic and International Studies, Washington, DC, August 4, 2009; and Steven Pifer et al., "U.S. Nuclear and Extended Deterrence: Considerations and Challenges," *Brookings Arms Control Series* no.3, May 2010.

6. See John Lewis Gaddis, *The Long Peace: Inquiries into the History of the Cold War* (Oxford, UK: Oxford University Press, 1989).

7. With two notable exceptions, of course: Great Britain and France. For the rationale behind that decision, see Thomas Devine, "Extended Deterrence and Nuclear Nonproliferation: Lessons from European and East Asian Regimes Applied to the Middle East," *Nuclear Scholars Initiative: Project on Nuclear Issues* (Washington, DC: Center for Strategic and International Studies, December 2011): 33–43.

8. Officially the "Treaty of Mutual Cooperation and Security between Japan and the United States of America," signed January 1960, http://www.mofa.go.jp/region/n-america/us/q&a/ref/1.html.

9. According to news reports, the secretary of state told the Japanese foreign minister, "Japan is a treaty ally of the United States, and . . . reaffirmed the U.S. commitment to the defense of Japan, including nuclear deterrents [sic]." Jim Garamone, "Secretary of State Clinton Meets Japanese Leaders on First Leg of Asian Tour," *Military News*, February 18, 2009, http://www.2010military.com/military-news-story.cfm?textnewsid=2747.

10. Office of the Press Secretary, The White House, "Readout of the President's Call with Japanese Prime Minister Shinzo Abe," 13 February 2013 at https://www.whitehouse.gov/the-press-office/2013/02/13/readout-presidents-call-japanese-prime-minister-shinzo-abe.

11. "The Withdrawal of U.S. Nuclear Weapons from South Korea," The Nuclear Information Project, http://www.nukestrat.com/korea/withdrawal.htm.

12. *Defense White Paper 2013: Defending Australia and Its National Interests* (Australian Defense Department, May 3, 2013), http://www.defense.gov.au/whitepaper2013/; also Richard Tanter, "Rethinking Extended Nuclear Deterrence in the Defense of Australia," *The Asia Pacific Journal: Japan Focus*, December 14, 2009, http://www.japanfocus.org/-richard-tanter/3269.

13. For further examination of the development of the NPR, see David Hoffman, "Obama's Atomic Choices: Inside the Making of U.S. Nuclear Policy," *Foreign Policy*, April 28, 2010.

14. *Nuclear Posture Review Report* (Washington, DC: Department of Defense, April 2010), vii. [Hereafter NPR.]

15. Ibid., viii–ix.

16. Ibid., iii.

17. Ibid., xii.

18. Ibid.

19. Ibid., 32.

20. It is unclear if the wording in the NPR was referring to the soon-to-be-retired TLAM-N, in storage in the United States, or more broadly to other NSNW, including B61 bombs.

21. NPR, 32–33.

22. "Sustaining U.S. Global Leadership: Priorities for 21st Century Defense," Department of Defense, January 2012, 2–3.

23. Ibid., 5.

24. Despite the lukewarm Alliance commitment made at the September 2014 Wales Summit to try and achieve the goal of defense budgets equal to 2 percent of each member state's gross domestic product within a decade.

25. The NPR made clear that "[t]hese decisions do not presume what NATO will decide about future deterrence requirements, but are intended to keep the Alliance's options open and provide capabilities to support other U.S. commitments," 35.

26. Ibid., 32.

27. Ibid.

28. Ibid.

29. One example of the previous phrasing, which appeared in every NATO document since 1990 through 2010, including the 1991 and 1999 Strategic Concepts: "the presence of US nuclear forces based in Europe, committed to NATO, reinforces the political and military link between the European and North American members of the Alliance." (*NATO/OTAN Handbook*, Brussels: NATO Office of Information and Press, 2001, 56). This exact wording was duplicated in the 2006 version of the *Handbook*. The 1999 NATO Strategic Concept, repeating the nuclear paragraphs from the 1991 version of that document, included this phrase: "The presence of United States conventional and nuclear forces in Europe remains vital to the security of Europe, which is inseparably linked to that of North America" (The Alliance's Strategic Concept, April 24, 1999, para. 42, www.nato.int/cps/en/natolive/official_texts_27433.htm).

30. "Active Engagement, Modern Defense: Strategic Concept for the Defense and Security of the Members of the North Atlantic Treaty Organisation," adopted by the Heads of State and Government in Lisbon, November 19, 2010, www.nato.int/lisbon2010/strategic-concept-2010-eng.pdf.

31. *Deterrence and Defense Posture Review*, para.12.

32. Amy F. Woolf, *Nonstrategic Nuclear Weapons*, *CRS Report for Congress*, RL32572 (Washington, DC: Congressional Research Service, February 2011), 26. See also Hans Kristensen, "Non-Strategic Nuclear Weapons," Federation of the American Scientists, May 2012, http://www.fas.org/_docs/Non_Strategic_Nuclear_Weapons.pdf.

33. Kristensen, "Non-Strategic Nuclear Weapons."

34. Woolf, *Nonstrategic Nuclear Weapons*, 24. See also Simon Lunn, "NATO Nuclear Policy—Reflections on Lisbon and Looking Ahead," draft chapter for *The NTI Study on Nuclear Weapons and NATO*, May 6, 2011; and Paul Shulte, "Is NATO's Nuclear Deterrence Policy a Relic of the Cold War?" *Policy Outlook*, Carnegie Endowment for International Peace, November 17, 2010.

35. For representative arguments about the European social situation and NATO nuclear policy, see Jeffrey A. Larsen, "The Future of U.S. Non-Strategic Nuclear Weapons and Implications for NATO: Drifting Toward the Foreseeable Future,"

Final Report from the 2005–06 Manfred Wörner Fellowship, NATO Headquarters, December 2006, www.nato.int/acad/fellow/05-06/larsen.pdf; Lunn, "NATO Nuclear Policy"; and Bruno Tertrais, "Extended Deterrence: Alive and Changing," *The Interpreter*, Lowy Institute for International Policy, February 2, 2011, www.lowyinterpreter.org/post/2011/02/02/Extended-Deterrence-Alive-and-Changing.

36. My thanks to a former office director for clarifying some of the relationships and recent changes within NATO's nuclear-planning structure.

37. "NATO's Nuclear Forces in the New Security Environment," *NATO Issue Brief*, NATO Headquarters, Brussels, June 2004. In addition, during the Cold War two US air bases in the United States—Cannon, New Mexico, and Seymour-Johnson, North Carolina—had responsibilities to train for and support the DCA role in Europe, but that is no longer the case.

38. David Yost reviewed these distinctive views and outlined the key questions under debate in "The U.S. Debate on NATO Nuclear Deterrence," *International Affairs* 87, no. 6 (2011): 1401–38.

39. Steven Pifer, "NATO, Nuclear Weapons, and Arms Control," *Arms Control Series* no. 7, The Brookings Institution, July 2011; and Steven Pifer, "The United States, NATO's Strategic Concept, and Nuclear Issues: Perspectives and Proposals in the NATO Policy Debate," Arms Control Association and British-American Information Committee, May 2011.

40. Woolf, *Nonstrategic Nuclear Weapons*, 25.

41. Ronald Reagan, "Address to the Nation on Defense and National Security," March 3, 1983, http://www.atomicarchive.com/Docs/Missile/Starwars.shtml.

42. "Wales Summit Declaration Issued by the Heads of State and Government participating in the meeting of the North Atlantic Council in Wales from 4 to 5 September 2014," para. 52, http://www.nato.int/cps/po/natohq/official_texts_112964.htm.

43. Portions of this section were previously published in Jeffrey A. Larsen, "Future Options for NATO Nuclear Policy," *Issue Brief*, The Atlantic Council, August 2011, http://www.acus.org/publication/future-options-nato-nuclear-policy.

44. Similar arguments have been made by Karl-Heinz Kamp and Robertus C. N. Remkes in "Options for NATO Nuclear Sharing Arrangements," *Nuclear Threat Initiative*, November 17, 2011, http://www.nti.org/analysis/articles/options-nato-nuclear-sharing-arrangements/; and Karl-Heinz Kamp, "NATO's Nuclear Weapons in Europe: Beyond 'Yes' or 'No,'" NATO Defense College Research Division, Research Report no. 61, September 2010, http://www.ndc.nato.int/research/series.php?icode=1.

45. In 1997, NATO made a political commitment to Russia that if it expanded its membership, the Alliance would have "no intention, no need, and no plans" to deploy nuclear weapons on the territory of the new member states. See "Founding Act on Mutual Relations, Cooperation and Security between NATO and the Russian Federation signed in Paris, France, 27 May 1997," http://www.nato.int/cps/en/natolive/official_texts_25468.htm; and Michael Rühle, "NATO and Nuclear Weapons," in *Understanding NATO in the 21st Century: Alliance Strategies, Security, and Global Governance*, ed. Graeme P. Herd and John Kriendler (London: Routledge, 2013).

46. Robert S. Gates, "The Security and Defense Agenda (Future of NATO)," as delivered by Secretary of Defense Robert M. Gates, Brussels, Belgium, June 10, 2011, http://www.defense.gov/speeches/speech.aspx?speechid=1581.

47. Author interview, NATO conference on the future of nuclear policy, Rome, June 2012.

48. These arguments have been diminished since early 2014, of course, by Russia's aggressive behavior in Eastern Europe, the Ukraine crisis, and Moscow's belligerent stance against the Alliance. Still, not all NATO member states have given up the dream of a nuclear-free Europe.

49. The MLF episode is a well-studied case study within NATO history. For example, see Wilfrid Kohl, "Nuclear Sharing in NATO and the Multilateral Force," *Political Science Quarterly*, (March 1965): 88–109.

50. "Speech by Jacques Chirac, President of the French Republic, to the Strategic Air and Maritime Forces at Landivisiau/L'Ile Longue, January 19, 2006," in "News in Review: Chirac Reasserts French Nuclear Weapons Policy," The Acronym Institute, Spring 2006, http://www.acronym.org.uk/dd/dd82/82chirac.htm.

51. "Sustaining U.S. Global Leadership: Priorities for 21st Century Defense," The White House, January 2012, http://www.defense.gov/news/Defense_Strategic_Guidance.pdf.

52. Thoughts on alternative models come from multiple sources, including Richard C. Bush, "The US Policy of Extended Deterrence in Asia: History, Current Views, and Implications," *Arms Control Series* no. 5, The Brookings Institute, February 2011; Kelley Saylor, "2011 Nuclear Policy Conference Summary: Extended Deterrence and the 21st Century," CSIS, April 4, 2011, at http://csis.org/blog/2011-nuclear-policy-conference-summary-extended-deterrence-and-21st-century; Hillary Clinton, "America's Pacific Century," *Foreign Policy* (November 2011): 56–63; and Kurt Campbell and Brian Andrews, "Explaining the US 'Pivot' to Asia," *Americas 2013/01 paper*, Chatham House, August 2013, http://www.chathamhouse.org/sites/files/chathamhouse/public/Research/Americas/0813pp_pivottoasia.pdf.

53. "Sustaining US Global Leadership."

54. Ibid., 4.

55. Ibid., 5. For more discussion on the international challenges facing the Obama administration, particularly with respect to nuclear policy and forces, see Christopher F. Chyba and J. D. Crouch, "Understanding the U.S. Nuclear Weapons Policy Debate," *The Washington Quarterly* (July 2009): 21–36; Keith B. Payne, "Maintaining Flexible and Resilient Capabilities for Nuclear Deterrence," *Strategic Studies Quarterly* (Summer 2011): 13–29; and *National Security Strategy*, The White House, May 2010, http://www.whitehouse.gov/sites/default/files/rss_viewer/national_security_strategy.pdf.

56. *National Security Strategy*, 41–42.

57. 2010 NPR, iv. See also Obama Prague Speech, April 5, 2009.

PART II

NATO'S NUCLEAR WEAPONS POLICY

CHAPTER 3

The Nuclear Straitjacket

AMERICAN EXTENDED DETERRENCE AND NONPROLIFERATION

Benoit Pelopidas

IN THIS CHAPTER, I discuss the future of US extended nuclear deterrence and the possibility of change in nuclear weapons and alliance policies. While several chapters in this book document and analyze the limits of extended deterrence arrangements, the goal of this chapter is to take a step back and look at the understanding of history that frames possible and desirable change in US nuclear weapons policy and submit it to historical critique based on European case studies.[1] I start by asking a specific question: Does the historical record suggest that extended nuclear deterrence has been a relevant tool for nuclear nonproliferation? To answer it, I identify a common and problematic framing of the question, the nuclear straitjacket, and analyze its policy implications before focusing on two European case studies: the United Kingdom and France.[2]

The nuclear straitjacket frames the requirements of national security as a binary choice between nuclear security guarantees from an ally and the quest for an independent nuclear deterrent. I call it the nuclear straitjacket because it limits itself to two ultimate security guarantors, both of which are nuclear. Most important, it does not leave any room for a third understanding of national security that would not rely on nuclear weapons.

To assess the nuclear straitjacket, negative security guarantees will be set aside and the focus will be on the positive ones.[3] In other words, the security guarantees coming from a nuclear-weapons-free zone (NWFZ) membership or a non-nuclear status under the nonproliferation treaty (NPT) are outside the realm of this analysis. The relationship that will be tested as a decisive component of the nuclear straitjacket is based on a strategy of extended nuclear deterrence.[4] This strategy introduces a relationship among three types of actors: the protector, the protégé, and the potential aggressor.[5] It is worth highlighting that these are categories of actors and not single actors; thus, the number of actors in each category can be more than one.

The nuclear straitjacket assumes a specific type of this relationship based on the idea that extended nuclear deterrence is a necessary tool for nuclear nonproliferation and disarmament, which are two modalities of renunciation of nuclear weapons.[6] It significantly affects the relationship I have just depicted. Classical extended deterrence is a promise of action from the protector that is expected to deter the potential aggressor from attacking the protégé. If you consider that these weapons have to play a role in nonproliferation policy or, more broadly, in a policy producing incentives to give up nuclear weapons ambitions, the assumptions about the relationship among the three types of players become much more demanding. The protector is still threatening to use its weapons to deter the potential aggressor from attacking but, in addition, this move from the protector is supposed to have an impact on the protégé and deter it from producing its own nuclear weapons. It is now clearer how the notion of the nuclear straitjacket is based on the idea that a commitment of extended nuclear deterrence is at least a necessary condition for renunciation of nuclear weapons.

In this chapter, I will demonstrate the importance of identifying and investigating the nuclear straitjacket and test the version of the nuclear straitjacket that assumes that positive nuclear security guarantees are both necessary and sufficient conditions across cases for states to give up nuclear weapons. Even though there is less commentary implying that nuclear security guarantees are sufficient because of the credibility issue, it is worth showing that even when they were as credible as possible, they were still not sufficient to prevent proliferation.[7] This is why I focus on the United Kingdom and France before 1957–1958: They were founding members of NATO and close US allies, in a context in which only few other states possessed nuclear weapons and the protector's homeland was not yet vulnerable to a massive nuclear retaliatory strike from the potential aggressor, which made its pledge of using nuclear weapons against the aggressor of an ally as credible as possible. To do so, I will show that (1) the nuclear straitjacket is implicit in the mainstream paradigms of international relations (IR) theory dealing with proliferation issues, and (2) it has political effects on the framing of possible and desirable nuclear weapons policies in the United States even though (3) it is not supported by the historical record and does not adequately portray the way French and British leaders conceived of the nuclear choices they could make.

The Nuclear Straitjacket and Nuclear History in Mainstream International Relations

In international relations theory, the most famous proponents of structural realism, area studies specialists inspired by it, and even critical voices have formulated forecasts and policy recommendations based on the nuclear straitjacket, even if their analytical assessments are often formulated in probabilistic terms.[8] Major proponents of structural realism argued that the protection offered by the two superpowers during the Cold War was the essential cause of nuclear nonproliferation during that period. This led to a series of proliferation forecasts about the post–Cold War period.[9] Benjamin Frankel offers the clearest formulation of this alternative when he writes that "there is an inherent contradiction between welcoming the end of bipolarity and deploring the spread of nuclear weapons" and "it is precisely the large size and sophistication of the superpowers' nuclear forces, and the avowed willingness of the superpowers to threaten to use them on behalf of their clients, . . . that have prevented a more pervasive weapons proliferation."[10] Most recently, Michael Horowitz phrases the nuclear straitjacket in terms of likelihood when he writes that "[i]n a world where progress towards arms reductions reverses, some states with civilian nuclear power might begin to prepare quietly for a world where they need to build their own small nuclear arsenal. Such an outcome might become likely if the economic struggles in the United States lead the country to pull back significantly from its international obligations, including its extended deterrence umbrella."[11]

A similar tendency can be identified in works of area studies specialists inspired by structural realism. Beyond the works of John Mearsheimer on the necessity of an independent nuclear deterrent in Ukraine, Fiona Hill and Pamela Jewett can be mentioned.[12] A few months before Kiev decided to give its weapons back to Russia, it insisted on the protection that these weapons would offer against a Russia depicted as expansionist, notably because of the remaining Russian minority in Eastern Ukraine.[13] Similarly, Yair Evron accepts the idea that the end of bipolarity created additional incentives to get nuclear weapons.[14] Some interpretations of the German case and, more broadly, of nuclear abstinence inside the European community tend to rely on the nuclear straitjacket.[15] Most recently, Andrew Kennedy argued that "implicit nuclear umbrellas" and disarmament diplomacy were key drivers of Indian nuclear restraint until 1998.[16]

Even critical voices like Glenn Chafetz, who intends to build an "alternative to the neo-realist perspective" for the post–Cold War world, ends up transposing the argument of the nuclear straitjacket at the level of perceptions. In his view, what matters for forecasting proliferation is not whether the protector will maintain its security guarantee but if the protégé believes the protector will do so.[17] This approach leaves room for the possibility that the protégé could misinterpret the intentions of the protector and decide not to go for the bomb even though the protector has not made a sincere credible pledge. Thus, the protégé in this instance would not go nuclear because it believes that the protector's defective pledge of extended nuclear deterrence is valid. The fact that the protégé makes a mistake should not mask that its supposed reasoning remains the same.[18] Most recently, Francis Gavin argues that the resolve to strike as a foundation of a credible nuclear security guarantee might have created incentives to go for the bomb for countries to which the deterrent pledge is not extended, but he does not criticize the efficacy of extended nuclear deterrence as a nonproliferation tool.[19]

The latest instance of the nuclear straitjacket can be found in the contemporary studies of the Saudi case in the context of the Iranian nuclear crisis. The two sides of the nuclear straitjacket now appear as prominent voices in the discussion: Either Saudi Arabia will receive a nuclear security guarantee from the United States, or it will develop its own nuclear arsenal in the near future.[20] The nuclear straitjacket, defined as an alternative between nuclear positive security guarantees and the quest for an independent nuclear deterrent, seems to be an implicit understanding of nuclear choices for more than just structural realist IR theorists. Let us now examine the impact of this view on contemporary debates related to nuclear weapons.

The Political Effects of the Nuclear Straitjacket on Contemporary US Debates

The Russian Federation and the United States possess more than 90 percent of the nuclear warheads on Earth, and these two states are still using some form of extended nuclear deterrence inherited from the Cold War.[21] The Russian military doctrine of 2000 read that:

> The Russian Federation will not use nuclear weapons against states party to the Nonproliferation Treaty that do not possess nuclear weapons except in the event of an attack on the Russian Federation, the Russian Federation Armed Forces or other troops, its allies, or a state to which it has security commitments that is carried out or supported by a state without nuclear weapons jointly or in the context of allied commitments with a state with nuclear weapons.[22]

The doctrines published in February 2010 and December 2014 repeat the same idea.[23] The Russian commitments under the Tashkent Treaty (also known as the Collective Security Treaty) suggest, however, that an attack against one member of the alliance is tantamount to an attack against all, and this in turn suggests a commitment that is close to the concept of extended nuclear deterrence.[24] Even if that is the case, and given that it is not the essential mission assigned to Russian nuclear forces, the United States is the only country that cites the requirements of extended nuclear deterrence as justifying the size of its arsenal.[25]

The other nuclear weapons states, whose arsenals are considerably smaller, adopt three different attitudes toward extended nuclear deterrence, all of which have one thing in common: None of them use the criterion of the imperative to protect allies to justify the size of the national arsenal. Some offer an extended nuclear deterrence of some sort to other states without legally binding agreements, a second group does not offer extended nuclear deterrence at all, and a third group not only refrains from offering it but publicly criticizes the United States and Russia for their extended deterrence commitments.

In the 2008 and 2013 *White Books on National Defense and Security*, France reaffirms that its strategic nuclear forces contribute to the security of the EU and NATO. This builds on the 1974 Ottawa Declaration, which states that its nuclear forces are "capable of playing a deterrent role of their own contributing to the overall strengthening of the deterrence of the Alliance."[26] It does not refer to extended deterrence to justify the size of its nuclear arsenal. The 2008 *White Book* insists on the independence of the national nuclear forces vis-à-vis NATO and the fact that the engagement of French forces in any case would not be automatic.[27] Thus, "France will keep on maintaining its nuclear forces at a level of strict sufficiency. Paris will adjust them constantly at the lowest level compatible with its security."[28] Compared to the American case, what can be called a French extended deterrence is offered to allies that do not necessarily demand it or might even be opposed to it.[29] Except for the Lisbon Treaty, these French commitments are not legally binding. In spite of the first comments that were given, the defense agreement between France and the United Arab Emirates signed in 2009 cannot be considered as an extended deterrence agreement. The assessments stating that France was committing itself to guarantee the security of the Emirates with all means at its disposal, including nuclear weapons, have been denied by the French authorities.[30]

In the second category, the United Kingdom, India, Pakistan, and North Korea simply do not offer any form of extended nuclear deterrence.[31] Israel obviously does not do it either because one of the requirements of an extended deterrence pledge is that the protector has to convey the message clearly both to the protégé and the potential aggressor. Israel's official policy of not being the first nation to introduce nuclear weapons in the Middle East does not make this possible.[32]

Finally, in the third category, China sticks to the notion of minimum deterrence.[33] It does not practice extended nuclear deterrence and has issued several proposals to give incentives to the United States and Russia to give up this practice.[34]

With respect to contemporary positive nuclear security guarantees, the United States is thus an exceptional case because it both offers positive nuclear security guarantees and defines the size of its nuclear arsenal based on the perceived requirements of these guarantees. This suggests that it is necessary to focus on the US case in order to assess the historical record of the nuclear straitjacket. The nuclear straitjacket has three consequences: justification of past extended deterrence policies as successes in nonproliferation, denial of the possibility for the protector to give up nuclear weapons, and limitation of the possible reduction of its arsenal in the name of nonproliferation.

Since the beginning of NATO, US positive nuclear security guarantees have been part of a policy of reassurance toward its allies, one that has continued after the end of the Cold War.[35] On October 18, 2006, less than ten days after the first North Korean nuclear test, US secretary of state Condoleezza Rice went to Tokyo and declared publicly that "[t]he United States has the will and capability to meet the full range—and I underscore full range—of its deterrent and security commitments to Japan."[36] Three days later, US secretary of defense Donald Rumsfeld reaffirmed US support for South Korea who, he said, was still included under a US "nuclear umbrella."[37] His successor, Robert Gates, made a similar move on October 21, 2009, five months after the second North Korean nuclear test.[38] The United States has long made similar declarations with respect to the Atlantic Alliance in Europe and, at least until the 2010 Nuclear Posture Review (NPR), its extended deterrence commitments have represented positive nuclear security guarantees that included potential first use of nuclear weapons to protect an ally that would be attacked with chemical, biological, or nuclear weapons.[39]

Beyond the goal of reassurance, this practice of offering positive nuclear security guarantees is now presented as a nonproliferation tool and it has been retrospectively declared successful in that respect. This is the first political effect of the nuclear straitjacket. In December 2008, the Report of the Secretary of Defense Task Force on DOD Nuclear Weapons Management stated that "[t]he United States has extended its nuclear protective umbrella to 30-plus friends and allies as an expression of commitment and common purpose as well as a disincentive for proliferation."[40] This report also quotes the 1998 annual defense report stating that "[n]uclear forces remain an important disincentive to nuclear, biological, and chemical proliferation."[41] The exact same idea is expressed in the May 2009 report to the US Congress in preparation for the Nuclear Posture Review. "During the Cold War," it said, "proliferation was strongly inhibited by the relationships of extended deterrence established by the United States (and also by the Soviet Union)."[42] One can argue that during the Cold War, the politics of the two blocs were based on the nuclear straitjacket.[43] The classical formulation of this approach is William Walker's notion of a nuclear order based on a "managed system of deterrence" and a "managed system of abstinence."[44] The meeting between French president Charles de Gaulle and US secretary of state John Foster Dulles on June 5, 1958, offers an explicit illustration of the nuclear straitjacket as a framework of the early US nonproliferation policy.[45] On the one hand, de Gaulle affirmed that France was becoming a nuclear power and intended to proceed to a test soon. As a consequence, the United States limited its nuclear cooperation with France in the name of nonproliferation. Washington argued that its resolve to protect Europe and its openness to share its strategic forces should deter the Europeans from developing autonomous nuclear arsenals.[46]

This dual role assigned to nuclear weapons—where they act both as a security guarantee for the United States and allies and as a nonproliferation tool—has another major effect beyond the justification of past extended deterrence policy as a success of nonproliferation: It limits the possible reductions in size of the US arsenal, to say nothing of complete disarmament. This reasoning has been expressed in preparatory reports leading to the 2010 Nuclear Posture Review as well as in the final document itself and in several public speeches by US officials. The report to Congress is consistent with the view previously quoted and repeats that "the United States will need to sustain a deterrent for the indefinite future."[47] This echoes several official speeches delivered by Barack Obama before and after he took office as well as by Secretary Gates. For example, in his interview with *Arms Control Today* in December 2008, president-elect Obama said the following: "I have made it clear that America will not disarm unilaterally. Indeed, as long as states retain nuclear weapons, the United States will maintain a nuclear deterrent that is strong, safe, secure, and reliable."[48] At the same time, Secretary Gates was explaining that "the nuclear arsenal is vital because the future cannot be predicted."[49] The 2010 *Quadriennal Defense Review* restated the need to maintain a nuclear arsenal for reasons including the security of allies: "We will maintain a safe, secure, and effective nuclear arsenal to deter attack on the United States, and on our allies and partners."[50] The May 2009 Report to Congress is particularly interesting because it articulated explicitly the link between extended deterrence and the limitation of nuclear arms reduction: "A policy agenda that emphasizes unilateral reductions could weaken the deterrence of foes and the assurance of allies."[51] If even the political goal of unilateral deep reductions is described as contradictory to the US commitments in terms of extended deterrence, complete unilateral nuclear disarmament is pushed even further into the realm of the impossible. This argument about the limitation of possible arms reduction relies on the assumption that the requirements of extended deterrence justify the existence of a larger arsenal than the one that would have been assigned to the defense of the national territory only. This is articulated most clearly in the Council on Foreign Relations April 2009 report entitled *U.S. Nuclear Policy.*

> Although the United States does not need nuclear weapons to compensate for conventional military weaknesses, other states are not in a similar position—they may consider acquiring nuclear weapons to deter attacks. The United States has the responsibility to assure allies through extended deterrence commitments. This assurance helps convince many of these allies not to acquire their own nuclear weapons. . . . A related pillar, necessary to maintain the credibility of the U.S. nuclear deterrent for as long as it is needed, is to ensure that the U.S. nuclear arsenal is safe, secure and reliable.[52]

The text of the May 2009 report to the US Congress in preparation for the Nuclear Posture Review explicitly echoes this reasoning.

> [The United States] must continue to safeguard the interests of its allies [. . .]. Their assurance that extended deterrence remains credible and effective may require that the United States retain numbers or types of nuclear capabilities that it might not deem necessary if it were concerned only with its own defense.[53]

The final text of the Nuclear Posture Review restates the same two arguments about the role of extended nuclear deterrence. It is meant to reassure the allies as well as to deter them from acquiring their own nuclear weapons.

> The United States will retain the smallest possible nuclear stockpile consistent with our need to deter adversaries, reassure our allies. . . . By main-

> taining a credible nuclear deterrent, . . . we can reassure our non-nuclear allies and partners worldwide of our security commitments to them and confirm that they do not need nuclear weapons capabilities of their own.[54]

The last formulation is worth noting because it relates to the formulation of the nuclear straitjacket in terms of a necessary condition: Extended nuclear deterrence helps to convince other actors not to go nuclear but is not perceived as sufficient for preventing them from doing so. Other conventional security guarantees should be added to constitute an effective nonproliferation architecture.[55]

Now that the three political effects of the nuclear straitjacket—justifying past extended deterrence policies as successes in nonproliferation, denying the possibility for the protector to give up nuclear weapons ambitions, and limiting the possible reduction of its arsenal—have been identified, it is time to assess its historical accuracy.[56]

The Nuclear Straitjacket in France and the United Kingdom

This section will shed light on the two European nuclear weapons states as parts of a broader investigation of one side of the nuclear straitjacket: Could a positive nuclear security guarantee be a sufficient condition for giving up nuclear weapons ambitions?[57] If one admits that both the United States and the Soviet Union also committed their nuclear weapons to the protection of their allies through the Atlantic Alliance and the Warsaw Pact, any successful proliferater coming from any of these alliances should be considered an anomaly.[58]

To strengthen my critique of the positive nuclear security guarantee as a sufficient condition for giving up nuclear weapons ambitions, I test this argument against cases in which it should be easily established. To that effect, I focus on cases in which the protector's pledge is most credible, the relationship between protector and protégé is deep and well-established, and the presence of nuclear-armed powers considered as potentially hostile to the protégé is minimal. Regarding the first condition of the highest credibility of the pledge, I assume that the credibility has to do with the expected costs of keeping the pledge, and those costs are lowest when the protector is not vulnerable to a massive nuclear retaliatory strike from the protégé's expected aggressor and when the number of potential nuclear-armed aggressors is lower.[59] Those are not the only factors but, for the purpose of this essay, I will consider them as the most important ones. So I will focus on the first years of the nuclear age, until 1957–1958, which, as shown below, meet all criteria.

At least until the successful launch of *Sputnik* in October 1957, which suggested that the Soviet rocket program was more advanced than had been expected, the French and British realized that the US homeland was not vulnerable to a massive Soviet nuclear attack.[60] There is no evidence that the earlier American concerns of the vulnerability of their homeland were communicated to their allies.[61]

On the French side, retrospective assessments suggest that a few strategists raised questions before *Sputnik*, but it did not really change the conversation.[62] We know that on November 15, 1957, four members of the new French government had a confidential meeting about the consequences of *Sputnik*, about the consequences of the increasing threat of Soviet intercontinental ballistic missiles (ICBMs) on the US homeland, and on the US commitment to deploy troops in Europe.[63]

On the British side, even *Sputnik* did not make much of a difference. Before *Sputnik*, British intelligence assessed that the trial tests of Soviet ICBMs would not be completed before 1962 and that operational quantities would not be available before 1964. After *Sputnik*, the Joint Intelligence Council maintained that it did not mean a greatly increased Soviet capacity in the near future. It never believed that there was a missile gap and, as late as January 1958, it wrote that it was "most improbable that sufficient stocks of ICBMs are now available to enable the Soviet leaders to launch a massive attack on the US, or that they will be in a position to do so for some time to come."[64] Summarizing the US and British intelligence on the issue, Michael Goodman concluded that "there were never any serious beliefs that the USSR would launch a nuclear offensive largely because the means did not exist to effectively threaten the American mainland."[65] The expected reputation costs of using nuclear weapons also increase with time if you accept the existence of a taboo or tradition of nonuse of nuclear weapons. So the costs of keeping the extended deterrence pledge were lower prior to 1958.

One might object that the doctrine of massive retaliation, publicized in January 1954, made a credible extended deterrence pledge more difficult than a doctrine that would involve using nuclear weapons later in the conflict. However, this theoretical objection is irrelevant as it does not match the perception of the European allies at the time. Reflecting in 1983 on the debate on alternatives to massive retaliation in the early 1960s, Raymond Aron offers the best summary of why the allies did not see them as improving the credibility of the US extended deterrence pledge. He writes: "Valid in the abstract, this theory [that the use of nuclear weapons becomes more credible when it is contemplated only as a last resort, after all other means have been used] never convinced the Europeans for two main reasons: they did not accept the great battle, waged on their soil [and] they did not consent to the effort in terms of conventional weaponry which was asked of them."[66] Not only is this theoretical objection irrelevant to the actors at the time. Even if it was, it would not compensate for the fact that until 1958, the United States did not need to fear a Soviet nuclear retaliation or large reputation costs and that the allies realized it.[67]

So the credibility of the US pledge to retaliate with nuclear weapons if one of its allies is attacked is at its peak before 1957–1958 because the costs of keeping it are lower than ever and the allies know it: The US homeland is not yet vulnerable to a massive nuclear strike from the Soviet Union and there is no other nuclear-armed enemy. So if extended nuclear deterrence was a sufficient condition for nonproliferation, as assumed by the variant of the nuclear straitjacket tested here, it should be easier to establish in this period. Even then, however, the United Kingdom and France appear as two major anomalies, which will be analyzed below.[68]

Both nations are founding members of NATO and, before going nuclear, the United Kingdom had developed a special relationship with the United States: The relationship between the former imperial power and its former colony significantly improved after the First World War. I will show that, in both cases, the nuclear straitjacket does not accurately portray the set of choices available to British and French leaders as they saw it at the time.

The United Kingdom

The United Kingdom has had a strategic and nuclear partnership with the United States since the beginning of World War II, when the Crown sent Sir Henry Tizard and his scientific team to the United States to share information on nuclear energy.[69] However, London did test an A-bomb in the Monte Bello Islands on October 3, 1952, and an H-bomb in 1957–1958. This represents a strong anomaly for the variant of the nuclear straitjacket tested here for the following reasons.

First, a deep alliance between the United States and the United Kingdom has developed since the 1940s, even before the foundation of NATO. The fact that the Mutual Defense Agreement between the two countries was not signed before July 3, 1958, should not lead one to neglect the depth of cooperation since World War II.[70] The signing of the Québec Agreement, which included Canada as a third party, on August 19, 1943, made the cooperation official and added a military component.[71] This agreement shaped technical cooperation as well as the sharing of information and ideas.[72] In addition, the three states agreed not to use the bomb against one another or to provide information to a third entity without the consent of the other two.[73] As for the bilateral US-UK relationship, which is my focus here, an interesting fact is that the British authorities were asked to approve the use of nuclear weapons on Hiroshima before the bombing took place.[74] It is true that the US Congress did pass the Atomic Energy Act, also known as the McMahon Act, in August 1946, and it put an end to the exchange of information related to nuclear weapons among the three parties of the Québec Agreement. However, there was room for restored cooperation in 1948, when the British committed to provide uranium to the United States if it offered nuclear assistance in return.[75] This was difficult in the late 1940s and early 1950s because of the scandals of espionage involving British scientists and high-level diplomats.[76] However, the alliance remained and the 1946 Spaatz-Tedder Agreement had since authorized the United States to use British air bases in peacetime.[77] In August 1948, after the Berlin blockade, the first US bombers able to reach the Soviet Union were deployed in the United Kingdom. In September, the chief of the US Air Force, General Norstad, informed the British allies that a group of B-29 bombers would be stationed in the United Kingdom permanently from this moment on.[78] So post–World War II tensions should not hide the depth of the alliance between the United States and the United Kingdom, which included a military dimension that was built and consolidated before the creation of NATO.

Second, this military alliance could be perceived as based on a positive nuclear security guarantee before the United Kingdom decided to test a nuclear device. It is true that President Truman did not allow the deployment of nuclear weapons abroad before April 1951.[79] The bombers previously deployed in the United Kingdom were able to carry and deliver nuclear weapons, but they were originally deployed without those weapons. However, the cooperation between the Royal Air Force and the US Air Force increased to such an extent that the British were convinced a positive nuclear security guarantee did exist.[80] Prime Minister Attlee was also convinced that the United States would consult him before using the nuclear weapons stationed in the United Kingdom, and this conviction is based on no official written document.[81] From the summer of 1956, the V-bomber force, which was able to carry fission bombs, entered service. From that moment on, the United States has shared part of its strategic planning with the United Kingdom.[82] After a period of tension following the Suez crisis, detailed agreements were signed in 1957–1958 between the Strategic Air Command and its British counterpart.[83] So the presence of US nuclear weapons on British soil, the cooperation between both the British and US air forces, and the personal convictions of Prime Minister Attlee suggest that an implicit nuclear security guarantee was perceived to be in place. The British conviction that the United States was ready to extend its nuclear deterrent to the United Kingdom was therefore in existence from the end of the 1940s.[84]

Third, in spite of this military alliance and the shared perception that it included a positive nuclear security guarantee, on January 8, 1947, Attlee decided that his country had to build an independent nuclear deterrent, and the additional guarantees given after that date did not change the course of British nuclear history.[85] The 1957 and 1958 White Papers insisted on the independence of the British "deterrent": the first one emphasized that Britain required "an appreciable element of nuclear deterrent power of her own" and that of 1958 proclaimed that Britain's nuclear force "in itself constitutes a formidable deterrent."[86] In spite of the strength of the ties between the two countries and the British project to include the national deterrent in a "deterrence in concert" with the United States, not only did the US positive nuclear security guarantee never convince the British to give up their weapons but plans for the use of nuclear weapons on a strictly national basis were elaborated in parallel in case the NATO security guarantee was withdrawn.[87]

Finally, the variant of the nuclear straitjacket tested here does not grasp the thinking of the British decision makers. The causes of the 1947 decision have almost nothing to do with US extended nuclear deterrence. Rationales focused on possessing an independent capability in case of a conflict; restarting a nuclear effort in order to restore the nuclear cooperation with the United States, which had stopped in 1946; and an "instinctive" desire to possess the newest weapons.[88]

Even if one superimposes the nuclear straitjacket onto decision making at the time, it becomes clear that it never really convinced because the nuclear alternative to an independent nuclear weapons system was not believed to be credible enough. The existing scholarship on British nuclear history shows that doubts about the credibility of the US nuclear security guarantee emerged among the chiefs of staff as early as 1957–1958, with the debate on "nuclear sufficiency."[89] But one can find traces of those doubts even earlier. In the very early 1950s, the British chief of staff subcommittee on air defense already anticipated the coming vulnerability of American cities and its impact on the credibility of the extended deterrence pledge: "Retaliation does not provide a global defence, it can only defend those places that are completely integrated politically. When New York is vulnerable to attack the United States will not use her strategic weapon in defence of London. The United Kingdom must, therefore, have its own retaliatory defence. Similarly, however, we will not be prepared to sacrifice the United Kingdom in the defence of say Darwin, and eventually each political unit must have its own means of retaliation."[90]

Other rationales were developed afterward, and they still remained incompatible with the variant of the nuclear straitjacket tested here. On March 1, 1955, for instance, Churchill made a military case for British nuclear weapons as capable of hitting targets of relevance that US weapons might not give adequate priority to.[91] More generally, since the Global Strategy Paper of June 1952, the alternative to an independent nuclear deterrent was not the US positive security guarantee but the development of conventional forces.[92] In spite of the effect of the Korean War, which created an incentive for conventional rearmament, the long-term trend of British military planning consisted of decreasing military spending and increasing reliance on the US security guarantee.[93] This reasoning, shared by the Labour and Conservative parties, never included the possibility of giving up an independent deterrent.[94] Instead, it was perceived both as a way to save money on conventional military spending and as a power multiplier when combined with the US security guarantee.[95]

So British nuclear history appears as a strong anomaly for the variant of the nuclear straitjacket tested here. The independent national deterrent and the positive security guarantee from the ally, both of which were nuclear, became combined in British thinking. The same can be said for France.[96]

France

France is a founding member of the Atlantic Alliance in 1949 and of the associated organization the year after. As such, it benefitted from the implicit positive nuclear security guarantee that protects all the members. American and Canadian bases as well as the Supreme Headquarters of Allied Powers Europe were even installed on French soil.[97] However, France did test its first A-bomb in the Reggane Desert in Algeria in February 1960, and its nuclear capability became fully operational in October 1964 when the Mirage IV bombers entered service.[98] France then tested its H-bomb in August 1968.[99] For reasons explained above, though, the analysis presented here will not cover the period after 1958.

I previously demonstrated that the US authorities approached the French case with the nuclear straitjacket logic in the late 1950s. However, France is another strong anomaly for the variant of the nuclear straitjacket tested here, even though it is sometimes neglected because of the misleading identification of the French nuclear program with the personality of Charles de Gaulle.

It is true that the degradation of the relationship between France and NATO as well as the acceleration of the French nuclear weapons program coincided with de Gaulle returning to power in May 1958. Indeed, the room for negotiation between France and NATO somewhat disappeared in 1959 when de Gaulle warned Germany and the United States that France intended to withdraw from the Alliance's operational structure after the settlement of the Algerian crisis or the US presidential elections.[100] And on March 17 of this same year, the defense council gave the nuclear weapons program (known as the *force de frappe*) "absolute priority."[101] However, interpreting this simultaneity is not as easy as it seems and should not reconcile the French case with the nuclear straitjacket or with the idea that a positive nuclear security guarantee could be sufficient for states to give up nuclear weapons ambitions.

First, the acceleration of the program or the change in the level of priority does not mean that there was no previous desire to acquire these weapons. Such an assessment would neglect the decisive roles of Pierre Mendès-France and Félix Gaillard in advancing the program, an attempt at cooperating with Italy and Germany, as well as fund transfers from the defense budget to the Atomic Energy Commission before de Gaulle returned.

As early as 1954, Prime Minister Pierre Mendès-France authorized significant progress in the militarization of the program.[102] On October 26, he signed a secret decree that created a superior commission for military applications of atomic energy as well as a committee dedicated to nuclear explosives. The commission never met, but the committee did begin working in secret as soon as it was created on November 4, 1954.[103] On December 26, Mendès-France, president of the Council of Ministers, also participated in a meeting at the Foreign Ministry during which some analysts believe the final decision to build the bomb was made.[104] On December 29, the *Commissariat à l'Énergie Atomique* (CEA; Atomic Energy Commission) created the *Bureau d'Études Générales* (Office of General Studies), which would later become the *Direction des Applications Militaires* (Direction of Military Applications).[105] A few days later, Mendès-France reconsidered the decision of December 26 and only wanted to leave the option open. Afterward, he always tried to underplay his role in French nuclear history.[106]

Beyond the personal role of Pierre Mendès-France and of the institutions that were created during his time in office, signs of a persistent will to develop an independent nuclear weapons capability can be traced back to the period between the fall of the Mendès-France cabinet and the return of de Gaulle. Major money transfers to fund the weapons program took place during that period.[107] On May 20, 1955, the minister in charge of atomic energy, Gaston Palewski, signed a secret protocol with his counterparts in the ministries of National Defense and Finance to fund the activities of the CEA for the period 1955–1957. The protocol stated that 20 billion francs would be transferred from the French defense budget to fund the activities of the CEA, including the building of a nuclear-powered ship. It included reciprocal measures suggesting that the sections of the three armies dedicated to nuclear issues could also receive money to fund activities in which both the CEA and the Ministry of Defense considered they would best perform. This possibility to transfer funding to the armies would prove crucial at the time of testing because that phase was delegated to them.[108] Physicist and chief scientist at the CEA Yves Rocard claims that around 1957, 100 billion francs were transferred from the defense budget to the CEA to fund all the military experiments except testing.[109] And in the defense budget for 1957, 37 billion francs were allocated to studies and prototypes of a nuclear-capable aircraft, which was at the time considered the most promising delivery vehicle for a nuclear payload to reach a target beyond the Iron Curtain.[110]

Beyond secret money transfers and financial provisions, parliamentarians started acting explicitly in favor of a military program, even before the Suez crisis. For instance, within the context of the Euratom debate, eight French senators feared that treaty commitments might impose restrictions on the development of an independent nuclear force. So, on April 17, 1956, they tabled a bill proposing a modification of the 1945 order (*ordonnance*) giving birth to the Atomic Energy Commission to create a military division within it.[111]

The attitude of the French representatives during the negotiations of the 1957 Euratom Treaty and vis-à-vis their European partners is also very telling of their military ambitions. They lobbied for the construction of power plants fueled by natural uranium *as well as* a European enrichment plant. They did not seem to want to use the enriched uranium as fuel, so the logical explanation for the French position is that the enriched uranium would be used to build weapons.[112] As Colonel Charles Ailleret, commander of "special weapons" in charge of organizing the first French nuclear test, remembers, "by January 1, 1957, one could consider that the practical decision to build and detonate the national atomic bomb was made and that the means to start the operations to this end were already at the disposal of the authorities."[113] In 1957 and 1958, the French authorities went so far as to sign a bilateral agreement with Germany and multiple trilateral agreements with Germany and Italy for future cooperation regarding the Pierrelate uranium enrichment plant as well as nuclear-weapons-related cooperation. Even if several aspects of this story remain unclear, the French drive for cooperation to speed up the national nuclear weapons program, and its desire to keep it secret from the United Kingdom and the United States and to make sure that it would benefit from it are yet other clues of a nuclear weapons project that was meant to be independent from the United States and, as such, incompatible with the variant of the nuclear straitjacket tested here.[114] Most important, in April 1958, former Prime Minister Felix Gaillard made the decision to test a nuclear device at the beginning of 1960 and antedated the document to April 11, before the fall of his government.[115] De Gaulle only confirmed it. Even before the strongest moments of the crisis between NATO and France that would coincide with the return of de Gaulle and the increasing level of priority given to the nuclear weapons program, Pierre Mendès-France's role, several money transfers, creations of institutions, and Felix Gaillard's decision to authorize the testing of a device show that the drive toward nuclear weapons in France predates de Gaulle and the degradation of French relations with NATO.

Third, neither de Gaulle nor Mendès-France ever thought about the independent national deterrent in terms of the nuclear straitjacket.[116] The key problem was not about the credibility of the nuclear security guarantee; it was about the risk of losing independence. In spite of their ideological differences, Mendès-France and de Gaulle shared this sense that "France's independence had to be defended against the United States."[117] The same could be said for Defense Minister Jacques Chaban-Delmas.[118] US nuclear weapons could be accepted as possibly strengthening the Alliance and saving some money, but they could not be an alternative to an independent national deterrent. Several explicit statements were made to that effect. On January 24, 1958, French minister of national defense Jacques Chaban-Delmas told *Le Monde* that "it is impossible for France to give up the bomb. . . . It would give up its rank of world power."[119] De Gaulle was as explicit in his exchange with Dulles in June 1958 when he told him "this is why we will not refuse your weapons."[120] It is true that France perceived a threat from the Soviet Union and was afraid of the prospect of Germany rearming. The Soviet threat helps to understand why France participated in NATO and the Union of Western Europe; the German threat accounts for the rhythm of the national program as well as the support from Mendès-France.[121] However, nuclear weapons appeared above all as instruments of independence and prestige, and the nuclear straitjacket does not approach them as such. Under the Fourth Republic, they were supposed to strengthen the French voice in NATO and the Union of Western Europe. The period following the Suez crisis of October 1956 radicalized this approach and made the nuclear weapons program an instrument to affirm the independence of France from the NATO Allies as well as from any other power. De Gaulle, who showed little interest in the subtleties of nuclear deterrence, personified this understanding of the purpose of the French nuclear program after he returned to power.[122]

The memory of the Suez crisis should be reinterpreted along this line. The nuclear straitjacket reads the crisis as a sign that the United States was not an unconditional ally, which decreased the credibility of its positive nuclear security guarantee and therefore created an additional incentive to go for the bomb. Instead, Dominique Mongin convincingly shows that Suez was a step toward the officialization of a policy rather than a window of opportunity for change at the level of policymakers; it was only decisive vis-à-vis the public opinion.[123] Once you take into account the primacy of the quest for independence, the crisis reveals that "the security of France is entirely dependent on the American alliance."[124] Indeed, the integrated command between the French and the British in the operation *Mousquetaire* proved to be a total failure. It deprived both parties of the ability to take initiatives at critical moments and ended up with the British yielding to US demands to withdraw troops from Egypt.[125] Therefore, the reasoning went, in the name of national independence, a national nuclear deterrent had to be built. Even the reasons for the crisis with NATO at the beginning of the de Gaulle era, which are often presented as supporting the nuclear straitjacket, point to this fundamental driver. The heart of the crisis was that de Gaulle wanted the French to control the US weapons stationed on their soil. This demand eventually led to the withdrawal of the French Mediterranean fleet from NATO integrated command and the expulsion of US nuclear forces on French soil.[126]

In sum, a careful reading of French nuclear history shows that the nuclear straitjacket was not successful as a policy and was so far away from the mind-set of the leaders that it did not provide much leverage.[127] This critique of the nuclear straitjacket is all the stronger in cases having strong relationships with a protector whose territory is not yet vulnerable to a massive nuclear retaliation, in a world of few potentially hostile nuclear weapons states. In such circumstances, the promise of extended nuclear deterrence should therefore be as credible as possible so the hypothesis of the nuclear straitjacket should be easier to confirm. Instead, both the British and the French cases indicate that a positive nuclear security guarantee is not a sufficient condition for all states to give up nuclear weapons and, most important, that the nuclear straitjacket does not capture adequately the options available at the time to the leaders. For French and British leaders, the decision to go nuclear was not a matter of extended nuclear deterrence or of its degree of credibility.

Conclusion

The behavior of two of the closest allies of the United States, the United Kingdom and France, shows that extended nuclear deterrence did not prevent them from developing their own national nuclear arsenals. This was the case in a world composed of only a few potentially hostile nuclear-armed states against which the protector would have had to act, a world in which the tradition of nonuse was still in its early years and, most important, a world where their protector was not yet vulnerable to a massive nuclear retaliatory strike. Since the European allies were not convinced of the higher credibility of alternatives to massive retaliation, the pre-1958 context made the US pledge of nuclear retaliation in case of an attack against a protégé as credible as it ever was. In spite of those conditions, which are particularly favorable to the variant of the nuclear straitjacket tested here, the British and French cases remain anomalies and developed their own nuclear arsenals.

The British and the French cases also illustrate the ways in which the nuclear straitjacket mischaracterizes the set of policy options available to decision-making elites. Nuclear-weapons-related choices are not only dependent on a subjective measurement of the credibility of a pledge based on nuclear weapons capabilities, which is why this critique should not be misinterpreted as a case for the inevitability of proliferation. On the contrary, the number of non-nuclear-weapons states whose security strategies do not depend on an extended nuclear deterrent underlines the widespread existence of a non-nuclear understanding of security that is also incompatible with the nuclear straitjacket. Indeed, a number of states that have tried to acquire nuclear weapons systems for a long time or have managed to acquire them after a long and costly effort have given up without receiving a pledge of extended nuclear deterrence.[128] For instance, in the post-Soviet states, during the negotiations that would lead to the renunciation, the strongest emphasis was laid on the independence of the state and the respect of its sovereignty, separate from the nuclear instrument.[129] Similarly, Libya put an end to an effort of more than thirty years, and South Africa dismantled its nuclear arsenal and neither received anything close to an extended nuclear deterrence pledge.

This has important implications for historians, analysts, and policymakers: The belief in the nuclear straitjacket as a principle working throughout nuclear history creates an overestimation of the role of extended deterrence, of the need to make the pledge credible, and of the successes of past policies based on it. More broadly, neglecting a political approach of nuclear choices—which gives room for the possibility of radical peaceful change over time and accepts the possibility of a non-nuclear understanding of security—could lead to misguided policies. As I have shown in the case of the nuclear straitjacket, rigid and structural approaches unduly oppose renunciation of nuclear weapons on the part of the protector, the reduction of its arsenal beyond a given size, and consequently the feasibility and desirability of a world without nuclear weapons. Most important, they induce policymakers to continue a nonproliferation policy based on a partial understanding of nuclear history and discourage policy innovation outside the proliferation paradigm.[130]

Notes

1. See Hans M. Kristensen's chapter in this book.

2. For a more complete analysis of the "nuclear straitjacket," see Benoit Pelopidas, "A bet portrayed as a certainty" in *The War that Must Never be Fought.*, eds. George P. Shultz and James E. Goodby (Stanford, CA: Hoover Press, 2015).

3. Nuclear security guarantees are usually presented as positive or negative, depending on the kind of action expected from the actor offering them. The provider of positive security guarantees commits itself to act in a certain way to protect the beneficiary of the guarantees; the provider of negative security guarantees commits itself not to act in a given fashion, in this case, not to use or threaten to use nuclear weapons against the other party. What matters for my argument here is that negative security guarantees only limit the nuclear threats coming from *one* actor, whereas positive security guarantees can cover actions against *several* sets of threats coming from different actors.

4. I am aware of the fact that resolutions 255 and 984 of the United Nations Security Council, passed on June 19, 1968, and April 11, 1995, respectively, also include security guarantees that are said to be positive. I do not include them because they take effect after a nuclear strike only, and are indirect, conditional, and very limited. The relevant part of resolution 984 reads as follows: "in case of aggression with nuclear weapons or the threat of such aggression against a non-nuclear-weapon State Party to the Treaty on the Nonproliferation of Nuclear Weapons, any State may bring the matter immediately to the attention of the Security Council to enable the Council to take urgent action to provide assistance, in accordance with the Charter, to the State victim of an act of, or object of a threat of, such aggression; and recognizes also that the nuclear-weapon State permanent members of the Security Council will bring the matter immediately to the attention of the Council and seek Council action to provide, in accordance with the Charter, the necessary assistance to the State victim."

5. I borrow the categories from Paul K. Huth, "Extended Deterrence and the Outbreak of War," *American Political Science Review* 82, no. 2 (June 1988): 423–43.

6. On the importance and policy implications of this notion, see Benoit Pelopidas, "Renunciation: Restraint, Reversal and Rollback," in *Routledge Handbook of Nuclear Proliferation and Policy*, ed. Joseph Pilat and Nathan Busch (London: Routledge, 2015).

7. For a complete treatment of the issue of the nuclear straitjacket, see Pelopidas, "A bet portrayed as a certainty": 30–39; and Benoit Pelopidas, *Renoncer à l'arme nucleaire: La seduction de l'impossible?* (Paris: Presses de Sciences Po, forthcoming).

8. Jeffrey Knopf's recent edited volume offers a welcome counterpoint in which he makes explicit that assurances are not a "silver bullet" and that their impact on nuclear weapons acquisition is "modest" rather than "decisive." See Jeffrey W. Knopf, "Introduction," in *Security Assurances and Nuclear Proliferation*, ed. Jeffrey W. Knopf (Stanford, CA: Stanford University Press, 2012), 6.

9. See John Mearsheimer, "Back to the Future: Instability in Europe after the Cold War," *International Security* 15, no. 1 (Summer 1990): 5–56; John Mearsheimer, "The Case for a Ukrainian Nuclear Deterrent," *Foreign Affairs* 72, no. 3 (Summer 1993): 50–66; Benjamin Frankel, "An Anxious Decade: Nuclear Proliferation in the 1990s," *Journal of Strategic Studies* 13, no. 3 (September 1990): 1–13; Benjamin Frankel, "The Brooding Shadow: Systemic Incentives and Nuclear Weapons Proliferation," in *The Proliferation Puzzle: Why Nuclear Weapons Spread (and What Results)*, ed. Zachary Davis and Benjamin Frankel (London: Frank Cass, 1993); Steven Van Evera, "Primed for Peace: Europe after the Cold War," *International Security* 15, no. 3 (Winter 1990–1991): 7–57. Kenneth Waltz did reply that a general theory of international politics like structural realism cannot predict proliferation. See Kenneth Waltz, "A Reply," *Security Studies* 4, no. 4 (1995): 803. For a detailed critique of the evolution and inconsistency in Waltz's discourse on nuclear weapons, see Daniel Deudney, "Dividing Realism: Structural Realism and Security Materialism on Nuclear Security and Proliferation," *Security Studies* 2, no. 3/4 (1993): 5–36.

10. Frankel, "An Anxious Decade," 6–7.

11. Michael C. Horowitz, "Nuclear Power and Militarized Conflict," in *The Nuclear Renaissance and International Security*, ed. Adam Stulberg and Matthew Fuhrmann (Stanford, CA: Stanford University Press, 2013), 308–09.

12. Mearsheimer, "The Case for a Ukrainian Nuclear Deterrent."

13. Fiona Hill and Pamela Jewett, *Back in the USSR: Russia's Intervention in the Internal Affairs of the Former Soviet Republics and the Implications for United States Policy Toward Russia*, Occasional Paper, Strengthening Democratic Institutions Project, Belfer Center for Science and International Affairs, Harvard University, John F. Kennedy School of Government, Cambridge, MA, 1994, 89.

14. Yair Evron, *Israel's Nuclear Dilemma* (Ithaca, NY: Cornell University Press, 1994), ix and chapter IV.

15. For a very prudent statement along this line, see David Yost, *The U.S. and Nuclear Deterrence in Europe*, Adelphi Paper no. 326 (Oxford: Oxford University Press, 1999), 25–27. See also the works by Bruno Tertrais, "Nuclear Proliferation in Europe: Could It Still Happen?" *Nonproliferation Review* 13 no. 3 (November 2006): 570. One has to recognize, however, that Tertrais' argument is slightly different. He tends to explain the absence of nuclear proliferation in Europe with the US nuclear security guarantee. However, on the one hand, he considers all the cases of nuclear temptations and not only the successful ones, which tends to give the nuclear security guarantee a role that goes beyond what the nuclear straitjacket assumes. On the other hand, the progress of the European construction is part of the explanation he provides. Along the same lines and more recently, he considers that the removal of the US extended nuclear deterrence would increase the Saudis' incentive to develop their

own nuclear weapons. Bruno Tertrais, "The Illogic of Zero," *The Washington Quarterly* 33, no. 2 (April 2010): 130–31.

16. Andrew B. Kennedy, "India's Nuclear Odyssey: Implicit Umbrellas, Diplomatic Disappointments and the Bomb," *International Security* 36, no. 2 (Fall 2011): 120–53. One has to note that the argument about "implicit nuclear umbrellas" was strongly criticized, emphasizing the key problem of credibility to which I will return. See Gaurav Kampani, Karthika Sasikumar, Jason Stone, and Andrew B. Kennedy, "Correspondence: Debating India's Pathway to Nuclearization," *International Security* 36, no. 2 (Fall 2012): 183–96, in particular 183, 185–91.

17. Glenn Chafetz, "The End of the Cold War and the Future of Nuclear Proliferation: An Alternative to the Neorealist Perspective," *Security Studies* 2, no. 3/4 (1993): 136.

18. This line of argument can be found among the opponents to a US shift to no first use of nuclear weapons. They say that the mere decrease of the credibility of the pledge of extended deterrence, let alone the removal of the pledge, would be enough to increase greatly the probability of proliferation. Tertrais expresses it very clearly when he writes, "If allies covered by the US nuclear umbrella saw such a policy shift as a reduction in the value of American protection, they could conclude that they should embark in their own nuclear programmes." Bruno Tertrais, "The Trouble with No First Use," *Survival* 51, no. 5 (October–November 2009): 25.

19. Francis Gavin, "Same as It Ever Was: Nuclear Alarmism, Proliferation and the Cold War," *International Security* 34, no. 3 (Winter 2009–2010), 27–28, 34.

20. Eric Edelman, Andrew Krepinevich, and Evan Braden Montgomery, "The Dangers of a Nuclear Iran," *Foreign Affairs* 90 no. 1 (January/February 2011): 70–71; and James A. Russell, "Nuclear Proliferation and the Middle East's Security Dilemma: The Case of Saudi Arabia" in *Over the Horizon Proliferation Threat*, ed. James J. Wirtz and Peter Lavoy (Stanford, CA: Stanford University Press, 2012).

21. This figure is based on the latest numbers published by the Ploughshares Fund. They are available at http://ploughshares.org/world-nuclear-stockpile-report.

22. Alexei Arbatov translated the 2000 Russian Military Doctrine into English, "The Transformation of Russian Military Doctrine: Lessons Learned from Kosovo and Chechnya," *German Center 2000*, appendix A, 36–37. http://www.marshallcenter.org/mcpublicweb/MCDocs/files/College/F_Publications/mcPapers/mc-paper_2-en.pdf

23. Nikolaï Sokov, "The New 2010 Russian Military Doctrine: The Nuclear Angle," http://cns.miis.edu/stories/100205_russian_nuclear_doctrine.htm; and Pavel Podvig, "New Version of the Military Doctrine," *Russian Strategic Nuclear Forces Blog*, December 26, 2014, http://russianforces.org/blog/2014/12/new_version_of_the_military_do.shtml.

24. On the commitments under the Tashkent treaty, interview with Nikolai Sokov, Monterey, California, March 19, 2010.

25. Sokov describes three main roles for these weapons in contemporary Russia: status symbol, existential deterrence in case of an attack from NATO forces, and deterrence of a conventional attack. Nikolai Sokov, "The Evolving Role of Nuclear Weapons in Russia's Security Policy" in *Engaging China and Russia in Nuclear Disarmament*, ed. Cristina Hansell and William Potter, Occasional Paper no. 15, James Martin Center for Nonproliferation Studies, Monterey, April 2009, 73–76. See also

Pavel Podvig, "Instrumental Influences: Russia and the 2010 Nuclear Posture Review," *Nonproliferation Review* 18, no. 1 (March 2011): 46–48. Those analyses still apply to the 2014 military doctrine since the nuclear paragraph is unchanged, as shown by Pavel Podvig in "New Version of the Military Doctrine." Jeffrey Lewis seems to follow a comparable line of argument when he writes that extended deterrence is "essentially an American phenomenon." Jeffrey Lewis, "From Extended Deterrence to Core Deterrence," *The Interpreter*, February 18, 2011, http://www.lowyinterpreter.org/post/2011/02/18/The-myth-of-the-nuclear-umbrella.aspx.

26. Translated and quoted in *Défense et sécurité nationale: le livre blanc* (Paris: Odile Jacob, 2008), 110. The 2013 White Book on Defence and National Security maintains a similar stance. See http://www.gouvernement.fr/sites/default/files/fichiers_joints/livre-blanc-sur-la-defense-et-la-securite-nationale_2013.pdf, 62. The original document can be retrieved at http://www.nato.int/docu/basictxt/b740619a.htm.

27. *Défense et sécurité nationale: le livre blanc* (2008), 110.

28. Ibid., 170. Author's translation.

29. The European allies that are also members of NATO do not wish to depend on a French or British nuclear guarantee, and both Sweden and Finland, members of the EU but not of NATO, want to delegitimize nuclear weapons in Europe. See David Yost, "Assurance and U.S. Extended Deterrence in NATO," *International Affairs* 85 no. 4 (July 2009): 761–62; Ursulla Jasper and Clara Portela, "E.U. Defense Integration and Nuclear Weapons: A Common Deterrent for Europe?" *Security Dialogue* 41, no. 2 (April 2010): 159–62.

30. See Isabelle Lasserre, "Moyen-Orient: la France se donne les moyens de riposter," *Le Figaro*, June 16, 2009; Régis Soubrouillard, "La France, parapluie nucléaire des Emirats Arabes Unis?," *Marianne 2*, June 17, 2009; Benoît Pelopidas, "French Nuclear Idiosyncrasy: How It Affects French Nuclear Policies Towards the United Arab Emirates and Iran," *Cambridge Review of International Affairs* 25, no. 1 (March 2012): 143–69.

31. The British 2008 National Security Strategy does not mention the notion of extended deterrence but only that of an "independent deterrent." Cabinet of the Prime Minister, *The National Security Strategy of the United Kingdom: Security in an Interdependent World* (London: Crown, 2008), 31, 44. William Walker confirms that "the U.K. does not practice extended deterrence on a bilateral basis. No other state shelters, formally at least, under a British nuclear umbrella." William Walker, "The U.K., Threshold Status and Responsible Nuclear Sovereignty," *International Affairs* 81, no. 2 (April 2010): 6.

32. On the Israeli relationship with its nuclear arsenal, see Avner Cohen, *The Worst-Kept Secret: Israel's Bargain with the Bomb* (New York: Columbia University Press, 2010).

33. I am aware of the debates about the modernization of Chinese nuclear forces, which might lead to a shift away from minimum deterrence. For the purpose of this argument, one has to recognize that the jury is still out on the issue and that the debate never really mentions the possibility that China will offer extended deterrence. See Jeffrey Lewis, "Minimum Deterrence," *Bulletin of the Atomic Scientists* (July–August 2008), http://www.newamerica.net/publications/articles/2008/minimum_deterrence_7552.

34. See "Recommendations for Achieving the Objective of Nuclear Disarmament and Nonproliferation of Nuclear Weapons," working paper submitted by China,

Disarmament Commission, United Nations, 2006 substantive session, April 10–28, 2006, A.CN.10/2006/WG.I/WP.3. See, more broadly, Jeffrey Lewis, "Chinese Nuclear Posture and Modernisation" in *Engaging China and Russia in Nuclear Disarmament*, ed. Cristina Hansell and William Potter, Occasional Paper no. 15, James Martin Center for Nonproliferation Studies, Monterey, California, April 2009, 40, 51. This remains true in spite of the false rumor spread by the *Washington Times* that Beijing had offered an extended deterrence pledge to Ukraine in January 2014. For a detailed analysis, see Jeffrey Lewis, "A Nuclear Umbrella for Ukraine?" *Arms Control Wonk Blog*, January 16, 2014, http://lewis.armscontrolwonk.com/archive/7019/a-chinese-nuclear-umbrella-for-ukraine.

35. On the case of the United States and the European allies during the Cold War, see Michael Howard, "Reassurance and Deterrence: Western Defense in the 1980s," *Foreign Affairs* 61, no. 2 (Winter 1982–1983): 309–324.

36. Quoted in Thom Shanker and Norimitsu Onishi, "Japan Assures Rice That It Has No Nuclear Intentions," *New York Times*, October 19, 2006, 14. I believe the umbrella analogy is seriously misleading, but this is not the right place to offer this critique in detail.

37. William Mann, "U.S. Reaffirms Promise to Defend South Korea," *Associated Press*, October 21, 2006.

38. Agence France Presse, "Robert Gates: les États-Unis n'accepteront jamais une Corée du Nord dotée de l'arme atomique," October 21, 2009.

39. Scott Sagan, "Shared Responsibilities for Nuclear Disarmament," *Daedalus* 138, no. 4 (Fall 2009): 163.

40. Report of the Secretary of Defense Task Force on DOD Nuclear Weapons Management, Phase II: Review of the DOD Nuclear Mission, 2008, iv.

41. Ibid., 7.

42. William Perry, James Schlesinger, et al., *America's Strategic Posture: The Final Report of the Congressional Commission on the Strategic Posture of the United States* (Washington, DC: United States Institute for Peace Press, 2009), 8.

43. Timothy Crawford, "The Endurance of Extended Deterrence: Continuity, Change and Complexity in Theory and Policy," in *Complex Deterrence. Strategy in the Global Age*, ed. T. V. Paul, Patrick Morgan, and James Wirtz (Chicago, IL: University of Chicago Press, 2009), 278; Bruno Tertrais, *La France et la dissuasion nucléaire: concept, moyens, avenir* (Paris: La Documentation Française, 2007), 24.

44. William Walker, "Nuclear Order and Disorder," *International Affairs* 76, no. 4 (October 2000); William Walker, *Weapons of Mass Destruction and International Order*, Adelphi Paper no. 370 (Oxford: Oxford University Press, 2004), chapter 2. See also Henry D. Sokolski (who does not explicitly list extended deterrence as a nonproliferation tool he explores in his book but whose remarks match the nuclear straitjacket perfectly) *Best of Intentions: America's Campaign against Strategic Weapons Proliferation* (London: Praeger, 2001), 5.

45. For an account of the meeting between De Gaulle and Dulles, see Bernard Ledwige, *De Gaulle et les Américains: conversations avec Eisenhower, Kennedy, Rusk, 1958–1964*. (Paris: Flammarion, 1984), 14–33. One should, of course, recognize the diversity of views within the US administration and the fact that in the early 1950s, the Pentagon tended to feel that the acquisition of nuclear weapons by France was inevitable and might even improve US security. See Shane Maddock, *Nuclear Apartheid:*

The American Quest for Nuclear Supremacy from World War II (Chapel Hill: University of North Carolina Press, 2010), 106; Jan Melissen, "Nuclearizing NATO, 1957–1959: The 'Anglo-Saxons,' Nuclear Sharing and the Fourth Country Problem," *Review of International Studies* 20, no. 3 (July 1994): 271–72.

46. Maurice Vaïsse, "Un dialogue de sourds: les relations nucléaires franco-américaines de 1957 à 1960," *Relations Internationales* 68 (Winter 1991): 421–22; Maurice Vaïsse, "Indépendance et solidarité 1958–1963," in *La France et l'OTAN 1949–1996*, ed. Frédéric Bozo, Maurice Vaïsse, and Pierre Mélandri (Paris: Éditions Complexes, 1996), 231, 233.

47. Perry, Schlesinger et al., *America's Strategic Posture*, 13, 17, 98, 123.

48. The Obama campaign website is also a valuable source in that regard: http://origin.barackobama.com/issues/foreign_policy/#nuclear.

49. Quoted in Isabelle Lasserre, "Les partisans du Global Zero misent sur Obama," *Le Figaro*, December 8, 2008.

50. US Department of Defense, *Quadriennal Defense Review Report*, Washington, DC (February 2010): 14.

51. Perry, Schlesinger et al., *America's Strategic Posture*, 15.

52. William Perry, Brent Scowcroft, and Charles Ferguson, *U.S. Nuclear Weapons Policy* (New York: Council on Foreign Relations, 2009), 5. These points are reaffirmed on pages 8, 14–16, 81, and 90–91.

53. Perry, Schlesinger et al., *America's Strategic Posture*, 13.

54. *Nuclear Posture Review Report*, April 2010, 7, 39.

55. The section I omitted in the previous quote expresses this point: "By maintaining a credible nuclear deterrent, and reinforcing regional security architectures with missile defenses and other conventional military capabilities, we can reassure our non-nuclear allies and partners worldwide of our security commitments to them."

56. David Holloway notes this lack of historical analysis of the role of extended nuclear deterrence in what he calls "the proliferation objection" to a world without nuclear weapons in "Deterrence and Enforcement in a World Free of Nuclear Weapons," in *Deterrence: Its Past and Future*, ed. George P. Shultz, Sidney D. Drell, and James E. Goodby (Stanford, CA: Hoover Institution Press, 2011), 353, footnote 19.

57. The other side of the problem, that is, extended nuclear deterrence being a necessary condition for nonproliferation, is considered in Pelopidas, *Renoncer a l'arme nucleaire*, chapter 4. In the deterrence theory literature, the problem has been addressed in terms of passivity of the protégé. Alexander George and Richard Smoke showed that the protégé is not passive in the relationship of extended deterrence. It can manipulate the pledge it has received, creating a classical problem of moral hazard. Alexander George and Richard Smoke, *Deterrence in American Foreign Policy: Theory and Practice* (New York: Columbia University Press, 1974), 370. This problem can explain why a positive security guarantee is not a sufficient condition for renunciation of nuclear weapons.

58. Given that the Warsaw Pact was a military alliance, the fact that it included a nuclear security guarantee was implicit but well known. Interview with Nikolaï Sokov, Monterey, California, November 13, 2009.

59. Deterrence theory recognizes that nuclear threats suffer from a major credibility problem, which is all the more important in the case of extended deterrence because the vital interests of the nation expected to retaliate with nuclear weapons

are not directly at stake. For an overview, see Crawford, "The Endurance of Extended Deterrence." During the May 17, 1956, meeting of the US National Security Council, President Eisenhower offered an exemplary statement of this problem. He said, "[I]n the defense of the United States itself we will certainly use nuclear weapons, but to use them in other situations will prove very difficult." *Foreign Relations of the United States 1955–1957*, vol. XIX, National Security Policy, document 79.

60. It is worth keeping in mind that first tests of Soviet ICBMs were not successful and the first of those missiles, an SS-6, actually became operational in early 1960. Even by the end of 1960, the Soviet Union had only two ICBMs. It is true that from 1956 onward, the Tu 95 (Bison) and 3M (Bear) strategic bombers were able to reach US territory and deliver nuclear weapons there, and by the end of 1959, the Soviet Union possessed 105 intercontinental bombers able to deliver 310 bombs. However, given the time it would take for those bombers to reach their target and the possibility to shoot them down, the American homeland was not vulnerable to a massive nuclear strike before at least 1959. See Natural Resources Defense Council, "Table of Soviet/Russian ICBM Forces," http://www.nrdc.org/nuclear/nudb/datab4.asp; Natural Resources Defense Council, "Table of USSR/Russian Strategic Bomber Forces," http://www.nrdc.org/nuclear/nudb/datab8.asp#fiftysix; and "Soviet and Russian Strategic Nuclear Forces," in *Russian Strategic Nuclear Forces*, ed. Pavel Podvig (Boston, MA: MIT Press, 2001), 4–5; and Georges Le Guelte, *Les armes nucléaires: mythes et réalités* (Arles: Actes Sud, 2009), 95–99.

61. Those concerns appear in the report by James Killian submitted in March 1955. The report recognized the shortage of good intelligence on Soviet intentions and capabilities but still offered estimates that the US nuclear superiority in megaton weapons would end as early as 1956. Michael Goodman, *Spying on the Nuclear Bear: Anglo-American Intelligence on the Soviet Bomb* (Stanford, CA: Stanford University Press, 2007), 194.

62. In a 2009 preface to his 1960 book *Stratégie de l'âge nucléaire*, Pierre Gallois claims that, as early as February 1956, he asked generals Montgomery and Norstad what would happen once the United States loses its "quasi-invulnerability" granted by two oceans. The loss of this invulnerability was, in 1956, still a problem for the future in his mind. In the book itself, written in 1959–1960, Gallois does note that in August 1957, the Soviet Union launched long-range (more than 10,000-kilometer) intercontinental ballistic missiles. Pierre-Marie Gallois, *Stratégie de l'âge nucléaire* (Paris: François-Xavier de Guibert, 2009), 12, 41. In his memoirs, *Le sablier du siècle*, he recounts how his interrogations were met with denials at the time at the French Ministry of Defense. Pierre-Marie Gallois, *Le sablier du siècle* (Lausanne: L'Âge d'Homme, 1999), 358. In 1973, when he published *La République impériale*, Raymond Aron reaches the exact same diagnosis: At least until 1956, the US homeland remains almost invulnerable. Raymond Aron, *La République impériale: les États-Unis dans le monde* (Paris: Calmann-Levy, 1973), 86. In his memoirs, Jacques Chaban-Delmas, who was Félix Gaillard's minister of national defense and a strong proponent of an independent nuclear force, claims that he told Eisenhower in Paris in 1952 that the Soviets would not possess the delivery vehicles capable of reaching the United States before two to four years. Jacques Chaban-Delmas, *Mémoires pour demain* (Paris: Flammarion, 1997), 216.

63. Georges-Henri Soutou, “Les accords de 1957 et 1958: vers une communauté stratégique nucléaire entre la France, l'Allemagne et l'Italie?,” *Matériaux pour l'histoire de notre temps*, no. 31 (1993): 6.

64. Huw Dylan, “Britain and the Missile Gap: British Estimates on the Soviet Ballistic Missile Threat, 1957–61,” *Intelligence and National Security* 23, no. 6 (December 2008): 784–86.

65. Goodman, *Spying on the Nuclear Bear*, 215. On the British intelligence on Soviet nuclear capabilities, see 189–98.

66. Raymond Aron, *Les dernieres annees du siècle*, (Paris: Calmann-Levy, 1984), 67. (My translation).

67. Ian Clark writes perceptively that “the launch of *Sputnik*, and development of associated ICBM technology, potentially neutralized the effectiveness of American nuclear guarantee to its allies.” Ian Clark, *Nuclear Diplomacy and the Special Relationship: Britain's Deterrent and America 1957–1962* (Oxford: Clarendon Press, 1994), 2.

68. If this chapter had been about the Soviet Union as a protector, China would have been the anomaly for the variant of the nuclear straitjacket argument tested here because it acquired nuclear weapons in spite of its 1950 agreement with the Soviet Union.

69. Alan Carr, “How It All Began: The Atomic Bomb and the British Mission,” in *U.S.-U.K. Nuclear Cooperation after 50 Years*, ed. Jenifer Mackby and Paul Cornish (Washington, DC: Center for Strategic and International Studies, 2008), 24–25. It would not be accurate to say that this collaboration was easy, among equal partners, and deprived of any component of rivalry. Mid-1942 can be identified as the moment when the American team overtook its British counterpart in nuclear research. However, the special relationship started in 1939 and was going beyond the nuclear aspect. See John Baylis, *Anglo-American Defence Relations, 1939–84: The Special Relationship* (London: Palgrave, 1984).

70. John Simpson and Jenifer Mackby, “The Special Nuclear Relationship: A Historical Chronology,” in *U.S.-U.K. Nuclear Cooperation after 50 Years*, ed. Jenifer Mackby and Paul Cornish (Washington, DC: Center for Strategic and International Studies, 2008), 12–15; John Baylis and Kristan Stoddart, “The British Nuclear Experience: The Role of Ideas and Beliefs (part I),” *Diplomacy & Statecraft* 23, no. 2 (2012): 333.

71. The original title of the agreement is: “articles of agreement governing collaboration between the authorities of the United States and the United Kingdom in the matter of Tube Alloys.” See Graham Farmelo, *Churchill's Bomb: A Hidden History of Science, War and Politics* (London: Faber and Faber, 2013), 240–44.

72. Béatrice Heuser, *NATO, Britain, France and the FRG: Nuclear Strategies and Forces for Europe 1949–2000*, (London: MacMillan, 1997), 63.

73. Simpson and Mackby, “The Special Nuclear Relationship,” 7; Carr, “How It All Began,” 26.

74. Jacques Hymans, “Britain and Hiroshima,” *Journal of Strategic Studies* 32, no. 5 (October 2009): 769–97.

75. Simpson and Mackby, “The Special Nuclear Relationship,” 4; Heuser, *NATO, Britain, France and the FRG*, 63.

76. At this time, a former communist, John Strachey, was appointed minister of war in the United Kingdom and, in February 1950, Klaus Fuchs, the person in charge

of theoretical physics in the British atomic energy program in Harwell, was identified as a spy working for the Soviet Union. Simpson and Mackby, "The Special Nuclear Relationship," 7; Andrew Brown, "Historic Barriers to Anglo-American Nuclear Cooperation," in *U.S.-U.K. Nuclear Cooperation after 50 Years*, ed. Jenifer Mackby and Paul Cornish (Washington, DC: Center for Strategic and International Studies, 2008), 44–45; Alex Danchev, "In the Back Room: Anglo-American Defense Cooperation," in *British Intelligence, Strategy and the Cold War 1945–1951*, ed. Richard Aldrich (London: Routledge, 1992), 229–30.

77. These bases were not only in the mainland but also in the islands of the British Empire, notably Okinawa in the South Pacific; the area from Cairo to Suez; and, until 1948, the region between Lahore and Karachi. Danchev, "In the Back Room," 225.

78. One has to recognize that the acceptance of those bombers was not without controversy. Lorna Arnold and Katherine Pyne, *Britain and the H-Bomb* (London: Palgrave, 2001), 36.

79. David Holloway, "Nuclear Weapons and the Escalation of the Cold War, 1945–1962," in *The Cambridge History of the Cold War. Volume I: Origins*, ed. Melvyn P. Leffler and Odd Arne Westad (Cambridge: Cambridge University Press, 2010), 381; Simon Ball, "Military Nuclear Relations between the United States and Great Britain under the Terms of the MacMahon Act, 1946–1958," *The History Journal* 38, no. 2 (June 1995): 443. The weapons were deployed in Guam.

80. Ball, "Military Nuclear Relations," 443–45; Simpson and Mackby, "The Special Nuclear Relationship," 15. See also Glen Segell, "Nuclear Delivery Systems Resulting from the MDA" in *U.S.-UK Nuclear Cooperation after 50 Years*, ed. Jennifer Mackby and Paul Cornish (Washington, DC: Center for Strategic and International Studies, 2008), 117–18.

81. Nicholas Wheeler, "The Attlee Government's Nuclear Strategy, 1945–1951," in *Britain and the First Cold War*, ed. Anne Deighton (New York: St Martin's Press, 1990), 138–39.

82. Brown, "Historic Barriers to Anglo-American Nuclear Cooperation," 41.

83. As soon as March 1957, President Eisenhower met with newly elected Prime Minister MacMillan in Bermuda to make sure that the Suez crisis did not damage the Alliance and to conclude an agreement on the transfer of Thor missiles to the United Kingdom. Simpson and Mackby, "The Special Nuclear Relationship," 9.

84. Wheeler, "The Attlee Government's Nuclear Strategy, 1945–1951," 130, argues that the guarantee has been in place since the deployment of the bombers in 1948.

85. See Peter Hennessy, *Cabinets and the Bomb* (Oxford: Oxford University Press, 2007), 55–59; Baylis and Stoddart, "The British Nuclear Experience," 333, 335–336. It is worth noting that when the Center for Nuclear Research was created in Harwell in September 1945, a discussion started about the number of reactors that needed to be built. At that time, the chiefs of staff had not yet submitted their report on the requirements of nuclear weapons. Attlee argued that the relevant number would be decided depending on the number of bombs the government would consider as needed. Wheeler, "The Attlee Government's Nuclear Strategy, 1945–1951," 132, 134. Andrew Brown argues that the United Kingdom acquired nuclear weapons because of the Soviet threat and distrust of the United States, and to keep its great power status. Brown, "Historic Barriers to Anglo-American Nuclear Cooperation," 46.

86. Quoted in Ian Clark and Nicholas J. Wheeler, *The British Origins of Nuclear Strategy 1945–1955* (Oxford: Clarendon Press, 1989), 241.

87. The expression "deterrence in concert" is used by the minister of defense talking to the prime minister on August 12, 1955. Quoted in Kristan Stoddart, "British Nuclear Strategy during the Cold War," in Matthew Grant (ed.), *The British Way in Cold Warfare: Intelligence, Diplomacy and the Bomb* (London: Continuum, 2009). Lawrence Freedman, *The Evolution of Nuclear Strategy*, 2nd ed. (Basingstoke: Macmillan, 1989), 283–330. This only underlines Britain's quest for independence and its postwar fear that the United States might become isolationist again. The US involvement in the 1948 Berlin crisis did not suffice to appease this British fear, and the behavior of the United States in Suez in 1956 only fed into it. Holloway, "Nuclear Weapons and the Escalation of the Cold War, 1945–1962," 389; Beatrice Heuser, *Nuclear Mentalities? Strategies and Beliefs in Britain, France and the FRG* (London: Palgrave, 1998), 32; Heuser, *NATO, Britain, France and the FRG*, 66.

88. This is derived from Margaret Gowing. She wrote about "something fundamentalist and almost instinctive—a feeling that Britain must possess so climacteric a weapon in order to deter an atomically armed enemy, a feeling that Britain as a Great Power must acquire all the major new weapons, a feeling that atomic weapons were a manifestation of the scientific and technological superiority on which Britain's strength, so deficient if measured in sheer numbers of men, must depend." Margaret Gowing, *Independence and Deterrence: Britain and Atomic Energy 1945–1952, Volume 1: Policy Making* (Basingstoke: St. Martin's Press, 1974), 84. Of course, one would need to recognize, following Richard Maguire's analysis, that there are multiple "nuclear cultures" in the United Kingdom. For the purpose of this analysis, I remain focused on the politico-military elites. Richard Maguire, "'Never a Credible Weapon': Nuclear Cultures in British Government during the Era of the H-Bomb," *British Journal of History of Science* 45, no. 4 (December 2012): 519–33. For an argument about how an independent nuclear weapons system was expected to fortify the alliance with the United States, see Nicholas J. Wheeler, "British Nuclear Weapons and Anglo-American Relations 1945–1954," *International Affairs* 62, no. 1 (Winter 1985–1986): 72.

89. See John Baylis, *Ambiguity and Deterrence: British Nuclear Strategy, 1945–1964*, (Oxford: Clarendon Press, 1995), chapter 8.

90. Defe 8/47, COS Air Defence Sub-Committee, Air Defence Working Party, 2 (54) 16, July 14, 1954.

91. "There are also big administrative and industrial targets behind the Iron Curtain, and any effective deterrent policy must have the power to paralyse them all at the outset, or shortly after. There are also the Soviet submarine bases and other naval targets which will need early attention. Unless we make a contribution of our own—that is the point which I am pressing—we cannot be sure that in an emergency the resources of other Powers would be planned exactly as we would wish, or that the targets which would threaten us most would be given what we consider the necessary priority, or the deserved priority, in the first few hours. These targets might be of such cardinal importance that it would really be a matter of life and death for us." March 1, 1955, http://hansard.millbanksystems.com/commons/1955/mar/01/defence#S5CV0537P0_19550301_HOC_281. See also Clark and Wheeler, *The British Origins of Nuclear Strategy, 1945–1955*, 231.

92. Clark and Wheeler, *The British Origins of Nuclear Strategy, 1945–1955*, 239.

93. Stoddart, "British Nuclear Strategy during the Cold War."

94. There was opposition to an "independent deterrent," particularly within the Labour Party, which came close to the nuclear straitjacket when it proposed that Britain would renounce its nuclear weapons if all others, excluding the two superpowers, did the same. But this never became British policy, not even when Harold Wilson, one of the critics of the so-called independent deterrent, became prime minister in 1964. David J. Gill, *Britain and the Bomb.* (Stanford, CA: Stanford University Press, 2014), 11, 41, 45, 48; and Peter Hennessy, *Cabinet* (London: Blackwell, 1986), 126.

95. Pelopidas, *Renoncer à l'arme nucleaire*, 277–79. See also Baylis, *Ambiguity and Deterrence*, 405–14; John Baylis and Alan Macmillan, "The British Global Strategy Paper of 1952," *Journal of Strategic Studies* 16, no. 2 (June 1993): 200–26; Holloway, "Nuclear Weapons and the Escalation of the Cold War, 1945–1962," 385; Heuser, *Nuclear Mentalities?*, 50–51; Stoddart, "British Nuclear Strategy during the Cold War."

96. Howard, "Reassurance and Deterrence," 313.

97. Maurice Vaïsse, "La France et l'OTAN: une histoire," *Politique Étrangère* 4 (2009): 862.

98. Marcel Duval, "Les décisions concernant l'armement nucléaire: pourquoi, comment et quand?" in *Armement et Vème République: fin des années 1950–fin des années 1960*, ed. Maurice Vaïsse (Paris: CNRS Éditions, 2002), 298; Philip Gordon, "Charles de Gaulle and the Nuclear Revolution," in *Cold War Statesmen Confront the Bomb: Nuclear Diplomacy since 1945*, ed. John Gaddis et al. (Oxford: Oxford University Press, 1999), 218.

99. The first thermonuclear test took place in Fangataufa in the Pacific on August 24, 1968. Duval, "Les décisions concernant l'armement nucléaire," 299.

100. Vaïsse, "Indépendance et solidarité 1958–1963," 225.

101. Duval, "Les décisions concernant l'armement nucléaire," 297; Jacques Chevallier, "La genèse de la force de dissuasion nucléaire française," *Armement et Vème République: fin des années 1950–fin des années 1960* (Paris: CNRS Éditions, 2002), 282. Maurice Vaïsse sees a shift to a "forced march" toward nuclear weapons in mid-1959: "Indépendance et solidarité 1958–1963," 230.

102. It is significant that key members of the government he composed in June 1954 were strong proponents of the development of French nuclear weapons: General (Marie)-Pierre Koenig, Minister of National Defense; Diomède Catroux, Secretary of State in charge of the air; and Jacques Chaban-Delmas, Minister of Public Works, Transport and Tourism. It is significant that Chaban-Delmas told Aline Coutrot he had explicitly conditioned his joining the government on pro–nuclear weapons measures. Aline Coutrot, "La politique atomique sous le gouvernement de Mendès France," in *Pierre Mendès France et le Mendésisme, l'expérience gouvernementale*, ed. François Bédarida and Jean-Pierre Rioux (Paris: Fayard, 1985), 310. In 1952, Antoine Pinay and Félix Gaillard had proposed the energy plan, which would guarantee the production of enough plutonium to consider military applications. Dominique Mongin, *La bombe atomique française. 1945–1958* (Brussels: Bruylant, 1997), 167, 295; Soutou, "Les accords de 1957 et 1958," writes about military ulterior motives for this energy plan already.

103. Georges-Henri Soutou, "La politique nucléaire de Pierre Mendès France," *Relations internationales* 59 (1989): 91–92.

104. Soutou, "La politique nucléaire de Pierre Mendès France," 99–100; Holloway, "Nuclear Weapons and the Escalation of the Cold War, 1945–1962," 390; Robert Frank, "De la puissance," in *Deux passions françaises: Pierre Mendès-France and Charles de Gaulle*, ed. Robert Frank and Eric Roussel, (Paris: CNRS Éditions, 2014), 309.

105. Soutou, "La politique nucléaire de Pierre Mendès France," 93–96. For more on the origins and development of this office, see Jean-Damien Pô, *Les moyens de la puissance: Les activites militaires du CEA (1945–2000)* (Paris: Ellipses, 2000), 58–68.

106. See Jean Lacouture, *Pierre Mendès France* (Paris: Seuil, 1981), 360–1. Several participants in the meeting gave contradictory accounts. See Coutrot, "La politique atomique sous le gouvernement de Mendès France," 309–16; Marcel Duval and Dominique Mongin, *Histoire des forces nucléaires françaises* (Paris : PUF, 1993), 32–36; Vincent Duclert, "Pierre Mendès France et la recherche scientifique," in *Le gouvernement de la recherche: Histoire d'un engagement politique, de Pierre Mendès France au Général de Gaulle*, ed. Alain Chatriot and Vincent Duclert (Paris: La Découverte, 2006), 48–49; Gabrielle Hecht, *The Radiance of France: Nuclear Power and National Identity after World War II* (Cambridge, MA: MIT Press, 1998), 76. In *Le mal français* (Paris: Plon, 1976), 288–91, Alain Peyrefitte offers a middle-ground interpretation when he crafts the analogy with a decision made under hypnosis.

107. On money transfers, see Duval, "Les décisions concernant l'armement nucléaire," 294.

108. Mongin, *La bombe atomique française*, 362–66; Chaban-Delmas, *Mémoires pour demain*, 218.

109. Yves Rocard, *Mémoires sans concession* (Paris: Grasset, 1988), 177.

110. Mongin, *La bombe atomique francaise*, 445; Claude Carlier, *L'aéronautique française 1945–1975* (Paris: Charles Lavauzelle, 1983), 204.

111. Mongin, *La bombe atomique française*, 411–13.

112. Grégoire Mallard, "L'Europe puissance nucléaire: cet obscur objet du désir," *Critique internationale* no. 42 (2009): 157–58; Soutou, "Les accords de 1957 et 1958," 2–3.

113. Charles Ailleret, *L'aventure atomique française* (Paris: Grasset, 1968), 226.

114. Soutou, "Les accords de 1957 et 1958"; Leopoldo Nuti, "The F-I-G Story Revisited," in Leopoldo Nuti and Cyril Buffet (eds.), *Dividing the Atom: Essays on the History of Nuclear Proliferation in Europe*. A Special Issue of the Journal *Storia delle Relazioni Internazionali* 13, no. 1 (1998): 69–100. Eminent members of the French foreign ministry and other government members did not see such cooperation as detached from US policy.

115. Mongin, *La bombe atomique francaise*, 453; Maurice Vaïsse, "Le choix atomique de la France," *Vingtième siècle: revue d'histoire* 36 no.1 (1992): 21; Maurice Vaïsse, "Jacques Chaban-Delmas ministre de la Défense nationale (novembre 1957–mai 1958)," in *Jacques Chaban-Delmas en politique*, ed. Bernard Lachaise, Gilles Le Béguec, and Jean-François Sirinelli (Paris: Presses Universitaires, 2007), 107; Aline Coutrot, "La création du commissariat à l'énergie atomique," *Revue française de science politique* 31, no. 2 (1981): 369.

116. Vaïsse, "Le choix atomique de la France," 23; Heuser, *NATO*, *Britain*, *France and the FRG*, 94; Heuser, *Nuclear Mentalities?*, 75; Scott Sagan, "Why Do States Build Nuclear Weapons? Three Models in Search of a Bomb," *International Security* 21, no. 3

(Winter 1996/97): 76–80. For the opposing point of view, see Bruno Tertrais, "Destruction assurée": The origins and development of French nuclear strategy," in *Getting MAD: Nuclear Mutual Assured Destruction, Its Origins and Practice*, ed. Henry Sokolski (Carlisle, PA: US Army War College, 2004), 56–58, in particular 56, footnote 19.

117. Frank, "De la puissance," 324, 326 (my translation).

118. Soutou "Les accords de 1957 et 1958," 5–7; Nuti, "The F-I-G Story Revisited."

119. Quoted in Vaïsse, "Jacques Chaban-Delmas ministre de la Défense nationale," 106, 110.

120. See Ledwige, *De Gaulle et les Américains.*

121. For an approach insisting on the prospect of Germany rearming and the role of Mendès, see Jacques Hymans, *Psychology of Nuclear Proliferation* (Cambridge, Mass: Cambridge University Press, 2006), chapter 4. On the importance of the prospect of Germany rearming, see also Vaïsse, "Le choix atomique de la France," 25; and Charles Cogan, "American-French Intelligence Relations and the French Nuclear Deterrent," *Journal of Intelligence History* 3, no. 1 (Summer 2003): 57–58. On the role of the Soviet threat of invasion as another reason for an independent nuclear arsenal, Frank, "De la puissance," 328.

122. Duval, "Les décisions concernant l'armement nucléaire," 297, 304. I imply here that this lack of interest in the discussions around nuclear deterrence suggests a distance vis-à-vis the nuclear straitjacket.

123. Mongin, *La bombe atomique francaise*, 442.

124. Note from Etienne de Croüy-Chanel, November 10, 1956, translated from the quote in Maurice Vaïsse, "Post-Suez France," in *Suez 1956: The Crisis and Its Consequences*, ed. W. M. Roger Louis and Roger Owens (Oxford: Clarendon Press, 1991), 338. De Gaulle would express this view of the peril of a US protectorate in public at a press conference on April 7, 1954, and again after that. He discussed it with General James Gavin, US ambassador to France, in an interview on May 26, 1962. With Gavin, he argued that France could see that the US were engaged and France did not fear potential US isolationism. He added that "it is rather the opposite that France fears, it is excessive intervention in the Western Alliance, i.e. an American hegemony" openly stated in the President's words, and which is destined to last and expand. The quote from the press conference can be found in Charles de Gaulle, *Mémoires d'espoir, suivies d'allocutions et messages sous la IVème et Vème République* (Paris: Plon 1999), 575–76, and the summary of the meeting with Gavin can be found in Archives of the Presidency of the French Republic, AG5(1)/720, folder "Etats-Unis," "Audience de M. Gavin, Ambassadeur des Etats-Unis le 26 mai 1962," 3–4 [my translation]. See also Vaïsse, "Indépendance et solidarité 1958–1963," 237. Admiral Marcel Duval supports this view of the primacy of independence regarding the American trusteeship in de Gaulle's views about nuclear weapons, "Les décisions concernant l'armement nucléaire," 297.

125. Vaïsse, "Post-Suez France," 338.

126. Vaïsse, "Un dialogue de sourds," 412–16; Maddock, *Nuclear Apartheid*, 130.

127. However, Jacques Chaban-Delmas seems to have used the nuclear straitjacket to convince Guy Mollet to support the project. Had the US positive security guarantee been durably credible, we would not have had to develop an independent nuclear force. Patrick and Philippe Chastenet, *Chaban* (Paris: Seuil, 1991), 214.

128. See Jacques Hymans, *Achieving Nuclear Ambitions: Scientists, Politicians and Proliferation* (Cambridge: Cambridge University Press, 2012).

129. William Potter, "Back to the Future: The Contemporary Relevance of the Nuclear Renunciation Decisions of Ukraine, Belarus and Kazakhstan," Paper for the Nobel Institute Conference on *The Spread of Nuclear Weapons: Past Experience and Future Challenges*, Oslo, 2009, 38.

130. For more on the proliferation paradigm, see Benoît Pelopidas, "The Oracles of Proliferation," *Nonproliferation Review* 18, no. 1 (Spring 2011). Another rationale supporting extended nuclear deterrence as a nonproliferation policy is that "the number of states seeking or obtaining the protection offered by the extended deterrent may increase as the size of nuclear forces providing that extended deterrent diminishes." David J. Trachtenberg, "U.S. Extended Deterrence: How Much Strategic Force Is Too Little?" *Strategic Studies Quarterly* 6, no. 2 (Summer 2012): 88.

CHAPTER 4

NATO's Protracted Debate over Nuclear Weapons

Paul Schulte

ALTHOUGH EXACT TOTALS REMAIN classified, it is generally accepted that there are some 160 to 200 US B61 nuclear bombs stored inside hardened vaults at six air bases in Europe and Turkey. These nonstrategic nuclear weapons (NSNW) are intended as payloads not only for American, but also, and most controversially, for nationally owned and crewed Belgian, Dutch, German, and Italian F-16 and Tornado dual-capable aircraft (DCA), available to the Alliance under NATO's unique system of nuclear sharing.[1] The B61 bombs represent the shrunken remnant of around seven thousand nonstrategic American nuclear weapons that NATO maintained at the height of the Cold War. Although it has been the Alliance's public position that the era of active nuclear antagonism is permanently over, NATO NSNW are routinely compared with deliberately uncertain numbers, an estimated one thousand to three thousand nonstrategic weapons owned by the Russian Federation.[2]

NATO NSNW make up fewer than 2 percent of the approximately 11,500 nuclear weapons now estimated to be on the planet.[3] Warhead for warhead, and very probably kiloton for kiloton, these have become the most internationally studied and debated nuclear weapons in the world.[4] Although far from a major political issue anywhere, they are the fervent concern of a relatively small number of technical military specialists and diplomats, political opinion makers, theorists of strategic stability, political commentators, and antinuclear activists.

This chapter examines the domestic-level and Alliance-level politics of extended deterrence, with a focus on NATO's nuclear weapons policy. It examines why the dispute has been so lengthy and inconclusive, and considers the intellectual judgements and sources of opinion on the different sides. This chapter also looks at four theoretical explanations for the differences and suggests possible outcomes and the dynamic factors that may determine them. Theoretically it does not assume that any one causative factor in any single explanation will be dominant. It emphasizes the difficulty of finding demonstrably objective reasons on which consensus could be reached, for or against, retaining NATO NSNW, and points out the importance and difficulty of the decision and implementation processes within the Alliance. But it also suggests a number of factors that can now be realistically identified as most likely to affect the NSNW issue. The uncertainty of their future interactions means that no firm predictions are yet plausible, although a range of possibilities can be usefully scoped out. Lastly, the complications created by the striking deterioration in relations between NATO and Russia since 2014 are considered, especially in relation to the difficulties which they will throw up for future NATO Nuclear Policy.

Historical Background

The question of US nonstrategic, tactical nuclear weapons in Europe has been alive and controversial since they began to arrive in the early 1950s.[5] NATO gratefully incorporated them into its deterrent strategy as potent free gifts from the US government, keeping the cost of deterring the Warsaw Pact down to politically affordable levels. But there has been a continuous aspiration among various European groups and political movements to remove nuclear weapons ideally from the whole of Europe but, if necessary, from Western Europe alone. This has been promoted as a morally desirable measure in its own right, a means of reducing risks, and of improving security relations with Russia. Up until the 1990s, the aspiration was fostered by Soviet "active measures."[6]

During the Cold War, as the number of NATO tactical nuclear weapons increased and became the main source of Alliance firepower (peaking at over seven thousand in the early 1970s), there were growing insider disagreements about the stage, during a Soviet attack, in which they would be used. These were conveniently minimized by the formulation of flexible response (in effect, as late as possible, as early as necessary) in 1967 and the creation of the NATO Nuclear Planning Group (NPG), which gave all allies (except France, which still remains outside) an opportunity to be consulted on nuclear policy and so, progressively, to develop a common deterrence culture within the Alliance.

Significant reductions in NSNW on both sides had already begun before the Cold War ended. Presidents George H. W. Bush and Boris Yeltsin both subsequently announced unilateral, unverified reductions, in 1991 and 1992, which came to be known as the Presidential Nuclear Initiatives and were seen as preludes to negotiations aimed at the elimination of all NSNW. Those negotiations never occurred but would have posed enormous verification problems if they had. Soon after Soviet forces returned all their nuclear weapons to Russia, NATO cancelled modernization programs and removed most of its remaining NSNW, leaving only several hundred B61 gravity bombs. The United States proceeded to eliminate nuclear artillery; short-range, surface-to-surface nuclear missiles; and tactical naval nuclear weapons from its global stockpile.

It is increasingly clear that the Russian Federation has persistently avoided making comparable NSNW reductions since the end of the Cold War.[7] The resulting asymmetry in Moscow's favor, widely accepted but not publicly entirely provable, is now long established and probably impossible to eliminate. In view of its shrunken military capabilities, and confronted with an expanded NATO (which it claims it had been promised would never happen), the Russian Federation has abandoned the Soviet Union's declaratory posture of no first use of nuclear weapons (NOFUN). Its military doctrine seems to rely significantly upon the trump card deterrent, which large numbers of NSNW can appear to offer, especially in scenarios where their use could deescalate potential military threats to the survival of a Russian state facing advanced sixth-generation warfare and NATO missile defenses.[8]

NATO's Deterrence and Defense Posture Review and the Chicago Summit

Among Western arms control proponents and antinuclear groups, however, hopes had been high in the last decade that NATO would move to withdraw all remaining US nuclear weapons from Europe. When the Alliance agreed in November 2010 to undertake a Deterrence and Defense Posture Review (DDPR), the political salience of nuclear weapons in Europe had increased. Germany's foreign minister, Guido Westerwelle, had recently called for the withdrawal of US nuclear weapons from its soil. This stemmed from a coalition agreement between the Christian Democratic Union and Free Democratic Party in October 2009, which was reached against the backdrop of President Obama's Prague Speech earlier that year, and the imminent 2010 Non-Proliferation Treaty review conference. The Dutch parliament had similarly declared that nuclear weapons in Europe were no longer needed to guarantee NATO's security. Despite political indications that

Germany would not purchase nuclear delivery capability for the successors to its Tornado fighter-bombers, Westerwelle subsequently promised that Berlin would coordinate decisions with NATO allies in a formal review and would not act unilaterally. Nevertheless, according to a think tank report issued in April 2012, German officials privately indicated that, although they remain loyal members of the Alliance, their objective of completing the denuclearization of the Luftwaffe had not changed and they do not expect it to change.[9]

The DDPR involved extensive consultations within and beyond NATO; strong political disagreements were expressed behind closed doors. This review process was denounced by antinuclear groups, who in general saw publicity as one of their key levers, as lacking "transparency and accountability."[10] Surprisingly for some, the result was the May 22, 2012 Summit Declaration announced in Chicago, which found that the Deterrence and Defense Posture Review "has reinforced Alliance cohesion and the continuing credibility of its posture." This posture of course included continued forward basing of US NSNW in Europe, and the logically linked long-term refusal of any NOFUN commitment. Work would continue to develop an optimally "appropriate mix" of forces to maintain deterrence and to ensure that Alliance nuclear weapons remained "safe, secure and effective," though NATO also stated that it hoped for gains in transparency and significant nuclear reductions through a reciprocated arms control process with Russia.

Reactions to Chicago: "Kicking the Can Further down the Road"?

This outcome predictably disappointed many antinuclear activists. Given their earlier expectations, opponents of continued NATO NSNW in Europe identified the proceedings as "kicking the can further down the road."[11] More broadly, they took it as evidence that real consensus could not be achieved by governments to the satisfaction of antinuclear movements.

For at least one commentator who has been consistently strongly sceptical of the Alliance's current nuclear posture and perhaps representative of a wider climate of opinion, the stakes were even higher because the Chicago decisions showed that "NATO's political mechanisms are deadlocked around the nuclear issue; allowing them to stay that way for much longer risks the very existence of the Alliance. For that reason, the US government must recognise the danger and act soon to save NATO from a nuclear implosion."[12]

On the other hand, the Chicago decisions undoubtedly caused relief in those countries that most strongly, but generally discreetly, wished to continue present nuclear arrangements. And the Chicago declaration seemed an ingenuously realistic diplomatic outcome to supporters of continued nuclear sharing. One strongly pronuclear expert emphasized that, "the [DDPR] review has shown that the Alliance's nuclear force posture currently meets the criteria for an effective deterrence and defence posture."[13] He pointed out that the DDPR also stated that the Allies would "develop concepts for how to ensure the broadest possible participation of Allies concerned in their nuclear sharing arrangements, including in case NATO were to decide to reduce its reliance on non-strategic nuclear weapons based in Europe."[14] He therefore argued that, for this purpose, "the Allies may conclude that it is difficult to surpass the advantages of nationally owned dual-capable aircraft within a NATO framework."[15] Whatever interpretations are advanced, the fact that consensus was reached among twenty-eight governments was itself an indisputably strong Alliance message. But for many, the issue remained and remains simply a problem deferred and, although the internal dispute is now temporarily less salient, no conclusion is in sight.[16]

The September 2014 NATO Summit in Wales was understandably preoccupied with immediate responses to annexation of Crimea and the proxy war in Ukraine. The seriousness of these events seemed to prevent any alliance member wishing to be seen to be weakening NATO's deterrent capability by pushing for dilutions of its nuclear posture. The resultant communiqué consequently maintained a tactful (or distracted) silence on nuclear issues, keeping to familiar, and by now formulaic, wording: "NATO will maintain the full range of capabilities necessary to deter and defend against any threat . . . .wherever it should arise. Deterrence, based on an appropriate mix of nuclear, conventional, and missile defence capabilities, remains a core element of our overall strategy. As long as nuclear weapons exist, NATO will remain a nuclear alliance. The strategic nuclear forces of the Alliance, particularly those of the United States, are the supreme guarantee of the security of the Allies." It would, nevertheless, be extremely unwise to assume that this represented the end of NATO's internal nuclear conflict.

Why Is It So Hard to Achieve Robust and Lasting Consensus over NATO NSNW?

Several overlapping explanatory hypotheses for the length and intractability of the dispute are worthy of examination.

> ***Explanation 1:*** *Especially since the end of the Cold War there has been pervasive uncertainty about the longer-term threats that might face NATO and what they might mean for robust extended deterrence. This uncertainty about NATO's future strategic environment leads to divisively different predictions of requirements, driven by expectations filtered through different strategic mind-sets.*

Given the unclassifiable, mutating, unforeseeable, unsatisfactory, but not hopeless, NATO-Russian relationship; the currently hostile enigma represented by the Islamic Republic of Iran; and the general, open-ended proliferation of nuclear and biological technologies, the world in which NATO's future role will be worked out remains unclear. As a consequence, it may be impossible to persuade others with strongly established positions about the relevance of nuclear weaponry.

Each concerned strategic player, group of players, or self-conscious strategic subculture within the Alliance is engaged in constructing a persuasive moral and intellectual case for determining the future of NATO deterrence that is intended to influence others. Almost all resultant arguments are safe from refutation given the intrinsic difficulty in demonstrating the consequences of a posture in which NATO's nuclear forces have been routinely described in Alliance publications as "no longer targeted against any country . . . their role is now more fundamentally political . . . are no longer directed towards a specific threat."[17]

> ***Explanation 2:*** *The complexity and obscurity of the (classified) politico-military role of NATO's NSNW in publicly unspecifiable scenarios inhibits any public process of clarification that might build shared understandings and eventual agreement.*

According to a detailed Carnegie/Brookings/RUSI assessment, the role of NATO NSNW has become deeply complex and disputable: "*an inseparable mix of operational and political utility*" and so extensively classified that it has proved impossible to explain (although this has provoked little public interest or concern).[18] The authors therefore set out their unofficially gathered collective impression, which has not been contested in numerous subsequent conferences or publications.

> Our understanding is that the role of [these] weapons is now seen within NATO as providing the Alliance with a limited and uniquely configured shared initial nuclear capability. . . . Such a use of nuclear weapons would involve a target, or targets, on the territory of an aggressor but could be observably limited. The preparatory and decision making steps leading up to such use would signal allied resolve to escalate further if necessary, while the com-

> bination of weapons and delivery systems would be least likely to be mistaken as forming part of a full-scale nuclear response with strategic forces. . . . In extreme circumstances of collective self-defense, the combination of DCAs with U.S. B61 bombs would allow NATO to decide, by consensus, to cross the nuclear threshold in a manner that was not purely demonstrative. . . . The collective nature of the initial nuclear response with nonstrategic nuclear weapons would be further emphasized by conventionally equipped aircraft from many Alliance nations flying to support it: the Support of Nuclear Operations with Conventional Air Tactics, or SNOWCAT, mission.[19]

Senior NATO officers have made numerous statements to the effect that NATO NSNW have no specific military role that other weapons could not undertake. Anti-NSNW campaigners repeat this. For proponents of NSNW, the objection misses the point: The essential purpose of these weapons is improved deterrence through demonstrable politico-military cohesion, through widespread allied military participation to conduct or assist the nuclear mission, rather than optimal nuclear war fighting. The cohesion enhanced by NSNW is judged to be particularly valuable in preserving what might be called a "nuclear militia" deterrence model for the Alliance. The implications are best understood in relation to Patrick Morgan's typology of five standard organizational models for collective actor deterrence, which also apply to nonmilitary actions, like sanctions.[20]

The first is the international hegemony model, which is characterized by bilateral guarantees from a superpower. This is also known as the Asia model, though its unbalanced dependence is progressively less attractive now to Japan, the Republic of Korea, and Taiwan. They seem to be investigating the possibilities of NATO-style joint planning, for example, by setting up extended deterrence policy committees. (Of course, NATO NSNW represent some elements of the hegemonic model because they are all donated by the United States, but it would have been hard for it to have been otherwise within the constraints of the Nuclear Non-Proliferation Treaty (NPT), which NATO nuclear sharing was designed to preserve.)

The second is the coalition of the willing model whereby some subset of the international community with coercive capabilities acts on its own, with or without UN authorization. This is an option for conventional operations, especially for expeditionary warfare, as seen with the coalitions that expelled Iraqi forces from Kuwait in 1991 and then toppled the Saddam Hussein regime in 2003. However, this model would be dangerously improvisational in the higher stakes, instantly fateful, nuclear sphere.

The third is the concert model. In this case, a few harmoniously interrelating dominant states manage international security by consensus. The

Concert of Europe avoided major war in the decades after 1815, but there is insufficient global harmony for it to apply in the twenty-first century, except perhaps in limited and special circumstances, such as the Six Party Talks on North Korean nuclear capabilities.

The fourth is the suprastate model, which is based on a central coercive authority, like proposals for UN armed forces. This has no near-term prospect of successful institution.

The fifth is the militia model. In this case, all members commit to contribute to the fullest extent when necessary, "although only a few would typically take much action. A decision-making body operates to identify when contributions are needed from the members of the coalition."[21] Although the analytical term is not used, the model it refers to has been rhetorically emphasized within NATO, especially during the Cold War, as the military embodiment of the Alliance choosing to act as "a shared community of fate" or *Schicksalsgemeinschaft*.[22]

The Chicago and Wales Summit declarations indicated NATO's intent to maintain the militia model as far as possible in the nuclear as well as nonnuclear sphere. Nevertheless, as Morgan points out, for collective actor deterrence, "considerable free riding, particularly over time, is typical, in part because . . . alliances have intrinsic free riding problems[:] under participation, delayed participation, bounded participation, and nonparticipation."[23] The question at the heart of the NATO NSNW debate is how far the Alliance can accept the wish of additional key allies to move toward "bounded participation" in the nuclear field. This would risk undermining progressively, though perhaps quite rapidly, the officially endorsed militia model. While nuclear *planning*, especially for the SNOWCAT mission, appears to have been Alliance-wide, nuclear *sharing* has never been unbounded within the Alliance. For example, Norway and Denmark always declined to host nuclear weapons in peacetime, Canadian forces gave up US NSNW in 1984, Greek forces in 2001 while US gravity bombs remained stored on USAF bases in the UK until 2006. Under the 1997 NATO-Russia Founding Act, NATO famously pledged that it had "no intention, no plan and no reason to deploy nuclear weapons on the territory of new members, and Turkey has unofficially indicated that it has given up training pilots for the nuclear delivery mission, although it is believed that it continues to store B61 bombs on its soil.[24]

Full participation in nuclear preparations can be complex, technically demanding, expensive, and potentially controversial. No concerted effort has been made to explain exactly how NATO governments see the role of NSNW in underpinning the Alliance nuclear posture and in maximizing allies' involvement (or, from an antinuclear perspective, complicity) in nuclear preparation and planning. Potential public anxieties within the Alliance seem too great for an information campaign, which would, at least initially, intensify political dispute over NSNW. The obscurity of the role of NSNW is therefore unlikely to change.

> ***Explanation 3:*** *NATO's issue over NSNW is a manifestation of underlying ideational disputes between sceptics and supporters of nuclear deterrence in Europe, a clash of strategic cultures and subcultures.*

The subcultural approach to understanding nuclear security choices pioneered by Jack Synder in the late 1970s offers another key to understanding the NSNW dispute. For Snyder, the term *strategic culture* referred to "the sum total of ideas, conditioned emotional responses and patterns of habitual behaviour the members of a national strategic community have achieved through instruction and in imitation with each other with regard to nuclear strategy."[25] A more recent definition, by Biava, Dent, and Herd, of "the set of beliefs, assumptions, attitudes, norms, world views and patterns of habitual behavior held by strategic decision-makers regarding the political objectives of war, and the best way to achieve [those objectives]" addresses a wider set of security issues in which nuclear matters necessarily nest.[26] It does not exclude the impact of dissenting groups, who are often committed to an antinuclear campaigning identity as an important social and political signifier for their members and who remain deliberately outside Snyder's more traditional and connected elite national strategic community. But those elite strategic communities can be kept usefully in mind in examining a dispute that is fundamentally connected with the internal Alliance sustainability of the nuclear doctrines developed, which they develop and propagate.

At its most fervent, the dispute provides an opportunity for various antimilitarist and antinuclear European national strategic cultures, and vanguard subcultures, to press for further change in NATO orthodoxy.[27] Overall, many wish to contest the prudence and moral acceptability of their country's deep involvement in a global system of nuclear deterrence largely extended from the United States.[28] In this dissenting project, personal moral imperatives to oppose the unbearable possibility of nuclear catastrophe, as part of what Max Weber would have called an ethic of authenticity, inner conviction, and "ultimate ends," collide with an ethics based on probable, traceable, secular consequences or "responsibility," as generally understood in the Alliance's mainstream politico-military discourse.[29] For many advocates of change, especially in Europe, NATO NSNW are the most accessible form of nuclear weaponry to be eliminated. Morally it may matter rather little to them whether doing so could in fact realistically be shown to create further benign disarmament consequences. But for many of their pronuclear opponents, proposals for withdrawing NATO NSNW amount to a wilful, unilateral choice to reduce Alliance security and ignore the lessons of nearly sixty years of collective nuclear deterrence.

The dispute is not quite between European Venusians and American Martians, as described by Robert Kagan.[30] Some NSNW sceptics have been senior military officers and accept the wider unavoidable predicament of nuclear deterrence, while opponents and proponents of NATO NSNW are to be found among both American and European experts. But European opponents of NSNW often appear more closely linked to left-wing or nationalist political parties, or nongovernmental organizations, which are themselves frequently sceptical about the costs and risks of dependence on the United States.[31] To maintain momentum in campaigning against NSNW, opponents need to portray themselves as potentially connected to sufficiently influential actors in national political systems to create a realistic possibility of ending NATO's current posture. Among NATO's European members that might require only a single decisive vote within a pivotal ally such as Germany, which could close down present basing arrangements or preclude nuclear modernization. Line-item financial vetoes in "parliamentary ambushes" during defense, foreign policy, or budgetary debates might offer opportunities for such far-reaching action. The risk of such ambushes, or preannounced barricades against spending on dual-use procurement, will persist for many years.

Proponents of the nuclear status quo, on the other hand, tend to be associated with existing bureaucratic or military structures and hope to exert their continuing influence within the Alliance and its collective arrangements to prevent major divergence from the consensus through individual eruptions of national domestic politics.

Mapping Strategic Subcultures

Each side can insist that their position on NSNW is rational and morally necessary rather than the result of any process of social conditioning. But here, at least as much as in any other field of social and political life, it is worthwhile trying to map the underlying assumptions and strategic cultures and subcultures that condition, but not determine, individual positions. The factors leading to active individual engagement over NSNW, on any side, are not random. Every strategic advocate tries to avoid cognitive dissonance, especially to prevent embarrassment in acrimonious policy dispute. The arguments, and their advocates, become familiar.

Sources of Opposition to NATO NSNW

The most notable and mutually reinforcing aspects of a polymorphous, shifting, but determined oppositional subculture can be located in the following arguments made in support of intellectual, social, and religious objections to NSNW. There is a very evident and acute concern with physical safety and with the security of warheads, terrorism, and accidental war that together make up the nuclear danger. This is felt to be a grave and technically unavoidable consequence of maintaining stocks of fissile materials in warheads in Europe and western Russia. It is therefore characteristic that for the 2013 elections the Social Democratic Party (SDP) in Germany tabled detailed questions about the fire resistance of B61 pits, Luftwaffe Tornados' recorded flying hours, and the technical requirements of extending their lives, all implying that the party supports the proposition that keeping Germany's dual-capable aircraft in service, particularly past 2025, could be physically dangerous. "Mixing anti-nuclear sentiment with safety concerns has already proven to be a potent recipe: Germany's phase-out of nuclear power by 2022 was sparked largely by the perception that 'nuclear power is unsafe.'"[32]

Fear of the nuclear danger mixes easily with intellectual scepticism about the role of deterrence, especially forward-based nuclear deterrence, in having historically kept the armed peace.[33] This perspective raises general doubts about the practical utility of nuclear weapons in the twenty-first-century security environment. Specifically, it leads to what might be called Alliance process scepticism, a judgment that NATO's requirement for consensus decisions would never allow even the operational preparation of NSNW as a form of signaling in a crisis. Such weapons cannot therefore be expected to contribute to NATO security, so resources and political attention should be directed to other priorities, including nonmilitary spending.

A further important cross-cutting source of opposition is religiously or morally inspired antinuclearism, especially in Protestant (or post-Protestant) strains of thought.[34] Activists animated by these religious, postreligious, or moral considerations frequently insist that any use of nuclear weapons would always be wrong, largely because it would, by definition, inject the irreducible and characteristic nuclear characteristic of pure violence with indiscriminate and permanently cataclysmic consequences.[35] A desire to end collusion with an intrinsically sinful and indiscriminate weapons category is often associated with sincerely held judgments that the irreducible nuclear danger from accident, miscalculation, or deterrence failure in Europe is in any case more significant than the worst predicted consequences of NSNW withdrawal.[36]

The moral antinuclear imperative often coexists with, or emerges from, progressive religious, intellectual, or political subcultures that reject the inevitability and human costs of various ugly and compromising aspects of the wider global technological, military, and economic system. A logically consistent recent initiative is therefore a renewed concern to press for "humanitarian nuclear disarmament."[37] The international campaign is still developing, and it is not clear how far its practical political consequences will go.

Similarly, there is a strong moral commitment to the achievement of early Global Zero and the frequently emphasized obligation from the NPT bargain for nuclear weapons states to disarm. The yearning for nuclear disarmament frequently translates into determination, as a first step, to end NATO's nuclear-sharing arrangements to which many non-nuclear weapons states object but were accepted by the Soviet Union as consistent with the treaty when it was concluded. The generalized, internationally sanctioned imperative of devaluing nuclear weapons endorsed in NPT Review Conferences creates a noticeable, quasi-Kantian indifference to questions about which specific states would become less likely to seek nuclear weapons capability if NATO ceased nuclear sharing, or how exactly the nuclear practices of India, Pakistan, or the Democratic People's Republic of Korea might change.[38]

Relatively optimistic strategic judgments of possible future adversaries also enter the equation. Above all, opponents of NATO NSNW tend (or need) to hold relatively positive views of Russia as unlikely, or unable, to take politico-military advantage of a total disparity in NSNW in its favor and as likely to respond positively to unilateral NATO disarmament measures, in ways that would promote positive political change in Western Eurasia in the direction of a Euro-Atlantic security community.[39] This is often combined with a determination to avoid discourses of "othering" by emphasizing mitigating contextual factors. It is a perspective which can lead to an empathic, though not necessarily wholly exculpatory identification with what is seen as Russia's almost tragic strategic predicament: historical trauma from repeated invasion, political encirclement, cultural problems related to building democratic legitimacy, demographic decline, absence of soft power, and economic weakness, all with consequent humiliating loss of power in the international system.

Similarly, there is an observable unwillingness to begin to refer to Iran as a potentially suitable object of future nuclear deterrence. Arguments encountered against this eventuality are that Iran does not really intend to develop its own nuclear weapons or, if it does, that it will be prevented or, if it is not, that the Iranian warheads would be negated by NATO missile defenses, which are morally superior to its nuclear capability. There is a similar reluctance to accept the possibility of other regimes that might unpredictably arise in NATO's increasingly volatile near abroad, in North Africa or the Middle East, as possible nuclear threats.

Backgrounds and Attitudes of Proponents of NATO NSNW

By contrast, proponents of the NATO nuclear status quo in Europe tend to display opposite characteristics. Most generally, they exhibit a markedly realist perspective that leads to support for a continuation of NATO nuclear-sharing arrangements as important instruments of assurance, crisis management, and deterrence.[40] The underlying judgments calling for this tend to be strengthened by prolonged socialization within nuclear specialties in official defense or research organizations or industry, in war or strategic studies departments in universities, or in conservative political parties. Doubts of the possibility of rapid improvements in present international security arrangements are frequently elaborated from first principles.[41]

As a consequence of this professionally sceptical worldview, NSNW proponents tend to see themselves explicitly and to argue, just as Snyder described, predominantly as insiders, "members of a national strategic community . . . achieved through instruction and in imitation with each other with regard to nuclear strategy."[42] Membership of expert national strategic communities deliberately interlinked within the Alliance is claimed by demonstrating a sophisticated understanding of the logic of nuclear strategy developed in Western doctrine since 1945, exemplified by the common deterrence culture shared within the Alliance, discreetly propagated by the Nuclear Planning Group. This common understanding has a slightly esoteric and initiated quality because it involves an appreciation that the remote but unextinguished possibility of nuclear escalation, even against non-nuclear attack, remains a key aspect of NATO nuclear strategy. Although not classified, this far-reaching truth is not widely appreciated by Alliance publics.

Second, proponents share a scepticism about the near-term attainability of Global Zero given the number of competing nuclear-dependent states, or its long-term desirability, if ever achieved.[43] Why hasten to put the Alliance at a permanent disadvantage by taking steps in the name of a temporarily fashionable vision that will falter and fail? They are concerned instead that, "while many in the West see nuclear weapons as instruments of the past, other actors tend to view them as weapons of the future" and that the world may be facing the dawning of a second nuclear age in which "new, innovative strategies are likely to develop.[44] Further modernization of nuclear forces and the spread of the bomb [are] likely."[45]

Third, proponents share an abiding respect for the unique and potentially fragile security community that NATO represents, especially with regard to the moral contribution of the militia model, the intrinsic solidifying value of NATO cohesion, the vital coupling with the US strategic nuclear arsenal, and the consequent need to hold to intra-Alliance commitments. They concede that the Alliance's present strategic situation is stable but stress that this cannot necessarily be relied on. For them, the major future risk is strategic and political destabilization, which might offer renewed incentives for miscalculated aggression. This is more significant than any intrinsic physical nuclear danger from the weapons or their platforms. With sufficient energy and professional excellence, NATO nuclear experts judge that these physical dangers can now be confidently minimized by sophisticated, well-proven warhead designs, permissive action links, storage facilities, guard forces exercises, and command and control arrangement. Russian nuclear forces may be less well provided for, but they too are seen as technically competent.

Fourth, they also share a concomitant trust in historical continuity and a conviction that deterrence policy prescriptions, which they judge to have avoided war successfully in Europe, should not be lightly discarded. Alliance process scepticism existed in the Cold War but was certainly not regarded as removing the deterrent utility of NSNW.

Fifth, they question whether Russian governments would consent to major changes in relations with NATO states, even if all NSNW were withdrawn to the continental United States. They tend to believe in the continuity of Russian strategic culture, including concepts such as the correlation of forces that was inherited from the Soviet era and generates attention to the peacetime political payoffs of military power.[46] This orientation is associated with concern about the intentions of the Putin regime and its unknowable successors, especially about scenarios of intimidation and limited intervention in what it regards as its sphere of privileged influence.[47] In states on NATO's eastern periphery, painful national historical experiences have left a strong sense of vulnerability to renewed Russian saber rattling, especially post-Euromaidan, which they fear might be encouraged by the Alliance-wide acceptance of a totally unbalanced disparity in a weapons category such as NSNW.

Sixth, proponents are concerned with the diffuse, nonkinetic, psychological, and political shaping effects of nuclear weapons in generating gravitational force fields of influence, cohesion, or inhibition. These would make it unwise for the Alliance to give up assets that, in the words of one senior NATO official "we use every day" and assume that the Russians try to do the same.[48] This vision of nuclear effectiveness is related to Robert Art's proposition that the "peaceful use of military power is akin to a gravitational field among large objects in space: it affects all motion that takes place, but it produces its effects imperceptibly."[49] In the mid-1950s, Paul Nitze had proposed a similarly shaping analogy, likening nuclear weapons to queens in chess: They may never move but their positioning determines how and where other pieces can safely advance.[50] But such considerations have to remain largely unvoiced. Official references to them would clash with the accepted and carefully scrutinized discourse of the NPT, which has come to emphasize the obligation on nuclear weapons states and their allies to lower the salience and systematically reduce the value of the weapons. Since these effects are largely intangible and sensed largely within national security elites, mentioning them publicly would be likely to attract horrified or derisive populist rebuttal from antinuclear commentators and activities.

Finally, there is apprehension over the long-term survivability of the Alliance if Europeans are seen to act as ungrateful financial and moral freeloaders, wanting the United States to take on sole responsibility for distasteful deterrent possibilities. This has been denounced as expecting the United States to agree in advance to act as nuclear executioner in order to preserve European self-conceptions as too spiritually advanced to be involved in the ugly business of contingency planning and training for thermonuclear war. To appreciate this fully, it is important to remember Robert Gates's gloomy departing warning about the necessity for a more equitable sharing of burdens if the Alliance is to be preserved, as mentioned in the introduction to this volume.[51] While resentment over inequitable moral burden–sharing has not yet entered US politics to a dangerous degree, many fear that it could in a toxically partisan atmosphere when the United States itself has, since March 1, 2013, faced reductions in every category of government spending following the application of deliberately painful budgetary sequestration.[52]

NATO NSNW on an Emerging Era of Nuclear Backed Russian Revisionism

The positions on Alliance nuclear policy presented in this chapter emerged principally during a 20-year period following the Cold War, during which NATO actively courted the Russian Federation to give up a relationship based upon deterrence and accept a genuine strategic partnership. This process came to an end with Putin's actions in 2014. Russia's open occupation and annexation of Crimea in March, and its subsequently denied but widely reported support for separatist rebels in Eastern Ukraine, were harshly criticized in the Wales Summit communiqué which set out a corresponding list of conventional responses, especially the creation of a new Spearhead Force (Very High Readiness Joint Task Force), which NATO judged necessary for the new threat environment.[53]

The dismemberment of a denuclearized Ukraine, violating formal assurances given under the 1994 Budapest Memorandum, carries very severe implications for the credibility of nuclear non-proliferation and disarmament arrangements.[54] Moreover, Russian statements since the occupation of Crimea have deliberately stressed the relevance of its formidable national nuclear capabilities and high-stakes determination, while denouncing NATO intentions in increasingly intemperate terms.

This deliberate Russian re-nuclearization of its relationship with NATO has taken various high-profile forms, all deliberately controlled by the central leadership.[55] *Nuclear signalling* has been bolstered by Putin's speeches, withdrawal from collaborative nuclear arrangements, as well as overflights by dual capable bombers with transponders sometimes turned off, to name a few examples.[56] In March 2015 the Russian ambassador, Mikhail Vanin, wrote openly in the Danish press to remind his hosts that Danish ships involved in (non-nuclear) NATO missile defense would become legitimate targets for Russian nuclear missiles.[57] In April 2015 there were revelations of an even more far-reaching and comprehensive attempt at *nuclear reshaping*. The recently published disclosures by the Elbe Group, a club of retired US and Russian generals and senior intelligence officials, were revelatory.[58] According to the account given to the London Times by a US participant, "the Russians flagged up at least three flashpoints that could lead to a direct, and possibly even nuclear, confrontation between the two nations:

- Crimea, where any attempt to return the annexed peninsula to Ukraine would be met forcefully including through the use of nuclear force;
- East Ukraine, where the supply of weapons by NATO to Kiev would be read as further encroachment by NATO to the Russian border;
- The Baltic States, where Mr Putin was ready to respond forcefully to any further NATO build-up in the Baltics . . . [with] . . . a spectrum of responses from nuclear to non-military."[59]

The Elbe Group warning seems to reveal Russia's nuclear backed aspirations to establish a permanently undisputed illegal annexation (in Crimea), a de facto protectorate over a provincial rebellion against a sovereign neighbor involving secessionist, proxy and clandestinely inserted Russian forces (in Eastern Ukraine), and an informally declared zone of heightened risk of nuclear confrontation comprising three entire independent countries (in the Baltic states). All this may amount only to a probe, a limited attempt to force the US at least to discuss unpalatable new "facts," or a means of maintaining the distracting strategic ambiguity (*maskirovka*) which seems to be a major feature of the new military Russian doctrine.[60] But, at worst, it could represent a developing (though very possibly improvised) attempt at revisionism to reshape the European security space, using semiformal nuclear threats to support covert sub-conventional interventions, and systematically inhibit the defensive choices of independent countries—reaching inside the borders of an opposing nuclear alliance.[61]

NATO has stayed silent about the Elbe Group warning and will probably remain so. This may be because, as very senior NATO military figures are prepared to admit, new Russian nuclear assertion requires some carefully considered NATO policy response, which has so far been largely inhibited by the sheer lack of political appetite among Allied governments for focusing public attention on nuclear issues given their upsetting electoral potential.[62]

As with so many aspects of NATO nuclear policy, collective official discretion is almost automatic. This is more than ever understandable. The Alliance faces a disturbing new conjunction: Moscow's fierce dissatisfaction with geostrategic and geo-economic trends in its self-declared zone of privileged interests around Russia's periphery. No clear-cut or reassuring policy response has so far been reported to be emerging within the Alliance. And anxieties about the immediate nuclear future have been further intensified by fears that Russian economic desperation, resulting from observable lack of reform, falling oil prices, and the paradoxically successful effect of sanctions, may lead to even more assertive or reckless Russian behavior.

At some stage, the Alliance nuclear policy will need to be comprehensively reconsidered, with special attention given to the role of NSNW. In the inescapable intra-allied policy debate (once again probably conducted as far as possible behind closed doors) the contending positions analyzed above are very likely to re-emerge, conditioned by the same persistent underlying nuclear dynamics—geopolitical divisions between and within Alliance members. Those differences will complicate the problems of achieving both analytical consensus and substantive agreement on implementation. Yet Mr Putin has now irrevocably raised the stakes for allied decisions. Outcomes, not only for NSNW, but for wider NATO nuclear strategy and indeed the nuclear world order beyond Europe will now have to be anticipated and managed against the more urgent and much less comfortable nuclear circumstances indefinitely facing the Alliance.

Conclusion

After Chicago, NATO committed itself to building a consensus capable of maintaining an acceptable comprehensive nuclear militia model in new conditions, including a largely contradictory anxiety to move toward Global Zero. This initially created interest in the idea of including NSNW in a comprehensive NATO position ("the whole enchilada") for conventional and nuclear arms control, and also missile defense.[63] No such comprehensive approach now seems feasible. The future of Alliance NSNW would be strongly affected by Russian willingness to come to the table for some form of agreement. But the possibility of opening such negotiations looked vanishingly small even before the dramatic deterioration of East-West relations in 2014. Russia has repeatedly announced that it will not negotiate over NSNW until all US nuclear weapons—which it points out are strategic in their ability to reach Russian targets—are withdrawn to the United States. It must therefore be expected that the Alliance will have to proceed without any prospect of Russian reciprocity over NSNW. The Ukraine crisis has made US-Russia talks over NSNW even less likely.

Alternatives for NATO NSNW will be hard to foresee, but there are at least four evident possibilities. In one optimistic transformative scenario, the interminable dispute would end by withdrawal of NATO NSNW to the continental United States as part of a comprehensive bilateral US-Russia treaty, accepted by the Alliance as a whole as an unavoidable precondition for sufficient, verifiable Russian concessions over nuclear numbers.[64]

Failing that outcome (which even its advocates concede would be politically and exquisitely difficult to bring off in a normal diplomatic atmosphere between NATO and Russia), the weapons would remain, but the issue could revert to its low normal salience (more kicking of the can), perhaps with slow progress toward a low-key, flexible, intra-Alliance compromise involving rebasing, transparency measures, and reductions in numbers. This would ideally be carefully linked with adequate reassurance measures for the most exposed and strategically apprehensive Alliance members.[65]

But there could instead be open and destructive political dispute within the Alliance over the NSNW question, most predictably because of antinuclear campaigning and political change in key basing countries, leading to a breaking of ranks over the Chicago decisions and giving up of any requirement for Russian reciprocation as a precondition. Cascading parliamentary refusals to maintain dual-capable roles or to create nuclear national replacements for F-16s or Tornadoes could repudiate the consensus achieved in Chicago. Considerable efforts would be made to avoid this scenario. They might involve face-saving assertions that more economically effective arrangements of some kind were available and that numbers of Russian NSNW or expensive delivery systems like dual-capable aircraft were on a falling trend anyway as a result of cost-constrained Russian military decisions and that this constituted sufficient reciprocation.[66]

A less divisive but still controversial alternative would be politically managed reduction, rebasing, and/or withdrawal of NSNW even without reciprocation. Compromise options such as the creation of a multinational European DCA wing might mitigate internal disagreements and anticipated loss of deterrence and reassurance.[67] But in the short term it would probably be impossible to avoid intra-Alliance dispute and distrust over such a symbolically entrenched and far-reaching nonconsensual change. Matters would be even worse if such changes had to be introduced despite active fears of aggression from Russia. The eventual consequences of further reduction in the salience of NATO NSNW in Europe would of course be fiercely disputed. There might be subsequent improvements in NATO-Russia relations, but these have been severely compromised following the annexation of Crimea.

If the issue turned into a serious intra-Alliance dispute surrounding a significant reduction of existing NSNW capabilities, there could even be calls for high-stakes recuperative moves intended to restore damaged US reassurance for anxious allies, including those watching closely from East Asia. One example might be rebasing US assets in the Baltic States, said to be under consideration as a potential future option in various congressional offices in Washington, DC in 2012.[68] Public suggestions of this kind to restore flagging US credibility would be of obvious concern to Russia and create perturbations in the Alliance.

Given the difficulty of reconciling contending positions and in view of the divisive underlying dynamics discussed in this chapter and throughout the book, sufficiently cohesive and successful handling within the Alliance may not be easy, although the Chicago Summit indicated widespread willingness to avoid major dispute.

At a minimum, successful handling is likely to require relatively unobstructed Alliance deliberations through the committee and planning processes in Brussels. This will mean a serious and prolonged collective attempt at objective analysis—without blockages or vetoes—of inconvenient and politically sensitive factors, such as the identity, location, form, and seriousness of imaginable future threats. It will also depend upon a willingness to turn conclusions from that horizon-scanning debate into investment, deployment, and declaratory language and, presumably, renewed contingency planning for nuclear strikes. Decisions of this kind will need a sufficiently objective calculation of the contribution of nuclear capabilities for both continuous shaping of NATO's international environment and support of nuclear options in particular contingencies.[69]

It will remain intrinsically difficult to agree on public statements about these factors. Even after Putin's actions in Crimea and Ukraine, there would be diplomatic sensitivities in naming *any* state as sufficiently threatening that nuclear deterrence would be required, together with political and media sensitivities over any apparent contradiction of Alliance and national commitments to devalue nuclear weapons and to contribute to a world without them. Deliberations within the Alliance will therefore again have to be conducted confidentially to offer the best chance of a durable consensus-building outcome. But it is true that the way NATO handles its NSNW choices will reflect its ability to reconcile and overcome potentially divisive intra-Alliance dynamics as spelled out in this chapter. NSNW decision-making processes and outcomes may therefore strongly influence the future tone, consultative style, internal levels of trust, and cohesive credibility of the system of transatlantic extended deterrence.

Notes

This chapter has benefited enormously and variously from advice, interaction, and debate over several years with Malcolm Chalmers, David Yost, Paul Ingram, Ward Wilson, Ian Kearns, Brad Roberts, Rebecca Johnson, Nick Ritchie, Nick Wheeler, Susan Martin, Mark Smith, Aaron Stein, Hugh Chalmers, Andrea Berger, Igor Sutyagin, Nikolai Sokov, Andrew Somerville, Patricia Lewis, Heather Williams, Camille Grand, Bruno Tertrais, the late Therese Delpech, Guillaume Schlumberger, Goetz Neunek, Tom Sauer, Laurens Hogebrink, Wilbert Van der Zeijden, Susie Snyder, Lukasz Kulesa, Jacek Durkalec, Paal Sigurd Hilde, Frank Miller, Jeffrey McCausland, David Hamon, Jeff Larsen, George Perkovich, James Acton, Steve Pfeiffer, Amy Woolf, Hans Kristensen, Hans Binnendijk, Isabelle François, Isabelle Williams, Paul Bernstein, Guy Roberts, Richard Weitz, Paolo Foradori, Sinan Ulgen, Mustafa Kibaroğlu, Kadri Liik, Greta Tuckute, Raimonds Rublovskis,

Marius Laurinavičius, Kathleen McInnis, William Walker, Sir Hugh Beach, Ted Seay, Oliver Meier, Anne Finger, Oliver Thranert, Ulrich Kuhn, Ursula Jasper, and a number of serving UK, US, Allied and NATO diplomats, officials and officers whom it might be invidious to name. Factual errors, misperceptions, misinterpretations, and obstinate disagreements are entirely my own.

1. Due to its special strategic position, Turkey's policies in this area are unique, deliberately low-key, and will not be specifically referred to again. But a convincing recent summary description has been offered by Aaron Stein: "Turkey values nuclear weapons for deterrence, believes they constrained Russian expansionism during the Cold War, and now believes that they help deter states in the Middle East. They are also an important symbol for a state perpetually wary of relying on verbal guarantees from its security guarantor—the US. . . . [Since the Cold War there has been] a noticeable drop in Turkish nuclear readiness. There are conflicting reports about whether or not Turkish F-16s can carry nuclear weapons. In all honesty, it does not really matter. The weapons can't be used quickly and, in the extremely unlikely scenario that these weapons would be used, the US would move assets into place. Turkish planes would likely serve as escort fighters. As for removing the weapons, Turks will tell you that they support the idea in principle, but only if it is agreed to by all NATO states—as we all know, this is a diplomatic dodge and a way for Turkey to hide behind the Baltic States and not reveal publicly just how happy Ankara is to keep the status quo." Aaron Stein, "Turkey, Tactical Nuclear Weapons, and Strategic Thinking," May 16, 2013, http://turkeywonk.wordpress.com/.

2. *Addressing Non-Strategic Nuclear Forces: Report of the Euro Atlantic Security Initiative Working Group on Non-Strategic Nuclear Weapons*, EASI Report, February 2012 (Washington, DC: Carnegie Endowment for International Peace, February 2013); George Perkovich, Malcolm Chalmers, Steven Pifer, Paul Schulte, and Jaclyn Tandler, *Looking beyond the Chicago Summit: Nuclear Weapons in Europe and the Future of NATO*. Carnegie Paper, April 2012 (Washington, DC: Carnegie Endowment for International Peace), 23; Igor Sutyagin, *Atomic Accounting: A New Estimate of Russia's Non-Strategic Nuclear Forces*, RUSI Occasional Paper, November 2012 (London: Royal United Services Institute, 2012).

3. Arms Control Association, *Nuclear Weapons: Who Has What at a Glance*, ACA Press Release, November 2012 (Washington, DC: Arms Control Association, 2012), http://www.armscontrol.org/factsheets/Nuclearweaponswhohaswhat/.

4. The UK nuclear deterrent, now at around 120 warheads, continues to generate profuse political debate, but this is in many ways an argument about British national identity and is largely confined to the British political class.

5. This was especially so in Germany. For a description of postwar reactions essential to the creation of German national strategic culture, see Beatrice Heuser, *Nuclear Mentalities? Strategies and Beliefs in Britain and France and the FRG* (Basingstoke, UK: Macmillan Press, 1998), 180–85; Western estimates of Russian military power at the start of the Cold War in the late 1940s, which led to the deployment of American nonstrategic nuclear weapons in Europe, were almost certainly exaggerated. See the impressive list of references compiled by Vojtech Mastny, "Imagining War in Europe," in *War Plans and Alliances in the Cold War: Threat Perceptions in East and West*, ed. Sven G Holtsmark and Andreas Wenger (London: Routledge, 2006), 16.

6. For discussion, see *Soviet Active Measures in the "Post–Cold War Era" 1988–1991: A Report Prepared at the Request of the United States House of Representatives Committee on Appropriations by the United States Information Agency* (Washington, DC: United States Information Agency, 1992).

7. A large international conference held in February 2013 in Warsaw on NSNW emphasized the scale of uncertainty. "Numbers of American and Russian NSNW in Europe have been considerably reduced since the end of the Cold War. However, there was a lack of transparency regarding numbers, location, operational status and levels of security. This created very evident disagreement over the true size of the Russian NSNW arsenal, which some participants believed still remained asymmetrically large, while others felt might in fact have fallen to levels much closer to the combined levels of NATO Allies, although this would require a calculation in which French and British strategic systems were added to American non-strategic weapons." "The Warsaw Workshop: Prospects for Information Sharing and Confidence Building on Non-Strategic Nuclear Weapons in Europe," *Polish Institute for International Affairs*, April 2013, 7, http://www.pism.pl/publications/reports/PISM-Report-The-Warsaw-Workshop-Prospects-for-Information-Sharing-and-Confidence-Building-on-Non-Strategic-Nuclear-Weapons-in-Europe.

8. Jacob W. Kipp, "Russian Doctrine on Tactical Nuclear Weapons: Contexts, Prisms, and Connections," in *Tactical Nuclear Weapons and NATO*, ed. Tom Nichols, Douglas Stuart, and Jeffrey D. McCausland (Carlisle, PA: US Strategic Studies Institute, 2012).

9. Perkovich et al., *Looking beyond the Chicago Summit*, 14.

10. Wilbert Van der Zeijden, *NATO Nuclear Weapons and the Defense and Deterrence Posture Review: A Non-Consensual Debate*, Open Security Reconciliation and Conflict, May 7, 2012, http://www.opendemocracy.net/opensecurity/wilbert-van-der-zeijden/nato-nuclear-weapons-and-defense-and-deterrence-posture-review/.

11. Wilbert van der Zeijden, Susi Snyder, and Peter Paul Ekker, *Exit Strategies: The Case for Redefining NATO Consensus on US TNW* (Utrecht: IKV Pax Christi, 2012); Rachel Oswald, "Arms Control Groups Accuse NATO of Keeping Nuclear Status Quo," *NTI*, May 22, 2012, http://www.nti.org/gsn/article/nato-failed-change-nuclear-status-quo-experts/.

12. Edmond E. Seay III, *Dissecting the DDPR, NATO's Deterrence and Defense Posture Review and the Future of Nuclear Sharing*, Arms Control Association (ACA), British American Security Information Council (BASIC), Institute for Peace Research and Security Policy at the University of Hamburg (IFSH). Nuclear Policy Paper No. 10, July 2012.

13. NATO Press Release 063, "Deterrence and Defense Posture Review," Section II. The Contribution of Nuclear Forces, issued on May 20, 2012, para. 8, http://www.nato.int/cps/en/natolive/official_texts_87597.htm?mode=pressrelease

14. Ibid, para. 12.

15. Quoted in David S. Yost, *NATO's Deterrence and Defense Posture after the Chicago Summit: A Report on a Workshop in Rome*, June 25–27, 2012 (Rome: NATO Defense College, October 2012), 4, http://www.ndc.nato.int/download/downloads.php?icode=356.

16. Hugh Chalmers, Malcolm Chalmers, and Andrea Berger (eds.), *A Problem Deferred? NATO Non-Strategic Nuclear Weapons after Chicago*, Whitehall Report 4–12 (London: Royal United Services Institute, 2012).

17. NATO, *NATO's Nuclear Forces*, http://www.nato.int/cps/fr/SID-02093EB1A95A4062/natolive/topics_50068.htm?blnSublanguage=true&selectedLocale=uk&submit=select (last updated October 27, 2010).

18. Perkovich et al. *Looking beyond the Chicago Summit*, 9.

19. Ibid.

20. Patrick M. Morgan, "Collective-Actor Deterrence," in *Complex Deterrence: Strategy and the Global Age*, ed. T. V. Paul, Patrick M Morgan, and James J. Wirtz (Chicago, IL: University of Chicago Press, 2009), 163–64.

21. Ibid., 164.

22. After rather different previous usages by Max Weber, Otto Bauer, and the Nazi Party, this term became noticeable in the internal German rhetorical struggles of the early Cold War to emphasize the moral and ideological significance of the truncated and threatened frontline Federal Republic's integration with the Atlantic Community. Peter Baehr, *Caesarism, Charisma and Fate: Historical Sources and Modern Resonances in the Work of Max Weber* (Piscataway, NJ: Transaction Publishers, 2008, and Google eBook), 117–53.

23. Morgan, "Collective-Actor Deterrence," 171.

24. Text of the Founding Act on Mutual Relations, Cooperation and Security between NATO and the Russian Federation, signed May 27, 1997, Section V: Political-Military Matters, http://www.nato.int/cps/en/SID-5766630B-56289618/natolive/official_texts_25468.htm.

25. Jack Snyder, *The Soviet Strategic Culture: Implications for Limited Nuclear Operations* (Santa Monica, CA: RAND, 1977).

26. Alessia Biava, Margiet Drent, and Graeme P. Herd, "Characterizing the European Union's Strategic Culture: An Analytical Framework," *Journal of Common Market Studies* 49, no. 6 (2011): 1227–48.

27. For an account of European demilitarization, see James J. Sheehan, *Where Have All the Soldiers Gone? The Transformation of Modern Europe* (Boston, MA: Houghton Mifflin, 2008).

28. This concern over the risks of over involvement with the US global nuclear role is quite compatible with explicit affection for Americans and American culture. The emphatic expression of these combined attitudes among antinuclear participants is a frequent trope at conferences and workshops on NATO nuclear issues.

29. Max Weber, "Politics as Vocation," in *The Vocation Lectures*, ed. David Owen and Tracy B. Strong, translated by Rodney Livingstone (Indianapolis, IN: Hackett Publishing Company, 2004).

30. Robert Kagan, *Of Paradise and Power: America and Europe in the New World Order* (New York: Alfred A Knopf, 2003).

31. The Scottish Nationalist Party's strongly antinuclear defense policy suggests that Scotland's national strategic culture has moved in a quasi-Scandinavian direction (although the party currently appears to wish to remain in NATO after secession). This may be illustrative of a general rule by which very small European states, except those on the frontline in the Baltic, will regard themselves as entitled to disengage from culturally controversial nuclear involvement.

32. Andrea Berger, "Playing It Safe: The German Election and Tactical Nuclear Weapons," January 18, 2013, http://turkeywonk.wordpress.com/2013/01/18/playing-it-safe-the-german-election-and-tactical-nuclear-weapons/.

33. For example, the "pragmatic historical skepticism" advanced by Ward Wilson, questioning the significance of Nagasaki and Hiroshima in causing the Japanese surrender, and the subsequent roles of nuclear weapons in major crises. These arguments are well presented on Wilson's website, http://www.rethinkingnuclear weapons.org/, and in Ward Wilson, *Five Myths about Nuclear Weapons* (Boston, MA: Houghton Mifflin Harcourt, 2013).

34. Pierre Hassner discussed the post-Protestantism thesis in his book, *Violence and Peace: From the Atomic Bomb to Ethnic Cleansing*, translated by Jane Brenton (Budapest: Central European University Press, 1997), 120–22.

35. Thomas C. Schelling, *Arms and Influence* (New Haven, CT: Yale University Press, 1966), 17.

36. As a striking indicator of major—and perhaps increasing—differences among the religious components of different national strategic cultures, it is worth noting that the Russian Orthodox Church has designated patron saints of Russian strategic nuclear forces. Mark Schneider, *The Nuclear Forces and Doctrine of the Russian Federation* (Fairfax, VA: National Institute Press, 2006), 2.

37. See Beatrice Fihn and Ray Acheson, "Moving towards a Ban on Nuclear Weapons," in *Report from the Conference on the Humanitarian Impact of Nuclear Weapons*, Oslo, March 4–5, 2013, http://www.reachingcriticalwill.org/images/documents/Disarmament-fora/oslo-2013/HINWreport.pdf. See also, in the same vein, Randy Rydell, "The United Nations and a Humanitarian Approach to Nuclear Disarmament," *Nuclear Abolition Forum*, no. 1 (October 2011).

38. The 2010 NPT Review Conference Final Document elaborated a sixty-four-point action plan that called on the nuclear weapon states "[t]o further diminish the role and significance of nuclear weapons in all military and security concepts, doctrines and policies."

39. For a wider context on this elusive international objective, see *Toward a Euro-Atlantic Security Community*, Euro-Atlantic Security Initiative Final Report, Carnegie Endowment for International Peace, Washington, DC, February 2012.

40. This term is often used interchangeably with *neorealism*, deriving from the work of Kenneth Waltz, certainly an important background influence on many involved in the nuclear debate. But others insist that their realism relies more on Thucydides than Waltz. Although they occur constantly in academic analysis, neither the term *realism* nor the term *neorealism* is noticeably employed within NATO, US, UK, or French government discourse.

41. For example, "neorealism posits that the anarchic structure of the international system conditions interstate relations and that conflict is an enduring possibility. In the absence of any supranational authority to ensure peace, states have no option but to adopt self-help strategies . . . by either internal efforts (moves to increase economic capability, to increase military strength, to develop clever strategies) and external efforts (moves to strengthen and enlarge one's own Alliance and shrink opposing ones." Another perennial feature identified in realist thought is the security dilemma, which exists when the military preparations of one state are viewed by another state as potentially threatening. It is thus said to be the "unresolvable uncertainty inherent in this domain." "Introduction," in *Neorealism Versus Strategic Culture*, ed. John Glenn, Darryl Howlett, and Stuart Poore, (Aldershot, UK: Ashgate, 2004), 5.

42. Jack Snyder, *The Soviet Strategic Culture: Implications for Limited Nuclear Operations* (Santa Monica, CA: RAND, 1977), 8.

43. Thomas C. Schelling, "A World without Nuclear Weapons?," *Daedalus* 138, no. 4 (Fall 2009).

44. Therese Delpech, *Nuclear Deterrence in the 21st-Century: Lessons from the Cold War for a New Area of Strategic Piracy* (Washington, DC: Rand Corporation, 2012), 10.

45. Paul Bracken, *The Bomb Returns for a Second Act*, Foreign Policy Research Institute Note, Philadelphia, 2012; and Paul Bracken, *The Second Nuclear Age, Strategy, Danger, and the New Power Politics* (New York: Times Books, 2012).

46. For an extensive account of the Correlation of Forces at its doctrinally optimistic height, see Richard E. Porter, "Correlation of Forces: Revolutionary Legacy," *Air University Review* (March–April, 1977).

47. The political and strategic costs and distortions for Russia involved in the concept of a privileged sphere of interests are discussed in Dmitri Trenin, *Post Imperium: A Eurasian Story* (Washington, DC: Carnegie Endowment for International Peace, 2011).

48. Guy Roberts, former head of the NATO WMD office, personal communication. The phrase was also used by a uniformed speaker at the 2013 Carnegie Endowment Nuclear Policy Conference, without challenge from the large and expert audience.

49. Robert J. Art, "The Fungibility of Force," in *The Use of Force: Military Power and International Politics*, 7th ed., ed. Robert J. Art and Kenneth N. Waltz (Lanham, MD: Rowman and Littlefield Publishers, 2009), 3.

50. See Paul Nitze "Atoms, Strategy and Policy," *Foreign Affairs* 34, no. 2 (1956).

51. Teri Schultz, "Robert Gates Blasts NATO Members in Final Speech" *Global Post*, June 10, 2011.

52. "Try explaining to a freshman Congressman why the US homeland should be subject to nuclear attacks to deter aggression against NATO while NATO allies are unwilling even to share the risk and burden of basing a very small part of the deterrent on their soil." Franklin Miller, "NATO's Nuclear Future: Self-Centered Policies Threaten Collective Security," remarks at the Brookings Institution on July 19, 2011, posted July 21, 2011, http://www.acus.org/natosource/nato's-nuclear-future-self-centered-policies-threaten-collective-security.

53. *Wales Summit Declaration: Issued by the Heads of State and Government participating in the meeting of the North Atlantic Council in Wales*, September 5, 2014, http://www.nato.int/cps/ic/natohq/official_texts_112964.htm

54. For an authoritative examination of the wider, and universally negative, implications of this far-reaching but underplayed event, see David S. Yost, "The Budapest Memorandum and Russia's Intervention in Ukraine," *International Affairs*, vol. 91, no. 3 (2015): forthcoming.

55. Nikolai Sokov "The 'Return' of Nuclear Weapons," *Open Democracy*, 28 November 2014, https://www.opendemocracy.net/od-russia/nikolai-sokov/'return'-of-nuclear-weapons

56. In December 2014 Moscow informed Washington, DC that Russia would no longer accept US help in protecting the Russian stockpiles of weapons grade uranium and plutonium. This effectively ended the Cooperative Threat Reduction Programme, one of the most successful fields of cooperation in the Post-Cold War period. Russia

also announced that it would not attend the 2016 Nuclear Security Summit in the US. Thomas Frear, Lukasz Kulesa and Ian Kearns, "*Dangerous Brinkmanship: Close Military Encounters Between Russia and the West in 2014*" European Leadership Network Policy Brief, November 2014. http://www.europeanleadershipnetwork.org/medialibrary/2014/11/09/6375e3da/Dangerous%20Brinkmanship.pdf

57. "*Russian Ambassador Warns Denmark Over NATO Missile Shield* "Agence France-Presse, March 22, 2015.

58. Kevin Ryan, "The Elbe Group: Meetings of Military Minds," *InFocus*, Winter 2014.

59. Ben Hoyle and Michael Evans, "Putin Threat of Nuclear Showdown over Baltics," *The Times*, April 2, 2015.

60. Dave Johnson "*Russia's Approach to Conflict: Implications for NATO's Deterrence and Defence*," NATO Defence College Research Division, no. 111 (April 2015) http://www.ndc.nato.int/news/current_news.php?icode=797

61. NATO will have to consider that the various moves in such a strategy are being conducted within a framework of "reflexive control," a formalized planning approach intended to interfere with enemy decision-making, often "by the use of disinformation, camouflage or some other stratagem." Within Russian military doctrine, reflexive control is defined "as means of conveying to a partner or opponent specially prepared information to voluntarily make the predetermined decision desired by the initiator of the action." See Timothy L. Thomas, "Reflexive Control Theory and the Military," *Journal of Slavic Military Studies* 17 (2004): 237–56.

62. Statement made under Chatham House rules at IISS high-level workshop on 'Meeting NATO's Future Ambitions', March 2015.

63. Tom Donilon, the national security adviser, announced that the Obama administration intends to seek, in the next round of negotiations with Russia, an agreement that would "include both non-deployed and nonstrategic nuclear weapons." Administration officials have taken to calling this approach the whole enchilada. Jeffrey Lewis, "Resuming SLCM Data Exchanges," *Arms Control Wonk blog*, July 10, 2012, http://lewis.armscontrolwonk.com/archive/5478/resuming-slcm-data-exchanges.

64. This is the ambitious prospectus of one final round of bilateral US-Russian reductions, which would include NSNW and cut numbers to around one thousand operationally deployed warheads on each side, proposed by Steve Pifer and Michael O'Hanlon in *The Opportunity: Next Steps in Reducing Nuclear Arms* (Washington, DC: Brookings Institution Press, January 2013).

65. Perkovich et al., *Looking beyond the Chicago Summit*, 20–26.

66. Igor Sutyagin at the Royal United Services Institute in London has repeatedly argued that such reductions in operationally available Russian NSNW has already been taking place to a greater extent than has been noticed or accepted in the West. But this assessment remains controversial.

67. David Yost, "The US Debate on NATO Nuclear Deterrence," *International Affairs* 87, no. 6 (November 2011).

68. Personal communication to the author.

69. For a useful explanation of how complicated this decision process could be, even for a single state, together with some "generic features of a good structure for supporting strategic level decisions," see Paul K. Davis, *Structuring Analysis to Sup-*

port Future Decisions about Nuclear Forces and Postures (Santa Monica, CA: RAND Corporation, 2011), http://www.rand.org/content/dam/rand/pubs/working_papers/2011/RAND_WR878.pdf. It is noteworthy that Davies contrasts "two stylized policy-level stances that bound the range of views" (pages 4–5) and that resemble the two opposing positions on nuclear weapons discussed in this chapter. He concludes that "most of the important issues cannot be accurately evaluated with reliably predictive models. To the contrary, the most important challenges are probably identifying appropriate test cases etc." This is partial corroboration of the improbability of reaching genuine consensus over the continuing need for NSNW in NATO force posture.

CHAPTER 5

Nuclear Weapons in NATO's Deterrence Posture

STATUS QUO OR CHANGE?

Hans M. Kristensen

IN TWO RECENT DOCUMENTS, the Strategic Concept adopted in Lisbon in November 2010 and the Deterrence and Defense Posture Review (DDPR) adopted in Chicago in May 2012, NATO and the United States have reaffirmed that nuclear weapons will continue to play a role in the Alliance's security doctrine as long as other countries have nuclear weapons. While the DDPR determined that the current nuclear posture is appropriate, both documents also commit NATO to work to create the conditions for reducing the number of weapons deployed in Europe, reducing the reliance on nuclear weapons in NATO strategy, and creating the conditions for a world without nuclear weapons.

These apparently contradictory commitments to the status quo and change create a somewhat dissonant nuclear policy with inherent conflicts for the Alliance's nuclear priority for the next decade and a half. The problem is more than academic. Proponents of the status quo and proponents of change are both likely to argue that these documents show that NATO has endorsed *their* position, thus potentially setting the stage for continued internal discord rather than unity on the priorities of NATO's nuclear policy. The dissonant policy reflects an internal need for mutual accommodation. It was more important for the authors of the documents to try to account for everyone's wishes within a growing Alliance and to avoid tackling the hard issues of the future role of nuclear weapons in Europe than it was to present a political vision for a new direction on nuclear policy.

Perhaps then it is symptomatic that the DDPR begins with five paragraphs on the contribution of *nuclear* forces, even though scenarios requiring the threat of use or employment of nuclear weapons are possibly the least likely to require NATO's attention in the foreseeable future. But addressing the security concerns of Eastern European allies need to be based on real reassurance that is credible in today's security environment rather than recycled nuclear doctrine from the Cold War. This need has deepened after Russia's invasion of Ukraine and NATO's subsequent efforts to reassure Eastern members of the alliance. In those efforts, the approximately 180 forward deployed US B61 nuclear bombs in Europe have been largely irrelevant and incapable of reassuring NATO allies, who instead have asked for reassurance from non-nuclear forces and operations.

Whether one believes that NATO's nuclear priority should be the status quo or change, the foreseeable future of the Alliance's nuclear posture seems to be anything but status quo. Significant modernizations are planned for both nuclear weapons and delivery platforms, and financial constraints are likely to challenge that modernization and the nuclear status quo even further. It is even possible that allied participation in the nuclear-sharing mission will be reduced. As a result, NATO's nuclear policy may soon be in need of an update.

Policy Contradictions: The Status Quo or Change

Before proceeding, it is necessary to address some of the policy issues that arise from the Alliance's two most important public documents: the Strategic Concept and the DDPR. Both documents raise the key issue of NATO's nuclear policy priorities. The Strategic Concept and DDPR were widely claimed by NATO officials as demonstrating Alliance cohesion and agreement about the direction for the future. Yet beneath surface platitudes, the documents contain policy statements and recommendations on NATO's nuclear posture that are contradictory. They appear to be the product of an attempt to reach a compromise among widely different perspectives within the Alliance rather than about clear leadership or thinking about the future role of nuclear weapons.

On the one hand, the documents reaffirm that nuclear weapons will continue to play a role in NATO's posture "as long as nuclear weapons exist," with "the broadest possible participation" in nuclear planning, basing, and command and control of nuclear forces, and that the "nuclear force posture currently meets the criteria for an effective deterrence and defence posture."[1]

These decisions appear to embrace the status quo, perhaps even indecision. On the other hand, much of the language that in earlier versions of the Strategic Concept explicitly highlighted the role and importance of US nonstrategic nuclear weapons (NSNW) in Europe is not included in the 2010 Strategic Concept. Gone is the previous language about the US non-strategic nuclear weapons providing "an essential political and military link" between Europe and North America, or that substrategic forces provide an escalation link with strategic forces.

Both documents pledge to further reduce the number of, and reliance upon, US nuclear weapons in Europe, and commit NATO to "create the *conditions for a world without nuclear weapons*" (emphasis in original). Indeed, the DDPR explicitly states that the North Atlantic Council (NAC) should "task the appropriate committees to develop concepts for how to ensure the broadest possible participation of Allies concerned in their nuclear sharing arrangements, *including in case NATO were to decide to reduce its reliance on nonstrategic nuclear weapons based in Europe*" (emphasis added).[2] These decisions appear to signal an intention to break with the status quo and begin preparations to that end. Granted, there have always been divergent views in NATO, and it is perhaps not surprising that NATO's eastward expansion to a total of twenty-eight countries will challenge the nuclear policy. Yet it is disappointing for an alliance such as NATO that two decades of post–Cold War developments and thinking have not generated a more visionary nuclear policy than is presented in the Strategic Concept and DDPR.

Adversaries and Numbers: Russia and Disparity

Just consider the question of who the adversary is and why. For two decades, NATO has insisted that US nuclear weapons in Europe were not directed against Russia or any other country and repeatedly reduced forces unilaterally. The Presidential Nuclear Initiatives of 1991 and 1992, which withdrew ground-launched and naval nuclear weapons from Europe and South Korea and offloaded nuclear weapons from ships and attack submarines, were unilateral initiatives that assumed (correctly) that Russia would follow the lead. The 1994 Nuclear Posture Review did not anticipate or require Russian reciprocity but nonetheless unilaterally denuclearized the entire US surface fleet, including those warships deploying to the European theater. In 2005 and 2006, the Bush administration quietly cut by more than half the stockpile of nuclear weapons in Europe, including the complete withdrawal of nuclear weapons from the United Kingdom and Ramstein Air Base in

Germany.[3] Both were unilateral reductions without any preconditions for Russian reciprocity or public arms control profile.

Both the Strategic Concept and DDPR declare that NATO does not consider any country to be its adversary. Yet at the same time both documents make further reductions in US nonstrategic nuclear weapons in Europe explicitly conditional on Russian reciprocity. They do not mention Iran or any other country by name. The Strategic Concept is the most explicit: "Any further steps must take into account the disparity with the greater Russian stockpiles of short-range nuclear weapons."[4] This apparent policy shift broke with the post–Cold War history of unilateral reductions and in effect reinstated Russia as the declared nuclear counterpart for the US nonstrategic arsenal in Europe. In reality, that has probably always been the main reason behind the scene, but now it is explicit. After the Russian invasion of Ukraine, NATO defense policy, including nuclear policy, is now being officially linked more directly to Russia.

This policy and the explicitness of its articulation has several potential implications. One is that officially declaring Russia as the nuclear counterpart for NATO's nonstrategic posture in Europe to some extent returns NATO's nuclear policy to the past, when the posture was directly aimed at the Soviet Union. Obviously this is not on the same scale or political context, but to link it explicitly further colors the current political context.

Another implication is that it plays into the counterproductive statements and exercises that Russia has delivered over the past few years, when we have seen officials making explicit nuclear threats against missile defense installations in Eastern Europe and simulated use of nonstrategic nuclear weapons in defensive exercises. This development began around 2008 but increased noticeably with the US decision to deploy missile defense systems in Europe and Russia's invasion of Ukraine.

Another potential implication is that it surrenders the initiative on nonstrategic nuclear weapons to Russian hard-liners, who have already rejected reductions on Russian nonstrategic nuclear forces as long as US nuclear weapons remain in Europe. As a result both sides have boxed themselves into positions of not doing anything until the other side does something. And in the current political crisis following Russia's invasion of Ukraine, progress seems highly unlikely.

Finally, by explicitly linking the US nuclear posture in Europe to Russia, NATO may be setting itself up for failure because Russia's nonstrategic nuclear posture is not determined by NATO's *nuclear* posture but as a way to compensate for Russia's inferior *conventional* forces. Neither side wants to reduce its nonstrategic forces because of disparity or to compensate for conventional inferiority, so NATO has been limiting itself to pursuing softer issues such as transparency and confidence-building measures. These are important and worthwhile steps, but they alone will not result in the reductions of the Russian nonstrategic nuclear weapons about which NATO now says it is so concerned.

It is worth mentioning that, although NATO policy now disavows unilateral reductions of nonstrategic nuclear weapons, one of the first decisions of the Obama administration curiously was to do precisely that by retiring (with NATO's blessing) the nuclear Tomahawk Land-Attack Missile (TLAM-N). Some of the TLAM-Ns had been supporting NATO scenarios since they were first deployed in 1983, even though they had been stored on land since 1992. No precondition was set for this retirement to urge Russia to retire its Tomahawski, the SS-N-21 Sampson or any other cruise missile.

This leads to the question, what does NATO mean by the terms *disparity* and *reciprocity*? The Strategic Concept and DDPR only mention four specific goals: First, seek Russian agreement to increase transparency on its nuclear weapons in Europe; second, relocate these weapons away from the territory of NATO members; third, any further steps must take into account the disparity with the greater Russian stockpiles of short-range nuclear weapons; and fourth, develop detailed proposals on and increase mutual understanding of NATO's and Russia's nonstrategic nuclear force postures in Europe.[5] Reduction of Russian nonstrategic nuclear weapons is not listed as an explicit goal.

Indeed, NATO is so unclear about how best to engage Russia that the DDPR itself directs the NAC to consider "what NATO would expect to see in the way of reciprocal Russian actions to allow for significant reductions in forward-based nonstrategic nuclear weapons assigned to NATO."[6] One would imagine that this question had been answered, or at least defined, before NATO decided to adopt disparity and reciprocity as potential roadblocks to further US reductions in Europe.

For example, when NATO says that it wants Russian nonstrategic nuclear weapons relocated away from the territory of NATO members, does that mean that it wants the delivery systems or only the *warheads* for those delivery systems moved? This ambiguity is critical because there is no reason to expect that Russia would agree to move aircraft and ships to other locations when these systems are also used for non-nuclear missions. As for the warheads, it is of little overall significance if Russia moves its warheads back. It would not change the military balance because the warheads could be returned quickly to the delivery systems if a crisis erupted. Is NATO referring only to a portion of the nonstrategic nuclear forces, such as nuclear-capable SS-21 and SS-26 short-range ballistic missile launchers in the Kaliningrad region, or to all non-strategic nuclear forces along the entire NATO-Russian border? The ambiguity of NATO's statements regarding Russia's NSNW is both misleading and damaging.

In fact, the significance of this disparity in nonstrategic nuclear forces between NATO and Russia is limited. Disparity also existed in 1994 when the United States denuclearized its surface fleet, it existed in 2005 when the Bush administration cut the deployment in Europe by half and withdrew nuclear weapons from the United Kingdom, and it existed in 2010 when the decision was made to retire the TLAM-N. If disparity existed but did not matter then, emphasizing it now does little to reduce the role of non-strategic nuclear weapons.

Conversely, does taking into account the disparity in Russia's larger stockpile of short-range nuclear weapons mean that NATO is advocating overall parity in nonstrategic nuclear weapons? If that is the case, how much disparity is acceptable? This should be clarified if NATO wants its nuclear weapons policy to have any leverage with Russia. Further, attention should be paid to which elements of the disparity matter. Russia and the United States have very different nonstrategic nuclear postures that are challenging to compare directly. Russia has an estimated 2,000 nonstrategic nuclear warheads assigned to naval, air, ground, and defense forces, with many more retired but still intact weapons awaiting dismantling. The United States has only an estimated 500 nonstrategic warheads left (approximately 180 Europe), all air-delivered bombs. After the nonstrategic B61-4 is modified into the new precision-guided B61-12, the B61-3 and B61-10 tactical bombs will be retired. And while Russian nonstrategic weapons are not deployed with their delivery systems, the US bombs in Europe are deployed in underground vaults a few meters from the aircraft, inside aircraft shelters, at six bases in five European countries.

NATO documents and statements make no distinction among categories of the various portions of the Russia nonstrategic nuclear posture. For the sake of clarity, a distinction should be made regarding overall numbers and those that are offensive. For example, NATO policymakers would do well to discuss whether the four hundred or so warheads that Russia is thought to have for arming nonoffensive air defense, missile defense, and coastal defense weapons systems are part of the disparity problem and consequently how a reduction might be envisaged. For its part, NATO does not have defensive nuclear weapons at all. If defensive nuclear forces are part of what NATO wishes to reduce, then it would have to engage the US Congress because the US Senate resolution that approved the New START treaty explicitly excluded such weapons from future negotiations: "it is the policy of the United States that such negotiations shall not include defensive missile systems."[7] This is yet another vexing contradiction that NATO should address.

Similarly, while Russia is thought to have a few hundred warheads for use by short-range ballistic missiles (SS-21 and SS-26), the United States and NATO have unilaterally eliminated all of their nonstrategic nuclear army weapons. Again, this makes a comparison on the disparity in army weapons very difficult in the NATO-Russia context. Likewise, with the retirement of the TLAM-N, the United States has unilaterally eliminated its entire inventory of nonstrategic naval nuclear weapons, a category that in 1987 included some 3,700 weapons for use by nearly 240 ships, attack submarines, and maritime aircraft.[8] Russia also has about 700 nonstrategic nuclear warheads assigned to its naval forces. Because the United States and Britain have unilaterally eliminated all its nonstrategic naval nuclear weapons, Russia's naval forces might also be counted against the disparity in nonstrategic nuclear weapons.

The only category where there is some degree of compatibility between Russian and US nonstrategic nuclear forces is air-delivered weapons. The United States has an inventory of approximately 500 gravity bombs left, compared with Russia's 730 estimated air-delivered weapons. But even in this category, the United States appears to be moving away from having specific nonstrategic nuclear bombs. There are currently three types of B61 bombs listed in the stockpile plan as *tactical* (B61-3/4/10); two other types are *strategic* (B61-7/11). But the planned life extension of the B61 bomb will convert the B61-4 to a hybrid bomb (B61-12) for use by both long-range bombers and fighter jets. After the B61-12 program is completed, there will no designated *tactical* bombs left in the stockpile. By the early 2020s, the nuclear mission in Europe will, if it is continued, be done with the same B61-12 bomb that will be assigned to the strategic B-2 bombers back in the United States.

In sum, NATO's policy on Russian disparity and reciprocity of nonstrategic nuclear weapons needs to be clarified and defined with an eye to what kind of changes the Alliance would like Russia to undertake. It should also address how NATO and US nonstrategic forces have developed and are likely to develop in the foreseeable future. As the disparity and reciprocity policy stands now, it seems retroactive and more like a roadblock than a basis for persuading Russia to reduce its nonstrategic nuclear weapons.

Nuclear Modernization

NATO's nuclear posture is scheduled to undergo a significant modernization over the next decade that involves upgrading both the nuclear weapons and delivery vehicles. The modernization will significantly increase the military capabilities of NATO's nuclear posture in Europe.[9] The first part of the modernization involves the B61 bomb, of which approximately 180 are deployed at six bases in five European countries. Over the next decade, the B61-3 and B61-4 bombs currently deployed in Europe will be shipped back to the United States as part of a life-extension program for the B61 bomb. The program involves consolidating four existing versions (B61-3, B61-4, B61-7, and B61-10) into one: the B61-12.[10] Disassembly of existing B61s will begin in 2016, and the first B61-12 is scheduled for delivery in 2020.

The increased military capability does not come in the form of a larger nuclear explosive yield—the new bomb will reuse the nuclear explosive package of the B61-4, which has four selective yields up to 50 kilotons. Instead, the B61-12 will be equipped with a new guided tail kit assembly that will increase the accuracy of the weapon compared with the weapons that are currently deployed in Europe.

The guided tail kit will have two primary effects. The first is that the 50-kiloton B61-12 will be able to hold at-risk targets that currently require the high yield of the 360-kiloton B61-7. In other words, the B61-12 will be a strategic bomb with significantly greater target kill capability than the B61 versions currently deployed in Europe. The second effect is that the B61-12 will be able to destroy smaller targets with lower yield selections than are currently needed to destroy the same targets today. For the strike planners, this creates a more usable weapon because they will be able to destroy targets with much less radioactive fallout than would otherwise be created by the higher yields needed for today's less accurate weapons.[11]

The B61-12 will be the first guided nuclear gravity bomb in the US arsenal. In 1992, the US Air Force tried to get approval for a guided bomb called the Precision Low Yield Weapon Design (PLYWD), but Congress rejected the proposal partly out of concern that combining precision with low yield could lead to more usable nuclear weapons. This and other low-yield weapons proposals triggered the Spratt-Fuerse Resolution that banned work on warheads with yields less than five kilotons. The resolution was later repealed by the Bush administration. The guided B61-12 will have two selectable low-yield options below five kilotons that, combined with the guided tail kit, will give the bomb capabilities that are similar to the PLYWD.

Getting NATO's approval for the B61-12 design apparently took some efforts and coordination but not because of concerns about improving the military capability of the nuclear posture in Europe. Early in 2010, US European Command (EUCOM) led a Department of Defense (DOD)–wide effort to resolve key issues with certain NATO allies. Finally, in April 2010—the same month the 2010 Nuclear Posture Review (NPR) was published and pledged that warhead life-extension programs would not provide for new military capabilities—the DOD and the NATO allies reached agreement on the key military characteristics of the B61-12, including the yield and its accuracy requirements when used on modern aircraft, and that it be capable of freefall (no parachute-retarded) delivery, that it employ a guided tail kit section, and that it have both midair and ground detonation options. The US Strategic Command (STRATCOM) later proposed a different yield for the weapon, which was approved by EUCOM and Supreme Headquarters Allied Powers Europe (SHAPE).[12]

DOD and NATO also agreed that the B61-12 would be capable of being carried by both existing and modernized fighter aircraft (F-15E, F-16, F-35A, and PA-200), and be compatible with the current weapons storage vaults in Europe. US officials said that getting approval from NATO was a significant achievement because, if the Europeans had opposed improving the accuracy with the guided tail kit, the whole plan to consolidate four weapons into one might not have worked.[13]

In addition to increasing the capability of the bombs in Europe, some of the delivery vehicles are also slated for a significant modernization. Starting in the early 2020s, the F-35A Lightning II, also known as the Joint Strike Fighter (JSF), will begin to replace the F-16 as carrier of the B61 nuclear bomb. The F-35A has a significantly better penetration capability than the F-16 due to its stealth features. Each F-35A will be able to carry two B61-12s internally (the F-16 can only carry the weapons externally). Three of the five European NATO allies that currently have national aircraft assigned to the NATO nuclear strike mission (Italy, the Netherlands, and Turkey)[14] are considering acquiring the F-35A to replace their aging F-15Es, F-16, and PA-200 (in the case of Italy) in the nuclear mission, although these programs could be threatened by cost overruns and the financial crisis. The US Air Force "intends to deliver nuclear capability to all JSFs in Europe in the 2020 time frame via the Block IV upgrade."[15] The first F-35As will be deployed to the Lakenheath air base in southern England.

The introduction of the B61-12 and F-35A in Europe has several implications. At the political level, the modernization seems to contradict the pledge made by the Obama administration in the Nuclear Posture Review that life-extension programs "will not provide for new military capabilities."[16] Yet the B61-12 clearly will have new military capabilities in the form of the guided tail kit and the increased accuracy and target kill capability this provides.

Government officials are aware of the dilemma and try to explain it by saying one of two things: either that the NPR reference to new military capabilities only refers to the warhead itself (it is acceptable to improve other components) or that the pledge must be measured across the stockpile (the maximum B61-12 kill capability already exists in the form of the B61-7).

Nevertheless, the improvements will enhance the military capability of NATO's nuclear posture, and this raises some important questions for NATO. One is how this will help in persuading Russia to reduce its nonstrategic nuclear weapons or whether NATO in effect is offering Russian hard-liners an excuse to justify modernizations of Russia's nonstrategic nuclear forces. Russian officials have already started pointing to NATO use of nuclear-capable fighters in Eastern NATO countries.[17] Another question is to what extent improving nuclear capabilities is compatible with NATO's policy to reduce the number and reliance on nuclear weapons and create the conditions for a world free from them.

Fiscal Realities

The implementation of these modernization plans will be influenced by the international financial crisis that has already resulted in significant cuts to military budgets in nuclear NATO countries. Yet it is clear that NATO and the United States plan to spend considerable resources on maintaining and modernizing the nuclear forces over the next decade.

Costs are escalating, with the estimate for the B61 life-extension program having more than doubled in the past two years, from $4 to $10 billion.[18] Part of this cost increase is due to attempts to incorporate new safety and security features into the new weapons beyond those that they already contain. These escalating costs will further increase the pressure on the program and questions about why it is needed.

All of the allies that currently participate in the nuclear-sharing mission have cut their defense budgets, and some are expecting significant additional reductions. Italy, for example, is planning a 30 percent cut in the overall operational, logistical, and headquarters network spending over the next five to six years. The number of new F-35s scheduled to replace the current fleet of Tornados (including nuclear mission aircraft) reportedly will be cut by about a third.[19] The air force's annual flying hours dropped from 150,000 in 1990 to 90,000 in 2010, and air force training reportedly declined by 80 percent, from €104.6 million (US$136.9 million) in 2005 to only €21.2 million (US$27.7 million) in 2011. Because the priority is on real-world missions such as Afghanistan, this means that training for other operations has been "pared to the bone," according to one defense official.[20]

The US Department of Defense estimates that "the annual operating costs for the United States to support forward deployed nuclear weapons in Europe is approximately $100 million per year." Beyond these costs, including the development of the B61-12 and the F-35A, and the costs carried by each host nation for housing US Air Force Munitions Support Squadrons (MUNSS) at the national bases with nuclear missions, NATO in 2011 spent another $14.7 million on a new weapons maintenance truck for all weapon sites, and in 2011 and 2012 spent $63.4 million on upgrading security at the weapons storage sites.[21]

The fiscal realities raise several issues. On the national level, some of the European countries that currently have a nuclear strike mission for their national aircraft will likely reconsider whether they will continue that mission. Although it has not yet said so, Germany appears to be on the way toward phasing out the nuclear mission. The Netherlands and Belgium might follow suit. And how will Italy be able to spend precious resources on maintaining nuclear-capable fighter-bombers when it cannot pay for their flying hours? For the United States, it raises questions about why it would spend more than $10 billion on extending the life of the B61 bomb that is intended partly for a mission in Europe that is likely to be phased out. Despite a NATO pledge to spend more on military forces following Russia's invasion of Ukraine, there is little appetite in European parliaments for increasing defense budgets and what additional funding is approved is likely to prioritize non-nuclear forces.

It might be advisable for NATO to address these issues head on and update the nuclear mission rather than having to pick up the pieces of the nuclear posture later, after countries begin to bail out for fiscal or political reasons. But more importantly, spending scarce resources on nuclear weapons in Europe may simply be bad defense planning.

Real versus Fake Reassurance

On the question of reassurance, some NATO allies continue to harbor security concerns that some say require the United States to keep nuclear weapons in Europe. This certainly was the case during the Cold War, when the imminent threat of a Soviet invasion and the tense nuclear frontline drawn through Europe triggered specific and extensive nuclear requirements for NATO. But today, even after Russia's invasion of Ukraine, the security concerns that NATO countries have are no longer related to those types of scenarios. Yet somehow we still hear arguments that US nonstrategic weapons need to be forward-deployed in Europe to reassure the allies.

But reassurance needs to be credible and based on real scenarios and capabilities that can actually be used. Whatever the security concerns of Eastern European NATO countries may be, they are certainly not about a Russian nuclear threat—despite belligerent statements made by some Russian officials. Put another way, if Russia eliminated all of its nonstrategic nuclear weapons tomorrow, what would Eastern European NATO countries say about their security concerns? Their position would most likely remain unchanged because their security concerns are not about nonstrategic nuclear weapons per se but about their borders; organized crime; and general uneasiness about Russian intentions in the region, especially after Russia's use of insurgents and "little green men" against Ukraine.

After being occupied by the Soviet Union for decades, some Eastern European countries have a deep-seated suspicion of Russian intentions. After all, these countries joined NATO in no small measure to get the ultimate security guarantee from the United States, and they naturally want to see clear signs of that security guarantee. Unfortunately, some officials still confuse nonstrategic nuclear weapons in Europe with that sign. But the reassurance they see—and the reassurance they are offered—has to be credible and linked to their actual security situation and the stakes at play in today's European security environment. Deployment of US nonstrategic nuclear weapons in Europe is the least credible form of reassurance because it is the least likely to be used under any foreseeable condition and the least usable capability to address their current security challenges.

That is not to say that nuclear weapons do not have any role whatsoever in reassuring those countries about being protected by the United States. But neither the Strategic Concept nor the DDPR assign that mission to nonstrategic nuclear weapons; both do assign that mission to *strategic* nuclear weapons: "The supreme guarantee of the security of the Allies is provided by the *strategic* nuclear forces of the Alliance, particularly those of the United States" (emphasis added).[22] Nor does the new Strategic Concept identify the role of nonstrategic nuclear weapons as providing the transatlantic link, a role that was included in the previous version from 1999.

Both the Strategic Concept and DDPR conclude: "The circumstances in which any use of nuclear weapons might have to be contemplated are extremely remote."[23] Therefore, and because of the immense destructive power and political sensitivity associated with nuclear weapons, they are not very useful as instruments of deterrence or reassurance for the type of security concerns that confront NATO today.

For these reasons, and because the second part of NATO's nuclear policy is to reduce the reliance on nuclear weapons and create the conditions for a world free of them, NATO and the United States are working on finding or strengthening non-nuclear means of deterring and reassuring. According to the US Quadrennial Defense Review (QDR) from 2009:

> To reinforce U.S. commitments to our allies and partners, we will consult closely with them on new, tailored, regional deterrence architectures that combine our forward presence, relevant conventional capabilities (including missile defenses), and continued commitment to extend our nuclear deterrent. These regional architectures and new capabilities, as detailed in the Ballistic Missile Defense Review and the forthcoming Nuclear Posture Review, make possible a reduced role for nuclear weapons in our national security strategy.[24]

NATO is already operating the Support of Nuclear Operations with Conventional Air Tactics (SNOWCAT) program specifically to enable non-nuclear countries to contribute actively and consult on the nuclear mission without requiring them to host nuclear weapons on their territories or assign aircraft to deliver US nuclear weapons. Moreover, to increase NATO participation in US overall nuclear force planning in support of the Alliance, NATO personnel have been established at STRATCOM, at Offutt Air Force Base in Nebraska, to allow for "substantive participation . . . on a daily and continuing basis . . . in OPLAN 8010 [the US strategic nuclear war plan, formerly known as SIOP] nuclear-related information in support of NATO operations."[25] All of these steps contribute to reducing the salience of deploying nuclear weapons in Europe while ensuring allied consultation in nuclear matters.

Conclusion

Extended nuclear deterrence in Europe received a facelift with the 2010 Nuclear Posture Review, 2010 Strategic Concept, and 2012 Deterrence and Defense Posture Review. NATO reaffirmed that nuclear weapons will continue to support the Alliance as long as nuclear weapons exist and that US nuclear weapons in Europe are—at least for now—just about right.

Over the next decade, NATO and the United States plan to spend well over $10 billion on modernizing and deploying a new nuclear bomb and fighter-bomber with increased military capabilities in Europe, and several allies are considering whether to upgrade their aircraft to continue the nuclear strike mission in the future. At the same time, however, NATO has also committed itself to creating the conditions for reducing the number of weapons deployed in Europe, reducing the reliance on nuclear weapons in NATO strategy, and creating the conditions for a world without nuclear weapons. These seemingly contradictory commitments have set the Alliance on a path where it is difficult to see what the priorities are, and where supporters of the status quo and modernization will continue to fight with advocates for changing and reducing the nuclear mission.

Funding for the nuclear mission will increasingly be seen as competing with conventional forces for scarce resources. Why would NATO require countries to spend money they do not have on maintaining a non-strategic nuclear mission for scenarios that most likely will never happen, compared to funding conventional forces and operations that are needed all the time for real-world scenarios?

To that end, it is fair to ask whether it is constructive for NATO to pin the security needs of new Eastern European allies on the promises of a non-strategic nuclear remnant from the Cold War that is probably the least credible form of reassurance in the security environment that NATO will face in the next decade—especially when the Strategic Concept says that it is the strategic nuclear weapons of the three nuclear NATO countries that provide the ultimate security guarantee for the allies. Indeed, the additional reassurances provided to Eastern NATO members after Russia's invasion of Ukraine have all been made with conventional forces and operations. Non-strategic nuclear weapons deployed in Europe have been irrelevant and impotent.

Several elements of the Strategic Concept and DDPR hint at a grab-bag nuclear policy borrowing heavily from Cold War arrangements and thinking. For the first two decades after the end of the Cold War, NATO did not seem to care at all about the disparity of the American and Russian inventories. But when bureaucrats were suddenly asked to think about nuclear weapons again (something they had not done very much for two decades) in preparation for the Strategic Concept, they intuitively reintroduced disparity with greater Russian stockpiles as the formal obstacle to further reductions in NATO nonstrategic nuclear forces. Yet disparity does not exist because Russia has increased its inventory of such weapons (in fact, it continues to decline) but because NATO and the United States have unilaterally reduced theirs significantly over the past two decades (because they decided then that disparity did not matter).

No one can explain why disparity suddenly matters now, except by referring to anonymous Eastern European officials who are said to prefer the status quo in NATO. A more careful analysis reveals that their interest is not nuclear weapons per se but reassurance. Nor do they believe US non-strategic nuclear weapons in Europe provide a very good—or appropriate—response to their own security issues. It is the American presence they are interested in, not the non-strategic nuclear weapons in Europe.

This creates a huge dilemma for NATO. If the Alliance emerges from the past two decades of not caring about disparity in nonstrategic nuclear weapons and now insists that nonstrategic nuclear weapons deployed in Europe are a credible guarantor of Eastern European member states' security concerns, and cannot be reduced further until Russia reduces its inventory, then how can NATO possibly create the conditions for a world free of nuclear weapons? What is clear is that this will certainly not happen if NATO upholds the status quo and continues to modernize and improve its nonstrategic nuclear capabilities in Europe. Reducing the reliance on nuclear weapons requires a break with the status quo and a bold political vision backed by action. NATO did not get to today's dramatically reduced nonstrategic nuclear forces level because it adhered to the status quo or worried about disparity and surrendered the initiative to Cold Warriors in the Kremlin, but because the political leadership ignored worst-case planners and former officials who argued against change. The new East-West crisis makes it imperative that NATO invests in non-nuclear forms of reassurance of eastern allies instead of wasting scarce resources on maintaining US non-strategic nuclear weapons in Europe.

Notes

1. North Atlantic Treaty Organization, "Active Engagement, Modern Defence: Strategic Concept for the Defence and Security of the Members of the North Atlantic Treaty Organisation," November 2010, sections 17–19; North Atlantic Treaty Organization, *Deterrence and Defense Posture Review*, May 20, 2012, sections 8–12.
2. North Atlantic Treaty Organization, *Deterrence and Defense Posture Review*, sections 12, 24.
3. Hans M. Kristensen, "U.S. Nuclear Weapons Withdrawn from the United Kingdom," *FAS Strategic Security Blog*, June 26, 2008, http://www.fas.org/blog/ssp/2008/06/us-nuclear-weapons-withdrawn-from-the-united-kingdom.php.
4. North Atlantic Treaty Organization, "Active Engagement," November 2010, section 26.

5. North Atlantic Treaty Organization, "Active Engagement," section 26; North Atlantic Treaty Organization, *Deterrence and Defense Posture Review*, section 25.

6. North Atlantic Treaty Organization, *Deterrence and Defense Posture Review*, sections 24, 27.

7. United States Senate, Resolution on Advice and Consent to the Ratification of the Treaty between the United States of America and the Russian Federation on Measures for the Further Reduction and Limitation of Strategic Offensive Arms, December 22, 2010, para. 12(ii).

8. Hans M. Kristensen, "US Navy Instruction Confirms Retirement of Nuclear Tomahawk Cruise Missile," *FAS Strategic Security Blog*, March 18, 2013, http://blogs.fas.org/security/2013/03/tomahawk/.

9. Russia is also modernizing part of its nonstrategic nuclear posture by deploying new nuclear-capable short-range ballistic missiles (SS-26 Iskander), possibly naval cruise missiles (SS-N-30 Kaliber), new warships with nuclear capability (Sverodvinsk-class attack submarine), possibly the SA-21 (S-400) air-defense interceptor (although evidence of its nuclear role is scarce), and the A-135 ballistic missile defense system around Moscow.

10. Note that the different B61 versions also have several lower yield options that can be selected depending on the mission.

11. For an analysis of the B61-12 capabilities, see Hans M. Kristensen, "B61 LEP: Increasing NATO Nuclear Capability and Precision Low-Yield Strikes," *FAS Strategic Security Blog*, June 15, 2011, http://www.fas.org/blog/ssp/2011/06/b61-12.php.

12. US Government Accountability Office, *Nuclear Weapons: DOD and NNSA Need to Better Manage Scope and Future of Refurbishments and Risks to Maintaining U.S. Commitments to NATO*, GAO-11-387, May 2011, 5.

13. Ibid. Note that, although the B61 life-extension program is officially said to be a consolidation of four existing versions, in fact the life of only one of the four warheads—the B61-4—is being extended. Instead, it will borrow selected components from the other three types, which will be retired.

14. Of the remaining two nuclear-sharing partners, Belgium has not decided whether it will acquire the F-35A or participate in the nuclear-sharing mission. Germany appears to have extended the service life of the aging PA-200 Tornado but has not announced whether the replacement—the Eurofighter—will have nuclear capability.

15. Joint Statement for the Record, the Honorable Madelyn Creedon, Assistant Secretary of Defense for Global Strategic Affairs, and the Honorable Andrew Weber, Assistant Secretary of Defense for Nuclear, Chemical, and Biological Defense Programs, on Fiscal Year 2013 National Defense Authorization Budget Request for Department of Defense Nuclear Forces Programs, before the Strategic Forces Subcommittee Committee on Armed Services, US Senate, March 28, 2012, 13, http://www.senate.gov/~armed_services/statemnt/2012/03%20March/Creedon-Weber%2003-28-12.pdf.

16. US Department of Defense, Office of the Secretary of Defense, *Nuclear Posture Review Report*, May 2010, xiv, 39.

17. Valda Kalnina (EPA), "Moscow suspects US of planning to deploy nuclear-capable frontline aviation near Russia," *TASS*, March 26, 2015, http://tass.ru/en/russia/785151.

18. Hans M. Kristensen, "B61-12: NNSA's Gold-Plated Nuclear Bomb Project," *FAS Strategic Security Blog*, July 26, 2012, http://blogs.fas.org/security/2012/07/b61-12gold/.

19. Luca Peruzzi, "Italian Force Cuts Its JSF Numbers," *Jane's Defence Weekly*, February 22, 2012, 14.

20. Tom Kington, "Training Cuts Could Hurt Italian Readiness," *Defense News*, November 29, 2010, 12.

21. James Miller, Principal Deputy Assistant Secretary of Defense, answer to Representative Loretta Sanches, Strategic Forces Subcommittee, House Armed Services Committee, November 2, 2011, 161, http://www.fas.org/irp/congress/2011_hr/nw-qfr.pdf.

22. North Atlantic Treaty Organization, "Active Engagement," section 18; North Atlantic Treaty Organization, *Deterrence and Defense Posture Review*, section 9.

23. North Atlantic Treaty Organization, "Active Engagement," section 17; North Atlantic Treaty Organization, *Deterrence and Defense Posture Review*, section 9.

24. US Department of Defense, Office of the Secretary of Defense, *Quadrennial Defense Review Report*, February 2010, 14. The description of new, tailored, regional deterrence architectures that make possible a reduced role for nuclear weapons is also included in the Ballistic Missile Defense Review. US Department of Defense, Office of the Secretary of Defense, *Ballistic Missile Defense Review Report*, February 2010, 23.

25. US Chairman of the Joint Chiefs of Staff, *Guidance for the Sanitization and Distribution of Information Pertaining to Nuclear Command and Control to Supreme Headquarters Allied Powers Europe (SHAPE); United Kingdom (UK) Liaison Office; US Strategic Weapon System Integrated Project Team; and UK Nuclear Operations and Targeting Centre in Support of North Atlantic Treaty Organization (NATO) Operations*, August 12, 2008, A-1 and A-2. Partially declassified and released under the Freedom of Information Act (FOIA).

PART III

THE POLITICS OF MISSILE DEFENSE

CHAPTER 6

From Offense to Defense?

EXTENDED DETERRENCE AND MISSILE DEFENSE

Oliver Thränert and Kerry M. Kartchner

MISSILE DEFENSE REPRESENTS A relatively new phenomenon in the extended deterrence discourse.[1] Today, the United States is still the main provider of extended deterrence; its European allies as well as Asian partners rely on security commitments within the framework of the Atlantic Alliance or within bilateral arrangements. Until recently, that obligation was underwritten almost exclusively by offensive means. However, as the result of a new and enduring consensus that has emerged over the course of the last three decades, missile defense is poised to make increasingly important contributions to underwriting not only central US strategic deterrence but also to supporting US extended deterrence and security assurance relationships.

In this chapter, we focus on the prospective implications of missile defense for extended deterrence and NATO, the primary beneficiary of US extended deterrence. We argue that, as opposed to the Cold War era, when conventional and nuclear capabilities were at the core of NATO's strategy and force planning, missile defense now is gaining ever more prominence for the Alliance. In a world where more countries possess or actively pursue weapons of mass destruction (WMD), not to mention their delivery systems, effective missile defense components are becoming ever more important to a viable security and extended deterrence strategy. In addition, NATO has come to acknowledge missile defense as an essential capability to support its core task of collective defense. At the same time, Alliance members agree that missile defense will be an important addition to NATO's capabilities for deterrence. The effective integration of offensive and defensive skills and capabilities represents an important challenge for the Alliance in the coming years.

Despite increasing tensions between NATO and Russia in the aftermath of the Ukraine crisis, today's NATO defense and deterrence planning is no longer focused solely on Russia. Rather, countries of concern such as Iran are gaining importance. While the likelihood of a direct attack on NATO territory seems low, Iran or another country equipped with ballistic missiles and weapons of mass destruction could act aggressively against its non-NATO neighbors. In such a case, NATO may want to act to reestablish regional order. The aggressor may then try to deter NATO from intervention. At this point, NATO missile defense would come into play. While a decision to intervene in such a contingency can be expected to be highly controversial within the Alliance, missile defense makes damage limitation options available and could help to keep military room for maneuver. At the very least, deliberately accepting vulnerability, as was the case during the Cold War, does not seem to be the appropriate approach under such circumstances.

Additionally, missile defense offers several important advantages. It influences the aggressors' calculations (deterrence by denial); enhances the credibility of extended deterrence; contributes to crisis stability; and, finally, minimizes the risk of coercion by proliferators. Nevertheless, missile defense is no panacea, and it is certainly not a substitute for nuclear deterrence, at least for the foreseeable future.

This chapter unfolds in four sections. First, we look back at nuclear deterrence and missile defense debates, with special emphasis on the 1991 Gulf War. Second, we explain where the Alliance stands today in terms of missile defense. Next, we analyze the changing strategic environment that is crucial for explaining the growing importance of missile defense. Finally, we discuss the relationship between missile defense and nuclear deterrence.

From Mutually Assured Destruction to Effective Missile Defense

Throughout the Cold War, the US as well as the NATO deterrence posture and force planning were based to a large extent on conventional and nuclear arms. Development and deployment of defensive systems were almost entirely neglected. Mutually assured destruction (MAD) became the mantra of a deterrence posture deliberately accepting vulnerability. Both the United States and the Soviet Union had been bound since 1972 by the Antiballistic Missile (ABM) Treaty, which, according to a 1974 protocol, limited both superpowers to one antiballistic missile site, each containing up to one hundred strategic ballistic missile defense interceptors.

Extended deterrence thus relied almost exclusively on the threat of punishment by retaliation. The respective strategies from massive retaliation during the 1950s and 1960s to flexible response throughout the 1970s and 1980s formed the bedrock of NATO's security. The United States guaranteed its European non-nuclear partners as well as Canada that its nuclear forces would not only counter a potential Soviet attack on the US homeland but also one on the territories of its allies. More specifically, a special arrangement called nuclear sharing was established. Some European allies on whose territories US nuclear systems were positioned prepared delivery systems and their crews to deploy those weapons in times of war. As a consequence of this policy, Europeans learned to live within the disquieting logic of nuclear deterrence.

Prior to the intensive public debate associated with NATO's double-track decision of 1979 and the stationing of nuclear-capable cruise missiles and Pershing IIs on NATO territory, only peace activists and a handful of left-wing politicians fundamentally opposed nuclear deterrence in Europe. In the United States, only a few intellectuals took issue with the MAD approach, and some of them belonged to the conservative camp. One vocal pundit was Fred Iklé, who in 1973 asserted that "our method for preventing nuclear war rests on a form of warfare universally condemned since the Dark Ages—the mass killing of hostages."[2] Ten years later, US president Ronald Reagan, a Republican, questioned the MAD doctrine. In his famous Star Wars Speech of March 23, 1983, he pointed out that the human spirit had to develop different ways of dealing with other countries than by threatening their existence. Therefore, he argued, defenses against nuclear-armed ballistic missiles should be developed.[3] In the United States as well as in Europe, critics of Reagan's Strategic Defense Initiative (SDI) lambasted the plans on the grounds that it would undermine strategic stability. In the end, SDI did not bear fruit; effective defense against the huge Soviet nuclear arsenal proved to be unrealistic in both technical and financial terms.

At the end of the Cold War, most experts expected any kind of missile defense effort to become obsolete. However, to the surprise of many and even prior to the collapse of the Soviet Union in 1991/1992, it became apparent that missile defense would gain more prominence, not less. In August 1990, Iraqi forces invaded and occupied Kuwait. Mandated by UN Security Council Resolution 678, a US-led international coalition in January 1991 began military operation Desert Storm to free Kuwait. In the course of this conflict, Iraq would launch some eighty ballistic missiles into Israel and Saudi Arabia, where US forces had been deployed. Not only did Iraqi president Saddam Hussein want to harm US army forces but, more importantly, he hoped to provoke Israeli retaliation against Iraq, thereby making it impossible for

Egypt, Saudi Arabia, and other Arab countries to remain part of the US-led coalition. Already by August 1990, US Patriot defense systems had been fielded in Saudi Arabia to protect US troops. As a consequence of the Iraqi missile attacks on Israel, US Patriots were immediately redeployed from Germany to Israel. The mission was to defend populated areas and prevent Israel from entering the conflict. Fear that Iraqi missiles carried chemical warheads added to the threat.

In February 1991, an Iraqi Scud missile hit a US military barracks in Dhahran, Saudi Arabia, leaving twenty-eight dead and ninety-nine wounded.[4] This catastrophic event invalidated certain previous assumptions about the adequacy of an offense-only strategy to confront the danger from regional ballistic missile attack. It had been assumed, first of all, that the Iraqis would be deterred from attacking coalition forces with ballistic missiles for fear of invoking an escalating and devastating offensive retaliation. This assumption proved false. The Iraqi leadership was not deterred from striking at coalition forces with the full range of ballistic missiles at its disposal. Second, it was assumed that formidable US air power could hunt down and preemptively eliminate the Scud missile launchers before they could be used to harm coalition forces. This assumption also proved problematic because the launchers turned out to be much more difficult to locate and target before launching their missiles. Third, many (but not all) subsequent missile attacks were successfully intercepted by forward-deployed Patriot missile defense batteries, proving that missile defense could contribute to defending coalition forces.

The impression during the conflict was that Patriots were effective in protecting Israel against Iraqi missiles. However, postwar analysis revealed that the Patriots did not perform as well as initially thought. Many times officials thought that an Iraqi missile was shot down by a Patriot when in fact the Iraqi missile had simply broken up into small fragments or gone far astray.[5] In spite of the fact that the Patriots intercepted only a few Iraqi missiles, however, the missile defense operation served its main strategic purpose: it helped the Israeli government remain outside the military confrontation so that Saddam's plans to extend the conflict and to split the international coalition did not succeed.[6] The 1991 Gulf War highlighted the missile proliferation threat. In hindsight, it represented the first case to underscore the value of missile defense in international interventions led by Western forces.

After the war, it became apparent that other countries of concern also showed an interest in ballistic missiles. As early as the 1970s, North Korea began purchasing Scud missiles with ranges of about 300 kilometers from Egypt and later the Soviet Union. Due to the severe economic crisis during the last years of the Soviet Union, Russian (and Ukrainian) ballistic missile experts left their country and settled in North Korea. It is believed that these missile engineers brought the complete blueprints to build the No Dong missile with them. The No Dong has a range of up to about 1,000 kilometers depending on the payload. In the late 1990s, North Korea began to export No Dong missiles to Pakistan, where they were labeled Ghauri, and to Iran, which named them Shahab-3 and developed them further into what is known as the Ghadr-1 missiles with an extended range of about 1,500 kilometers.

On August 31, 1998, North Korea launched a three-stage Taepo-Dong 1 missile. Although the test was not entirely successful, Pyongyang demonstrated for the first time the technical capability to handle the complicated multistage technology. In addition, the second stage passed over Japan before the third stage failed to separate. Given that North Korea was also working on a nuclear weapons program, the missile tests fueled concerns in Asia as well as in the United States. Only months before the missile launch, the Commission to Assess the Ballistic Missile Threat to the United States, also called the Rumsfeld Commission, an independent group of experts, was formed by the US Congress to evaluate the ballistic missile threat posed to the United States. The commission had concluded that Iran and North Korea could develop the capability to strike the United States within five years of a decision to pursue ballistic missile technology.[7] The North Korean launch was interpreted by many as validating the conclusions of the Rumsfeld Commission.

Despite these developments, the emerging missile proliferation threat did not motivate the Democratic Clinton administration to put much emphasis on missile defense due to its strong commitment to preserving the ABM Treaty. The Taepo-Dong launch complicated the Clinton administration's desire to suppress the development of missile defense in favor of shoring up the ABM Treaty, however, and ultimately led the US Congress to pass the so-called National Missile Defense Act of 1999, which remains US policy to this day. That act said in part that it shall be the policy of the United States "to deploy as soon as is technologically possible an effective National Missile Defense system capable of defending the territory of the United States against limited ballistic missile attack (whether accidental, unauthorized, or deliberate). . ."[8]

Nevertheless, the 2001 incoming Republican administration of George W. Bush, in which Donald Rumsfeld served a second term as secretary of defense, perceived missile proliferation as an urgent challenge. As a consequence, missile defense became an important element of the US defense posture. After repeated diplomatic attempts to convince the Russians to accept amendments or revisions to the ABM Treaty that would allow the United States to proceed with testing certain components of a ground-based, mid-course intercept system, President George W. Bush, in December 2001, announced his decision to withdraw from the ABM Treaty as allowed by Article XVI of the treaty. This decision took effect in June 2002.[9]

Furthermore, in its 2002 Nuclear Posture Review, the Bush administration supported the concept of a New Triad consisting of offensive strike forces (both nuclear and non-nuclear), defenses (including missile defense), and a robust nuclear infrastructure. In so doing, Washington reduced reliance on nuclear weapons while at the same time underscoring the value of missile defense for its deterrence posture.[10] In practical terms, beginning in 2004, three-stage ground-based interceptors (GBIs) were deployed in Alaska and California. These defenses were complemented with early warning radar sites upgraded to perform missile defense–related missions in Alaska, California, Greenland, and the United Kingdom as well as a command and control infrastructure. A third site (in addition to the ones in Alaska and California) was planned to be implemented in 2013; it included the deployment of two-stage GBIs in Poland and an X-band radar in the Czech Republic.[11]

Bush's missile defense plans caused a lot of criticism both inside and outside NATO. In particular, then and now Russian president Vladimir Putin warned that any effort to undermine Russia's nuclear second-strike capability would trigger a new nuclear arms race. However, Bush's Democratic successor, Barack Obama, showed in many ways continuity regarding missile defense. In fact, the new president shared many but not all of the threat perceptions of his predecessor. Therefore, in its Nuclear Posture Review of 2010, the new administration declared that "effective missile defenses are an essential element of the U.S. commitment to strengthen regional deterrence against states of concern."[12] But President Obama did not simply continue with what George W. Bush had begun. Rather, Obama changed the Bush plans so that the missile defense architecture would become more flexible and use only proven technologies. Therefore, Bush's planned GBI deployments in Poland as well as the plan to station a radar system in the Czech Republic were abandoned. Obama, in contrast to Bush, did not want to focus on cooperating with individual NATO members on a bilateral basis but on embracing NATO as a whole. As a result, in its 2010 Lisbon Strategic Concept, NATO declared that it would "develop the capability to defend our populations and territories against ballistic missile attack as a core element of our collective defence."[13] In part to assuage Russian concerns, the Alliance also announced that it would "actively seek cooperation on missile defense with Russia."[14]

Many of the missile defense programs initiated by the Bush administration had started to be deployed by 2008. As of the end of that year, the US missile defense system consisted of the following:

- Twenty-four GBIs placed in silos in Alaska and California
- Twenty-one Standard Missile-3 (SM-3) sea-based interceptors
- Seven Navy Aegis BMD destroyers configured for the long-range surveillance and track (LRS&T) mission
- Three Navy Aegis BMD cruisers and up to seven destroyers, armed with SM-3s
- Five hundred forty-nine Patriot Advanced Capability-3 (PAC-3) missiles
- A sea-based X-band (SBX) radar
- Active, upgraded early warning radars in California and the United Kingdom and an upgraded Cobra Dane radar in Alaska
- Two forward-based X-band radars operational in Japan and Israel
- A command and control battle management and communications (C2BMC) system online at three combatant commands.[15]

What is significant about this impressive list of deployed hardware is that almost none of it (except for some of the PAC-3 batteries) existed at the beginning of the Bush administration.

While the Bush administration compiled a formidable list of accomplishments in fielding actual hardware, the Obama administration surprised both missile defense critics and supporters when it announced the "Phased Adaptive Approach to European-based Missile Defense" in September 2009. Many had expected the Obama administration to revive an approach to missile defense similar to that of the Clinton administration, slashing the high Bush-era missile defense budgets, resurrecting some form of the ABM Treaty, and restoring MAD as the touchstone of strategic stability and the US-Russian relationship. But on September 17, 2009, President Obama announced:

> I'm committed to deploying strong missile defense systems which are adaptable to the threats of the 21st century. The best way to responsibly advance our security and the security of our allies is to deploy a missile defense system that best responds to the threats that we face and that utilizes technology that is both proven and cost-effective.[16]

The "Phased Adaptive Approach for European-based Missile Defense" would involve four deployment phases, and proceeding from one phase to the next would be contingent on developments in the threat, testing performance, and budgetary feasibility. According to the US Department of Defense:

> In Phase One, during the 2011 timeframe, the United States will deploy current and proven missile defense systems available in the next two years, including the sea-based Aegis Weapon System, the SM-3 interceptor (Block IA), and sensors such as the forward-based Army Navy/Transportable Radar Surveillance system (AN/TPY-2), to address regional ballistic missile threats to our European NATO Allies and our deployed forces;
>
> In Phase Two, during the 2015 timeframe, the United States will deploy a more capable version of the SM-3 interceptor (the Block IB) in both sea- and land-based configurations, and more advanced sensors, to expand the defended area against short- and medium-range missile threats;
>
> In Phase Three, during the 2018 timeframe, we will deploy the more advanced SM-3 Block IIA variant currently under development, to counter short-, medium-, and intermediate-range missile threats; and
>
> In Phase Four, during the 2020 timeframe, we will deploy the SM-3 Block IIB interceptor to counter medium- and intermediate-range missiles and the ICBM [intercontinental ballistic missile] threat to the United States.[17]

President Obama and his senior defense officials cited two primary considerations to justify the "Phased Adaptive Approach to European-based Missile Defense." First, they acknowledged that there were new technological opportunities. Over the past several years, US missile defense capabilities and technologies had advanced significantly, with this trend expected to continue. Improved interceptor capabilities, such as advanced versions of the SM-3, offered a more flexible, capable, and cost-effective architecture. And improved sensor technologies provided a variety of newly developed options to detect and track enemy missiles.

Second, there was a revised assessment of the threat. It was recognized that rogue state ballistic missile systems were becoming more flexible, mobile, survivable, reliable, and accurate, and were also increasing in range. The Obama administration was less concerned about the direct threat to the US homeland from North Korean–type threats, believing that there was some uncertainty about when and how potential Iranian and North Korean ICBM threats would mature. Instead the Obama administration concluded that the most critical ballistic missile threat to US deployed forces and allies around the world would come from short- and medium-range ballistic missiles.

The Obama administration conducted the "Ballistic Missile Defense Review" (BMDR), the results of which were released on February 1, 2010. This policy statement validated the mature role of missile defense in the US national security posture, aligned the US missile defense program with near-term regional missile threats, and provided the basis for allied participation and cooperation. The 2010 BMDR established the following missile defense priorities:

The United States will:

- Defend its homeland against limited ballistic missile attack.
- Defend against regional threats to US forces, allies, and partners.
- Deploy new systems only after their effectiveness and reliability has been determined through testing under realistic conditions.
- Develop new capabilities that are fiscally sustainable over the long term.
- Develop flexible capabilities that can adapt as threats change.
- Expand international cooperation.[18]

Phase one of the European Phased Adaptive Approach (EPAA) has already been implemented. Since March 2011, the USS *Monterrey*, which is equipped with the SM-3 Block IA missile interceptors, has been cruising the Mediterranean, and an X-band radar system was deployed to Turkey in late 2011.[19] Until 2020, the United States is planning to develop more advanced SM-3 interceptors in several phases to be deployed on additional Aegis ships. In addition, and beginning in 2015 and 2018, respectively, Aegis-Ashore versions of the SM-3 are to be deployed in Romania and Poland. Together with sensors and radars, some of which are located on European territories, such as Flyingdales/UK and Thule/Greenland, as well as communication links, this system would be capable of defending most parts of NATO Europe by 2020.

In March 2013, however, then US secretary of defense Chuck Hagel announced a significant change to the original EPAA. Due to technical difficulties as well as delays in congressional funding, the SM-3 IIB program was suspended. Instead of implementing this project, which was the essential element of Phase Four of the EPAA, Hagel explained that the United States would rather strengthen its homeland missile defense by deploying fourteen additional GBIs in Alaska.[20]

To complement the EPAA, NATO decided at Lisbon to extend the mission of its Active Layered Theatre Ballistic Missile Defence (ALTBMD), already in place since 2005, to the defense of populations and territories and to link it to the US EPAA for an effective NATO missile defense. Currently, ALTBMD's main feature is to provide protection for allied troops deployed in out-of-area operations. ALTBMD relies mainly on German, Spanish, Dutch, and Greek Patriot interceptors as well as French and Italian SAMP/T systems. Furthermore, ALTBMD includes sensors and radars as well as command and communication. ALTBMD elements will be integrated into a system of systems step by step.

In their Chicago Summit Declaration of May 20, 2012, the Heads of State and Government of NATO declared that the Alliance had achieved an interim NATO missile defense capability. In addition, the NATO Council also agreed on prearranged command and control rules. The Supreme Allied Commander Europe was designated commander for the ballistic missile defense mission. Only one day later, on May 21, 2012, the Headquarters Allied Air Command in Ramstein, Germany, took over the command and control systems required to exercise limited operational command of NATO's Interim Missile Defense capability.[21]

At its Wales Summit in September 2014, NATO Heads of State and Government reconfirmed that the Alliance's aim is to provide full coverage and protection for all NATO European populations, territories, and forces against the threat posed by ballistic missiles. The Summit Declaration welcomed the deployment of Aegis BMD-capable ships to Rota, Spain, and further noted that the deployment of Aegis Ashore systems was on track and expected to be completed in the 2015 time frame.[22]

A Different Strategic Environment

The integration of missile defense constitutes the most significant change in NATO's deterrence posture since the end of the Cold War. This growing significance of missile defense is consistent with tremendous changes in the international strategic environment. For more than forty years, NATO's deterrence posture focused on the Soviet threat.

In the course of the Ukraine crisis, NATO-Russia relations deteriorated. The Alliance continues to stress that its missile defense is not directed against Russia and will not undermine Russia's strategic deterrence capabilities.[23] However, NATO's missile defense plans are regarded in Moscow with great skepticism. Many in Russia, including government officials, claim that NATO's missile defense poses a threat to the national security of Russia because the final aim of these projects is to undermine Moscow's nuclear second-strike capability.[24]

In April 2014, NATO formally suspended its missile defense cooperation efforts with Russia as a consequence of Russia's actions in Ukraine.[25] Be that as it may, Russia is no longer NATO's sole force planning focus. Rather, the growing threat of the proliferation of modern delivery systems originating in rogue states, in particular a possible Iranian nuclear capability, becomes ever more important.[26]

We do not yet know whether the P-5 plus 1 (the US, Russia, China, the UK, France and Germany) process will be successful with its two-track approach of sanctions and incentives to stop Iran from developing a nuclear weapons option; however, encouraging political developments have occurred under the Rouhani presidency. Nor do we know whether military action will be taken to end Iran's controversial nuclear projects, nor what the result of such military operations would be. What we know is that an Iranian nuclear capability would definitely change NATO's security environment significantly, although it will never be comparable to the threat that the Soviet Union imposed during the Cold War. Not only would NATO partners at its southern flank feel less secure, but NATO itself could hardly be indifferent in a case where Israel, or one of the Arab countries that participate in NATO's Mediterranean Dialogue or the Istanbul Cooperation Initiative, became the victim of Iranian military pressure.[27]

In addition to the aforementioned Ghadr-1, which is believed to have entered military service sometime after 2007, Iran was developing a two-stage, solid-fueled Sajjil-2 missile with a maximum range of 2,000 kilometers. The missile has already undergone a number of tests, most of which have failed. Hence, the missile requires—according to expert analysis—at least another six tests. The fact that Iran continued to work on a relatively modern design of a multistage solid-fuel missile shows Iran's ongoing ambition; at the same time, however, experts believe that international trade sanctions slowed down the program significantly.[28] Those pundits portray the current Iranian missile threat as low. At the other end of the spectrum, though, other experts believe that Iran should not have any severe difficulties extending the range of the Sajjil-2 missile to hit targets all the way to the English Channel should negotiations break down.[29]

If Iran proceeds with its nuclear and missile projects, NATO would need to adapt its extended deterrence planning to the new situation. Extended deterrence in the face of a nuclear Iran would differ tremendously from extended deterrence in view of the former Soviet Union. During the Cold War, NATO feared that Warsaw Pact forces could begin a conventional offensive that could escalate to the nuclear level. Today, it is more than unlikely that Iran would attack the still most forceful military alliance on Earth, namely,

NATO. Such an attack would definitely result in an overwhelming retaliatory strike, ending the current regime in Tehran. Hence, it is inconceivable that Iran would initiate such an assault.

Still, extended deterrence with respect to a nuclear Iran can be expected to be meaningful for NATO. In his famous debate with Kenneth N. Waltz on the possible threats associated with the spread of nuclear weapons, Scott Sagan argued that further nuclear proliferation could result in aggressive behavior of new nuclear weapons states.[30] They could easily invade small (neighboring) countries if they assume that their new weapons would deter intervention by outside powers. This is exactly the situation we would have been faced with if Saddam Hussein had already developed nuclear weapons by the time he invaded Kuwait in 1990. As it turned out, in the course of International Atomic Energy Agency (IAEA) inspections after Operation Desert Storm, Iraq's nuclear program was more advanced than previously thought.[31]

Today, many states in the Middle East fear that a nuclear Iran might become more assertive. Leaders in Tehran may calculate that foreign invasion to counter their aggressive acts becomes less likely if Iran's nuclear and missile capabilities become more advanced. In any event, many observers believe that for Iran, nuclear weapons are weapons of deterrence *and* power projection.[32] Against this background, the issue is not whether the United States, NATO, or the international community could deter Iran from a nuclear attack. At stake is whether a nuclear Iran could deter international intervention aiming at reestablishing regional order against Iranian aggression or assertiveness.

During the Cold War period, the main idea of deterrence was not to use military force in a relatively stable situation. In the future—and in a world with more nuclear powers equipped with long-range ballistic missiles—countries and alliances, such as NATO, will have to face different decisions: Will they be willing to use their forces against aggression and for the protection of international order in a contingency that might result in severe damage caused by nuclear weapons used by the aggressor? Deliberately accepting one's own vulnerability, as the West did during the Cold War, does not seem to be the appropriate strategic approach in such a context. Instead, the security environment dictates that defensive competencies, in addition to offensive capabilities, are needed. Missile defense can work as a damage-limitation option and help to maintain some room for maneuvering against aggressive states.

Why Missile Defense?

In the United States, there is broad bipartisan support for missile defense. Most politicians agree that such defenses are needed in a world with more and more missile- and nuclear-capable states.[33] With NATO's Lisbon 2010 and Chicago 2012 decisions, missile defense has become part of the Alliance's force planning and deterrence posture. While missile defense is not controversial in principle, a number of issues remain. For some Europeans, it will still be important to make sure that NATO's missile defense projects do not alienate Moscow. Furthermore, it remains to be seen whether NATO's missile defense will trigger even more missile proliferation. This might be the case if opponents intensify their missile projects in an effort to overcome NATO's defenses. To be sure, certain defense systems, their technical characteristics, and particularly their price tag will remain hot topics in Alliance circles. Against the backdrop of an ongoing financial crisis and shrinking defense budgets, it may seem questionable whether NATO partners could afford to spend enormous amounts of taxpayers' money to defend against a threat that many do not perceive as urgent, while at the same time NATO has to tackle other urgent priorities such as the improvement of its rapid reaction forces to reassure allies in the face of a new conflict with Russia.

Finally, at least two still-controversial issues need further clarification. One concerns the fact that the Alliance needs to prioritize areas to be defended, a problem that is of particular relevance for NATO members close to countries of concern, such as Turkey. NATO cannot avoid debating this question—no matter how advanced future missile defense become—because attacking missiles might overcome the first line of defense so that point defenses would be needed to protect those areas that are deemed most significant. Second, an opponent might target a missile on NATO country A, the attacking missile would then be successfully intercepted over NATO member B, while NATO partner C would suffer from the debris that results from the successful intercept and drops on its territory. In fact, the little debris that does not burn up during reentry into the Earth's atmosphere would continue along its original ballistic trajectory and land near the original target. Regardless, the devastating consequences of a successful hit on a city by a warhead carrying a weapon of mass destruction such as a nuclear weapon would be overwhelming compared to the potential damage that may be caused by any debris that survives reentry into Earth's atmosphere. Whatever the technical reliability of future missile defense might be, this problem can hardly be overcome entirely and must be addressed.

Despite these shortcomings, missile defense also has several advantages. It is already widely accepted that missile defense is needed to protect forces in out-of-area operations against short-range missile attacks. In addition, missile defense can be expected to become ever more valuable for extended deterrence contingencies for a number of reasons, as detailed in the following paragraphs.

Most importantly, missile defense provides damage limitation should a missile attack occur. It is important to note, however, that missile defense will never be able to protect territories and populations reliably and comprehensively. Therefore, terms such as *missile defense shield* seem inappropriate. For the domestic audience, such wording implies erroneous expectations of an all-embracing protection. For the external audience, particularly Russia as well as China, the term *defense shield* would increase apprehensions that the final aim for the United States and NATO is to undermine the nuclear second-strike capability of these countries. But this is exactly *not* the purpose of the Alliance's missile defense. In fact, in a confrontation that involves large and modern ballistic missile arsenals, the role of missile defense, even for damage limitation, would be very limited.[34] Therefore, NATO's aim is to establish damage limitation options in the face of limited but growing missile threats from countries of concern such as Iran. For instance, in a conflict with a future Iran equipped with a few nuclear-tipped ballistic missiles, it would make a difference whether all of them would reach their targets (mostly densely populated cities) or whether it would be possible to intercept at least most of them.

In addition to damage limitation, missile defense has an important effect on the aggressor's calculations. Without missile defense in place, the attacking state may assume that all its ballistic missiles would reach their targets provided they work as planned. With missile defense deployed, the uncertainty on the part of the aggressor increases. War planning under such circumstances needs to take into consideration that some incoming missiles would be successfully intercepted and thus the effect of the attack would be reduced. This function of missile defense can be labeled as deterrence by denial.

At the same time, missile defense is important to help in maneuvering against aggressors equipped with ballistic missiles and weapons of mass destruction. If Saddam Hussein had developed a nuclear capability prior to his occupation of Kuwait, Operation Desert Storm to free Kuwait under a mandate of the UN Security Council might never have taken place. Populations at Europe's periphery would have been defenseless against nuclear-tipped Iraqi missiles, and thus the risk of a military operation directed against

Saddam would have been considered to be too high. If the United States and its allies would be confronted in the future with a nuclear and more assertive Iran that would put pressure on its neighbors, missile defense capable of effectively reducing the damage of an Iranian attack could help to convince both Western politicians and populations that an Iranian aggression must not go unpunished. To be sure, risk calculation would still be extremely difficult, but missile defense would add an important option.

Furthermore, missile defense has positive ramifications for the credibility of extended deterrence. During the Cold War, Europeans often questioned Washington's promise to escalate to the strategic nuclear level in case a conflict with the Soviet Union would occur. Countless books and articles have been published focusing on the coupling or decoupling effect of US nuclear forces deployed on European territories. In particular it was asked whether US nuclear weapons would be used in the first place if this could result in all-out nuclear war. Some pundits argued that the United States would be deterred against using its nuclear weapons, calling into question the credibility of NATO's deterrence posture: Why would the United States sacrifice New York City for Brussels?

Such self-deterrence would not apply to missile defense. These systems are not meant to provide for escalation dominance in conjunction with offensive threats. Rather, they are purely defensive and do not damage the aggressor. Nuclear escalation would not be imminent. Therefore, missile defense is much more likely to be used to defend allies.[35]

Missile defense also contributes to crisis stability. As long as territories and populations are defenseless against a potential nuclear aggressor, the United States and its allies would be required to take out the opponent's nuclear forces early in a crisis with offensive means to prevent a nuclear attack. If equipped with missile defense, the United States and its allies would not be under pressure to attack the opponent's nuclear weapons early in a crisis situation. If damage limitation through defenses becomes achievable, the need to reduce damage by attacking the opponent's offensive capabilities would decrease. Because the opponent would know this, it would not be forced to use nuclear weapons early in a use-them-or-lose-them mode. Hence, in the critical first hours of a severe crisis, the likelihood of escalation would diminish.

Finally, proliferators are motivated to acquire missiles as well as nuclear weapons in the hope that they can use them as instruments of coercion. For instance, the United States and its allies could be coerced by a nuclear Iran to lift sanctions. With its nuclear capability as a background, Iran could threaten to close the Strait of Hormuz, severely hampering the international oil supply. To be sure, it is highly questionable whether Iran would have the conventional military means to mine the Strait of Hormuz successfully in the face of superior Western navies present in the area. But such a contingency would become much more risky in terms of intended or unintended escalation if Iran possessed nuclear weapons and the respective delivery systems. Missile defense could help to reduce such risks.[36]

Can Missile Defense Substitute for Nuclear Weapons?

Missile defense can contribute to reducing the salience of nuclear weapons. But as long as nuclear weapons exist, defenses cannot become the sole backbone of a credible deterrence posture. Rather, missile defense can only complement nuclear deterrence.[37] A credible deterrence strategy needs to confront the opponent not only with a deterrence-by-denial component (the possibility that its attack can be effectively defended) but also with an increase in the costs of aggression to a point where it becomes unattractive for the deterred to attack; thus, the threat of punishment is essential. The opponent needs to be exposed to a massive retaliation so that it would not dare to use its nuclear forces first. To that end, nuclear weapons remain indispensable for the time being.[38]

If Iran were to attack NATO with nuclear-tipped missiles and if the Alliance were capable of intercepting all of them so that severe damage to NATO populations and territories could be avoided, there would still be the need to reestablish deterrence. The attacker would need to learn a lesson: Aggression must not go unpunished. Without retaliation, this might not be achievable. At the same time, such retaliation could be kept to the conventional level if NATO intercepts all the attacker's missiles. But if only one Iranian nuclear-tipped missile detonates over a European city, a nuclear retaliation could hardly be avoided. The more attacking nuclear missiles would overcome the defense, the more massive the retaliation would need to be. Missile defense can contribute to decreasing the salience of nuclear weapons for the deterrence posture, but a nuclear retaliatory capability needs to be maintained to make deterrence effective as long as nuclear weapons exist.

Some hoped that missile defense may, in the medium- to long-term, help to substitute for a particular component of NATO's nuclear deterrence, namely, US nonstrategic nuclear forces deployed in Europe.[39] The United States deployed nuclear forces in Europe for the first time in 1953 and 1954. Their numbers peaked in 1971 at around 7,300 nuclear warheads of thirteen different types. At that time, these weapons and, in particular, the practice of nuclear sharing, were perceived as an important symbol of the transatlantic link. Since the end of the Cold War, however, the number of US nuclear forces in Europe has been drastically reduced. Today, only 150 to 200 air-launched gravity bombs remain. They are stored in Germany, the Netherlands, Belgium, Italy, and Turkey and would be deployed by aircraft that are on extremely low-level alert.

It is widely acknowledged that in today's strategic environment, NATO's nonstrategic systems have little or no military operational relevance. The respective combat aircraft have limited flight ranges and would be vulnerable during combat operations when attacking well-defended targets. There are even concerns regarding the safe and secure storage of nuclear weapons at US sites in Europe: They could be targets of theft.

While the military utility of nonstrategic nuclear forces is called into question, US nuclear weapon deployments in Europe continue to be relevant in political terms. New NATO members in particular would interpret the removal of these assets as evidence that their security needs are not well taken care of within the Alliance. Central and East European NATO members would believe that such a nuclear withdrawal would only be the pretext of a complete American retreat from Europe, making them more vulnerable to Russian assertiveness and intimidation. This concern is of particular importance given that almost all European NATO partners are reducing their budgets for conventional forces.

Moreover, US nuclear forces in Europe are an essential link to US strategic forces and help maintain allied burden-sharing and solidarity. Some of the countries that host US nuclear bombs and participate in nuclear sharing are aware that, in so doing, they have a special status within the Alliance. The United States, for its part, welcomes the participation of allies in extended nuclear deterrence, including NATO's nuclear sharing, because the latter is an instrument of burden-sharing in terms of financial costs as well as political risks and responsibilities.[40]

One should also not forget that the stationing of US nuclear forces in Europe has always had a nonproliferation dimension. The concept of nuclear sharing was developed in the 1960s to convince the Federal Republic of Germany to renounce nuclear weapons. Today, only few believe that Germany would ever develop nuclear weapons of its own; in fact, Germany is legally bound by the Nuclear Non-Proliferation Treaty, as well as the two-plus-four treaty, handling German unification, to renounce nuclear weapons. But other NATO members might change their mind in case nuclear proliferation at NATO's periphery would take place. This particularly applies to Turkey. While a nuclear weapons program would not be an easy undertaking for

Ankara both politically and technically, some already fear that one of the reasons that Turkey is currently so eager to establish a civilian nuclear program is to keep the nuclear weapons option open.[41]

Despite these political arguments in favor of maintaining the current practice of deploying US nonstrategic nuclear forces in Europe, it is questionable whether those European countries that currently provide aircraft to deploy US nuclear bombs can be expected to modernize these aging delivery systems within the next ten years or so. A possible denuclearization by default could severely hamper the Alliance and weaken the transatlantic link. Missile defense could help to prevent such an unwelcome development.

To begin with, in the face of a nuclear Iran, missile defense that provides damage limitation in case of conflict would be much more valuable than European aircraft equipped with US nuclear bombs that could hardly reach Iranian airspace and hence would be of limited deterrence value. Instead, the United States could use more capable nuclear forces, such as strategic bombers, to deter Iran.

Missile defense can also have an important alliance dimension. In many ways, step-by-step missile defense could replace the importance that nuclear sharing has for NATO today. It could enhance transatlantic sharing of responsibility and reinforce the principle that security is indivisible. The NATO effort to establish missile defense keeps the United States committed to European defense. Allies could find new opportunities to participate in NATO force planning. Finally, missile defense would have a nonproliferation impact on allies. If well protected by missile defense, there would be fewer incentives for NATO allies at the periphery (such as Turkey) to establish their own nuclear deterrence in case of intensifying nuclear dynamics in the Middle East.

In sum, a NATO missile defense that includes a visible European footprint would result in a strategically much more valuable asset and stronger transatlantic link in the future compared to the aging and militarily redundant nuclear-capable delivery systems made available by European NATO allies today. At the same time, missile defense may contribute to reducing the salience of nuclear weapons, but missile defense cannot substitute for nuclear deterrence as a whole, as long as nuclear weapons exist.

Conclusion

Nuclear deterrence has never been an ideal strategy. If nuclear weapons were used, the result would be catastrophic. But it is also true that nuclear deterrence will remain a fact of life for the foreseeable future. During the Cold

War, efforts to overcome nuclear deterrence by establishing missile defences were unrealistic and counterproductive. They would have undermined the stabilizing principle of nuclear second-strike capabilities. Today, the strategic environment looks different. Against limited threats, effective missile defense seems possible. At the same time, it does not pose a threat to former opponents such as Russia and hence do not undermine strategic stability. However, NATO needs to convince Moscow through confidence- and transparency-building activities that this is indeed the case.

In a global context where missile and nuclear proliferation endures and where confrontation with a nuclear Iran remains possible, missile defense may be stabilizing and may make extended deterrence more credible—for both allies and adversaries. They add an important damage limitation option and thereby help to maintain room for military maneuver. Missile defense can also help to reduce the salience of nuclear weapons, but they cannot completely substitute for their deterrence function. The specific role that missile defense will play for NATO in the years to come depends on a number of factors. One is the evolution of the nuclear and ballistic missile threat. Another is the relationship with Russia and whether both sides will agree to build transparency and confidence in the missile defense realm. In addition, budget considerations as well as technical developments will come into play. In any case, we conclude that missile defense will play an increasingly important role in future deterrence and extended deterrence postures for many reasons.

Notes

1. The views and analysis contained in this chapter are those of the authors and should not necessarily be construed as representing the views of the Center for Security Studies, the US Department of State, or Missouri State University.

2. Fred Iklé, "Can Nuclear Deterrence Last out the Century?" *Foreign Affairs* 51, no.2 (January 1973): 270.

3. Ronald Reagan's Star War Speech of March 23, 1983, www.pierretristam.com/Bobst/library/wf-241.htm (accessed January 23, 2013).

4. R. W. Apple Jr., "Scud Missile Hits a U.S. Barracks, Killing 27," *New York Times*, February 26, 1991, http://www.nytimes.com/1991/02/26/world/war-in-the-gulf-scud-attack-scud-missile-hits-a-us-barracks-killing-27.html (accessed January 15, 2013); Bob Drogin and Patt Morrison, "Iraqi Missile Slams Into GIs' Barracks; 27 Killed," *Los Angeles Times*, February 26, 1991, http://articles.latimes.com/1991-02-26/news/mn-1889_1_scud-attack (accessed January 15, 2013).

5. Joseph Cirincione, "The Performance of the Patriot Missile in the Gulf War," An Edited Draft of a Report Prepared for the Government Operations Committee, US House of Representatives, October 1992.

6. Avi Shlaim, "Israel and the Conflict," in *International Perspectives on the Gulf Conflict, 1990–91*, ed. Alex Danchev and Dan Keohane (London: St Martin's Press 1994), 59–79, http://users.ox.ac.uk/~ssfc0005/Israel%20and%20the%20Conflict.html (accessed January 20, 2013).

7. Executive Summary of the Report of the Commission to Assess the Ballistic Missile Threat to the United States, July 15, 1998, www.fas.org/irp/threat/bm-threat.htm (accessed January 23, 2013); Mark Fitzpatrick, "North Korean Proliferation Challenges: The Role of the European Union," EU Non-Proliferation Consortium, *Non-Proliferation Papers*, no. 18 (June 2012).

8. Greg Thielmann, "The National Missile Defense Act of 1999," *Arms Control Today* 39 (July/August 2009), http://www.armscontrol.org/act/2009_07-08/lookingback (accessed January 20, 2013).

9. Lynn F. Rusten,"U.S. Withdrawal from the ABM Treaty," Center for the Study of Weapons of Mass Destruction *Case Study 2* (Washington, DC: National Defense University Press, January 2010), http://www.ndu.edu/press/lib/images/occasionalPapers/cswmd-cs2.pdf (accessed January 20, 2013).

10. Office of Public Affairs and Office of the Secretary of Defense, "Pentagon Briefing: 2002 Nuclear Posture Review," *Fact Sheet*, January 10, 2002.

11. US Department of State and US Department of Defense, "Proposed U.S. Missile Defense Assets in Europe," www.fas.org/irp/threat/missile/bmd-europe.pdf (accessed January 23, 2013).

12. US Department of Defense, *Nuclear Posture Review Report* (April 2010), 33.

13. *Active Engagement, Modern Defence. Strategic Concept for the Defence and Security of the Members of the North Atlantic Treaty Organization*, adopted by Heads of State and Government in Lisbon, November 19–20, 2010, 16.

14. Ibid.

15. Ibid.

16. Barack Obama, "Remarks by the President on Strengthening Missile Defense in Europe," September 17, 2009, http://www.whitehouse.gov/the-press-office/remarks-president-strengthening-missile-defense-europe (accessed January 23, 2013).

17. Deputy Assistant Secretary Frank A. Rose, "Challenges in Europe," Bureau of Verification, Compliance, and Implementation, Remarks at the 6th International Conference on Missile Defense (Lisbon: February 2010), http://www.state.gov/t/avc/rls/137991.htm (accessed January 23, 2013).

18. US Department of Defense, Ballistic Missile Defence Review Fact Sheet (March 2010), http://www.defense.gov/bmdr/docs/BMDR%20FACT%20SHEET%20March%202010%20_Final_.pdf (accessed January 23, 2013).

19. Tom Z. Collina, "Turkey to Host NATO Missile Defense Radar," *Arms Control Today* (October 2011): 41. http://www.armscontrol.org/act/2011_10/Turkey_to_Host_NATO_Missile_Defense_Radar (accessed January 15, 2013).

20. United States Department of Defense, Office of the Assistant Secretary of Defense (Public Affairs), Missile Defense Announcement as delivered by Secretary of Defense Chuck Hagel, The Pentagon, March 15, 2013.

21. Chicago Summit Declaration, Issued by the Heads of State and Government participating in the meeting of the North Atlantic Council in Chicago in May 2012.

22. NATO, Wales Summit Declaration, Press Release, Issued on September 5, 2014, para. 55–60.

23. NATO, Wales Summit Declaration, Press Release, Issued on September 5, 2014, para. 61.

24. Nikolai Korchunov (Acting Permanent Representative of Russia to NATO), "You Say Defense, We Say Threat," *New York Times*, June 6, 2012.

25. Statement by NATO Foreign Ministers, April 1, 2014, http://www.nato.int/cps/en/natolive/news_108501.htm, accessed December 14, 2014.

26. Bruno Tertrais, "A Nuclear Iran and NATO," *Survival* 5, no. 6 (December 2010–January 2011): 45–61.

27. Oliver Thränert, "Nuclear Arms and Missile Defense in Transatlantic Security," in *European Security and the Future of Transatlantic Relations*, ed. Riccardo Alcaro and Erik Jones (Rome: Istituto Affari Internazionale 2011), 79.

28. "Iran Sanctions Halt Long-Range Ballistic-Missile Development," *IISS Strategic Comments* 18, Comment 22, July 2012.

29. Uzi Rubin, "Showcase of Missile Proliferation: Iran's Missile and Space Program," *Arms Control Today* 42 (January/February 2012): 14–20.

30. Scott D. Sagan and Kenneth N. Waltz, *The Spread of Nuclear Weapons. A Debate* (New York: W.W. Norton, 1995), 129.

31. David Albright and Mark Hibbs, "Iraq's Bomb: Blueprints and Artifacts," *The Bulletin of the Atomic Scientists* (January/February 1992), 30–40: "[I]t is clear that by the mid-1990s Iraq could well have emerged with a small nuclear arsenal that would have fundamentally changed the Middle East," (40).

32. Eric S. Edelman, Andrew F. Krepinevich, and Evan Braden Montgomery, "The Dangers of a Nuclear Iran: The Limits of Containment," *Foreign Affairs* 90, no. 1 (January/February 2011): 67.

33. Kimberly Misher, "Why Obama Is Right on Missile Defense—What's Next?," *Carnegie Endowment for International Peace Policy Outlook* (September 2009), www.carnegieendowment.org/files/misher_missile_defense.pdf (accessed January 20, 2013).

34. Dean Wilkening, "Does Missile Defence in Europe threaten Russia?," *Survival* 54, no.1 (February/March 2012): 31–52.

35. In the vernacular of the nuclear discourse, this means that missile defense may raise the threshold of nuclear use rather than lower it, as some have argued.

36. Jeremy Stocker, "The Strategy of Missile Defence: Defence, Deterrence and Diplomacy," *RUSI Journal* 156, no. 3 (June/July 2011): 56–62; Oliver Thränert, "Europe's Need for a Damage Limitation Option," in *Readings in European Security*, ed. Michael Emerson (Bruxelles: Center for European Policy Studies/London: International Institute for Security Studies/Geneva: Geneva Center for the Democratic Control of Armed Forces/Geneva: Geneva Center for Security Policy, 2009), 62–77. NATO's Deterrence and Defense Posture Review of May 20, 2012, also highlights certain advantages as well as limits of missile defense in paragraph 20: "It is expected that NATO's missile defence capabilities would complicate an adversary's planning and provide damage mitigation. Effective missile defence could also provide valuable decision space in times of crisis. Like other weapons systems, missile defence capabilities cannot promise complete and enduring effectiveness."

37. Kerry M. Kartchner, "Missile Defenses and New Approaches to Deterrence," US Department of State, Office of International Information Programs, April 2002, http://www.nti.org/media/pdfs/203.pdf?_=1316623847 (accessed January 20, 2013).

38. NATO Defence and Deterrence Posture Review, May 20, 2012, paragraph 20: "Missile defence can complement the role of nuclear weapons in deterrence; it cannot substitute for them."

39. Oliver Thränert, "NATO, Missile Defence and Extended Deterrence," *Survival* 51, no. 6 (December 2009/January 2010): 63–76.

40. George Perkovich, Malcolm Chalmers, Steven Pifer, Paul Schulte, and Jaclyn Tandler, "Looking Beyond the Chicago Summit: Nuclear Weapons in Europe and the Future of NATO," *Carnegie Papers*, Carnegie Endowment for International Peace, Washington, DC, April 2012, http://carnegieendowment.org/files/beyond_chicago_summit.pdf (accessed December 16, 2014).

41. Sinan Ülgen, "Turkey and the Bomb," *Carnegie Papers*, Carnegie Endowment for International Peace, Washington, DC, February 2012.

CHAPTER 7

Ballistic Missile Defense in Europe

GETTING TO YES WITH MOSCOW?

Paul I. Bernstein

DEFENSE AGAINST BALLISTIC MISSILES is an increasingly salient element of Western security architectures, and the ongoing effort to develop and field ballistic missile defense (BMD) capabilities in Europe has become a major project for the United States and NATO. The previous chapter examined the potential for BMD to complement nuclear weapons as a core component of NATO's deterrent posture. This chapter focuses on a different aspect of the BMD challenge: Russia's perspective on missile defense in Europe, Moscow's continued opposition to US plans as embodied in the European Phased Adaptive Approach (EPAA), the struggle to address Russia's concerns without weakening US and NATO capability, and prospects for meaningful cooperation on missile defense.

From Star Wars to EPAA

The spread of regional ballistic missile capabilities has grown steadily as a security concern of the United States since the mid-1980s. The Iran-Iraq war of 1980 to 1988 witnessed the launch, by both sides, of hundreds of short-range ballistic missiles (SRBMs) targeted at cities in an effort to alter the political dynamics of the conflict. While this extension of strategic bombing tactics had little impact on the prosecution of the ground and air war, it is believed by some Western analysts to have affected Iranian morale later in the war, in part because of fears that these missiles would be used to deliver chemical weapons.[1] To the United States and others, the so-called Scud duel between Iraq and Iran demonstrated that regional powers saw ballistic missiles as potentially powerful instruments of warfare and that they were prepared to invest in them, and were able and willing to employ them with few inhibitions. The fact that ballistic missiles could be an effective means to deliver weapons of mass destruction (WMD) only reinforced concerns about their potential strategic and operational impact in future conflicts.

At the end of the Cold War—and on the eve of the first Gulf War—these concerns led the United States to begin reorienting its approach to missile defense to give greater weight to regional threats. In January 1991, President George H. W. Bush announced a major reconfiguration of the controversial Strategic Defense Initiative (SDI) to focus on limited missile threats from any source and thus include protection not just of the United States but also of US power projection capabilities, forward-deployed forces, and the territory of friends and allies.[2] The Gulf War underscored the rationale for a shift toward regional missile threats. Attacks by Iraqi Scud missiles on Israeli cities early in the war threatened to fracture the coalition assembled by Washington to reverse Iraq's aggression and led the United States to undertake extensive countermeasures, including the deployment of Patriot missiles configured to defeat SRBMs and a major operation to eliminate Iraqi Scud launchers. In addition to the political and psychological impact of successful ballistic missile strikes, there was growing concern about the potential military impact. The official Department of Defense report on the war observed the following about Iraq's Scuds: "Had they been more accurate or able to penetrate more successfully, they might have inflicted serious damage on military targets, including the large troop concentrations at Saudi ports at the start of the war."[3]

After the war, President Bush renewed his push for a program to provide protection against limited ballistic missile attacks and called on Russia to join in this effort. In January 1992, Russian President Boris Yeltsin proposed a "global protection system," and at the June 1992 summit the two presidents issued a joint statement launching a high-level working group to develop the concept and explore the potential for practical cooperation.[4] In September 1992, the United States tabled a draft protocol of the Antiballistic Missile (ABM) Treaty that called for a significant expansion of missile defense sites and interceptors, and the removal of limits on the development and testing of BMD systems and space-based sensors.[5]

Coming into power in early 1993, the Clinton administration opposed changes to the ABM Treaty and declared its intention to pursue BMD capabilities within the strict framework of the treaty. It proposed guidelines that would demarcate permissible "theater missile defense" systems from prohibited "national missile defense" capabilities.[6] And in the years following Desert Storm, the United States began to invest heavily in defensive systems designed to protect expeditionary forces and coalition partners from short- and medium-range ballistic missile threats. Technologies intended to defend the US homeland against long-range missile threats became a lesser priority based not only on the administration's intent to remain compliant with the ABM Treaty but also on intelligence assessments of the missile threat. Research and development programs initiated during this period have matured slowly but are now delivering capabilities that are gradually expanding US fielded BMD assets. This includes the sea-based system that provides the foundation for current US plans in Europe.

The national-level threat assessment underpinning the Clinton administration's emphasis on protection against shorter-range threats was increasingly challenged in the mid-1990s by those who believed the US intelligence community had underestimated the potential of regional powers to develop long-range missiles capable of threatening US territory. An independent commission concluded in 1998 that rogue states such as North Korea, Iran, and Iraq could in fact acquire such missile capabilities within just a few years of making a decision to do so, especially if they had foreign assistance.[7] Only weeks later, North Korea launched a Taepo Dong missile configured as a space launch vehicle (SLV). While the satellite that constituted the third stage of this missile did not deploy successfully, this launch demonstrated capabilities that could be applied to the development of a missile that could reach the United States.

A year later, in September 1999, a National Intelligence Estimate acknowledged this new reality: "Most intelligence community agencies project that by 2015 the United States most likely will face ICBM [intercontinental ballistic missile] threats from North Korea and Iran, and possibly Iraq—in addition to the longstanding missile forces of Russia and China."[8] These developments led the Clinton administration to reconfigure its BMD program; R&D activities in support of homeland defense heretofore categorized as a technology readiness effort would be placed on a track leading to deployment if warranted by advances in adversary capabilities. The principal national missile defense program was the Ground-Based Midcourse Defense System based on the Ground-Based Interceptor (GBI).

This system became the centerpiece of US efforts to defend the homeland from limited long-range missile attacks during the presidency of George W. Bush. An initial operational capability was fielded in late 2004 in Alaska and California, and was configured to defeat attacks from North

Korea. To address a potential long-range Iranian threat, the Bush administration sought a deployment site in Europe and initiated consultations with a number of European governments about hosting a missile defense complex. Formal negotiations with Poland and the Czech Republic began in February 2007. In August 2008, an agreement was reached with Warsaw for the basing of ten GBIs and with Prague for the fielding of sophisticated radar technology in the Czech Republic.[9]

Moscow strongly opposed the so-called Third Site initiative, arguing that it posed a potential threat to Russia's nuclear deterrent and constituted a further Western encroachment into Russia's traditional sphere of influence. As an alternative, Russian president Vladimir Putin offered to make available existing radar capabilities in Azerbaijan or construct a new radar complex in southern Russia and to place any Russia-based facility under the auspices of the NATO-Russia Council.[10] After these offers were rejected by Washington as a substitute for the Third Site program, Moscow issued numerous threats in an effort to derail the project, some directed at Poland and others at the United States, suggesting a return to Cold War tensions and highlighting compensatory steps it would be compelled to take. At the same time, Russia responded favorably to confidence-building and transparency measures offered by the United States at the 2008 Sochi summit, stating that such steps would address Russia's concerns to some degree.[11]

While the specific measures proposed by Washington have not been publicly released, the memoirs of former US senior officials and contemporaneous press accounts point to the following: greater transparency regarding US and NATO deployments, regular data exchanges, Russian observation of BMD flight tests, joint modeling and analysis, sharing of early warning data, joint monitoring of the Iranian missile threat, joint R&D, potential use of a Soviet-era radar in Azerbaijan, consultation on significant program changes, a pledge to avoid rapid expansion of BMD systems in Europe, visits by Russian officials to BMD-related facilities in Europe and the United States, and linking deployments and operational status to specific developments in the Iranian missile threat.[12]

The administration of Barack Obama came into office with different ideas about missile defense, and while fully committed to deploying US interceptors in Europe, it sought alternatives to the plan inherited from its predecessor. Just thirteen months after the Third Site agreement was announced, the United States declared that it no longer planned to go forward with it; instead, it would pursue a new architecture that would be based on different systems but still provide opportunities for participation by NATO allies. The EPAA was premised on a new assessment of the Iranian missile threat that saw short- and medium-range capabilities advancing more rapidly, and ICBM-type capabilities more slowly, than previously projected. It was also based on a judgment that certain missile defense technologies had progressed more than others and offered more flexible, reliable, and cost-effective counters to the threats of greatest concern.[13]

In effect, the homeland was adequately defended, at least for the moment. True, there was less confidence in the GBI as a homeland defense capability, but there was also time to develop a more robust solution. The new approach to missile defense in Europe would give priority to the most pressing threats while establishing a technology pathway to that solution. The EPAA relies principally on existing and more advanced future versions of the Standard Missile-3 (SM-3), the interceptor currently based at sea as part of the Aegis Ballistic Missile Defense System. The plan announced in September 2009, and later articulated in the 2010 Ballistic Missile Defense Review, envisioned four phases of development and deployment:

Phase One (2011 time frame): Use existing sea-based systems to defend against short- and medium-range ballistic missile threats to portions of southern Europe. Phase One relies on the initial version of the SM-3 interceptor (Block 1A) and a forward-based radar.

Phase Two (2015 time frame): Field an enhanced SM-3 interceptor (Block 1B) in both sea- and land-based configurations, and additional sensors, expanding coverage of SRBM and MRBM threats to a greater number of NATO allies.

Phase Three (2018 time frame): Add a second land-based SM-3 site, to be located in northern Europe, and field an improved interceptor (Block 2A) to extend coverage to all NATO allies, including against intermediate-range ballistic missiles.

Phase Four (2020 time frame): After development and testing are complete, deploy a version of the SM-3 (Block 2B) to provide greater area coverage against MRBMs and IRBMs, and some early-intercept capability against a future Middle East ICBM threat.[14]

Agreements reached subsequently with NATO allies have placed advanced radar in Turkey and will see the deployment of land-based SM-3 interceptors in Romania in 2015 and in Poland in 2018. It is important to note that Phases One, Two, and Three are configured to address short-, medium-, and intermediate-range threats; only the final phase of this architecture envisions a capability tailored to the threat posed by regional ICBMs. While hardly the only aspect of EPAA opposed by Moscow, the projected Phase

Four capability has been a major focal point of Russian anxiety about the potential of EPAA to put Russia's strategic deterrent at risk. The US announcement in March 2013 that it was, in effect, canceling Phase Four would seem to bear directly on this concern.[15]

The Roots of Russian Opposition

Throughout this period of BMD development by the United States, Russia repeatedly has raised concerns about concepts, technologies, and operational schemes perceived as challenging Russia's geopolitical position and posing a potential threat to Russia's nuclear deterrent. The roots of this opposition run deep and reflect far more than military-technical considerations. Russian fears with respect to US missile defense plans fit into a larger narrative defined by Moscow's disillusionment with the post–Cold War settlement in Europe, its sense of lost geopolitical power, and the primacy it attaches to nuclear weapons. Russian strategists offer a lengthy bill of indictment against the United States and NATO in this regard, including the arbitrary use of force in places like the former Yugoslavia and Iraq, NATO's eastward expansion, "degradation" of the nuclear arms control regime in the George W. Bush years (especially withdrawing from the ABM Treaty), US pursuit of destabilizing non-nuclear strategic capabilities, and general disregard of Russia's regional and global interests.[16]

Some Western observers have made similar arguments. Writing in the first year of the Obama presidency, scholars David Deudney and John Ikenberry suggested the causes and consequences of Russia's belief that the United States and NATO have reneged on key elements of the Cold War settlement:

> [W]hat most marks Russia's orientation to the world, and to the United States in particular, is a thick and toxic narrative of grievance. . . . The basic reason for Russian antagonism toward the United States is the widespread Russian perception that Washington has encroached upon legitimate and historical Russian national and security interests, which were accommodated in the settlement. Three issues dominate this narrative: two decades of NATO expansion into former Warsaw Pact and post-Soviet areas, and the prospect that Georgia and Ukraine could join as well; the termination of the Anti-Ballistic Missile Treaty and George W. Bush administration plans for deployment of missile-defence systems in Eastern Europe; and American efforts to orchestrate oil-pipeline routes from the Caspian Sea that circumvent Russia. These American moves underscore and exacerbate the deeper Russian malaise stemming from lost status and diminished influence.[17]

From Moscow's vantage point, the US missile defense project in Europe has compounded the problems posed by NATO expansion into the former Warsaw Pact by serving as a catalyst for US or NATO military deployments in these states and the forging of strong bilateral security relationships with Washington. For some Russian leaders and strategists, this is the principal danger represented by US missile defense plans: deeper encroachment embodied in the establishment of new military installations in a geographic zone close to Russia. It thus represents another phase in the steady loss of Russian dominance in its own region.

It also reinforces Russia's position of technological inferiority as the United States extends military systems into Russia's traditional sphere of influence that it cannot match and for which it has limited counters. Thus, as Deudney and Ikenberry note, while the post–Cold War settlement was bipolar, over the course of two decades "it became increasingly evident that the distribution of power between the two states was ever more unipolar" as US military capabilities advanced and Russia's stagnated, and as the United States took on the burden of new security tasks in Europe and other key regions.[18]

This sense of inferiority vis-à-vis US high-technology military capabilities is an important reason nuclear weapons remain so deeply ingrained in Russia's strategic mind-set, military doctrine, and conceptions of global stability. As US high-technology systems advance in ways perceived to pose a potential threat to Russia's interests, Moscow urgently seeks to preserve a status quo in which nuclear weapons continue to be the principal currency of strategic power. As Matthew Rojansky has observed, despite widespread recognition among Soviet experts that nuclear weapons are of limited utility in addressing the most pressing contemporary security challenges,

> . . . Russia's still dominant share of the global nuclear weapons pie continues to endow Moscow with substantial geopolitical leverage and means that Russian attitudes can also shape realities to some degree . . . there is no other resource in which Moscow comes close to holding such an influential stake. With this dominance in mind, Russian thinkers are naturally inclined to accentuate both the likelihood and negative consequences of behavior by other states that might degrade Russia's nuclear deterrent and thus compel Russia to take action. Doing so imbues Russia's position on every issue that can be plausibly connected to nuclear weapons and strategic stability with greater significance for the rest of the world. . . . Emphasis on strategic stability is a way for Russia to maintain some leverage over the world's dominant power, the United States, and by extension over other great powers who are fast eclipsing Russia in every other sphere.[19]

Thus, it is no surprise that even the potential for EPAA in its later stages to pose a threat to Russia's nuclear deterrent has been a source of alarm for Moscow. Of course, missile defense is only the most visible capability that threatens this Russian conception of stability. Russian strategists view a larger suite of emerging US systems—BMD, conventional prompt global strike, space systems, and perhaps offensive cyberweapons—as the leading edge of a new form of high-precision deterrence underwritten by capabilities that Russia cannot compete with and therefore threaten to create a permanent set of strategic force asymmetries that will leave Russia vulnerable to high-technology non-nuclear threats. Thus, rather than a continuing commitment to mutual deterrence or—as Russia claims to seek—a cooperative retreat from it, Moscow fears the United States is moving toward a posture of absolute security, complete invulnerability, or overwhelming superiority. Putin himself has given voice to this fear. Speaking in 2007, he observed the following:

> The United States is actively developing and already strengthening an anti-missile defense system. Today this system is ineffective but we do not know exactly whether it will one day be effective. . . . So hypothetically we recognize that when this moment arrives, the possible threat from our nuclear forces will be completely neutralized. . . . The balance of powers will be absolutely destroyed and one of the partners will benefit from the feeling of complete security. That means that its hands will be free not only in local but eventually also in global conflicts.[20]

Recognizing that it lags significantly in precision and space technologies, it is no surprise that Russia actively seeks to forestall the emergence of non-nuclear strategic asymmetries and keep concepts of stability, deterrence, and parity firmly anchored exclusively in the nuclear realm. This likely will remain the logic of Russian strategic thinking as long as nuclear weapons remain a preeminent source of national power and Russia remains noncompetitive in other measures of capability and influence, both military and nonmilitary.

For Moscow, then, US plans for missile defense that are not organized around some integration of American, NATO, and Russian capabilities that respects Russia's geographical sphere of influence pose a grave threat to strategic stability. The widely held view in Russian leadership, strategy, and military circles that no credible long-range missile threat from Iran is likely to emerge any time soon only reinforces the fear that US plans are directed at Russia. And if the stakes are high for Russia, then Moscow also seeks to convey to Washington the risks in not taking appropriate account of its interests. Thus, in the last few years, both senior officials and prominent strategists routinely have framed Russia's position—publicly and privately, at working and senior levels—in the language of crisis and transformation. Pursued without Russian participation or some accommodation to Russia's interests, BMD will create a crisis in relations with the West, generate a new arms race, and put at risk further progress on arms control and cooperation on nonproliferation. In his annual state of the nation address in November 2010, immediately preceding the NATO Lisbon summit, then president Dmitry Medvedev stated openly "that over the next decade we are facing the following alternative: either we reach an agreement on missile defense and create a fully-fledged joint mechanism of cooperation or, if we fail to reach a constructive agreement, a new round of the arms race will start and we shall have to take decisions on the deployment of new strike equipment."[21] By contrast, it is argued, an approach to missile defense that respects Russia's strategic interests and accommodates Russia's active participation will fundamentally transform relations, enabling an orderly transition from mutual deterrence to cooperative strategic security.

Medvedev's reference to the deployment of new strike systems was intended to indicate the steps Russia would take to compensate for Western BMD deployments not constrained by some understanding with Moscow. For example, Russia is working to develop its own version of a prompt global strike system based on hypersonic propulsion technologies against which existing BMD systems could be far less effective.[22] Speaking at a conference on missile defense in Moscow in 2012, a senior Russian military official provided a list of other potential compensatory measures in the event that US- and NATO-deployed BMD assets posed a growing threat to Russia's strategic nuclear forces. These include improving the penetration capabilities of ICBMs, taking steps to ensure destruction or disruption of opposing BMD mobile and fixed assets, enhancing nuclear force readiness, increasing the protection of fixed launch sites, and maximizing concealment of mobile launchers.[23]

EPAA Anxiety

It is not difficult to see how US and NATO missile defense plans serve to reinforce the basic narratives that underpin Russia's contemporary strategic outlook. The grievances and fears that define these narratives can be discerned in the specific concerns articulated by Moscow about the EPAA: unilateral deployment and operation, open-ended architecture, and political geography.

Unilateral Deployment and Operation

Moscow's core proposition is that European missile defense cannot be solely an American or NATO project but must be developed and operated jointly to ensure that it is not directed against any one member of the European security community. It asserts as a "matter of principle" an "equal right to participation" in the system: hence Russia's emphasis on alternative approaches intended to give Moscow some degree of control over the design and operation of the BMD architecture. This is the source of Russia's initial proposal to adopt a sector concept of operations that would allocate the missile defense mission along geographic lines, thus ceding to Russia sole responsibility for protecting against threats in its traditional region of influence. It is also the source of Russia's subsequent proposal to establish some type of dual-key or dual-control arrangement that would provide for joint planning and command and control of missile defense operations—what some have referred to as "a finger on the button."[24] Both these alternative approaches have been rejected as inconsistent with EPAA and more broadly with NATO principles of collective defense.

Open-Ended Architecture

Also central to Russia's calculations is the view that EPAA is a program whose end-state cannot be described definitively with respect to the number of systems that may be fielded and where they may operate. Thus, what is characterized as limited by Washington in fact has almost unlimited potential from Moscow's perspective.[25] This concern has largely been focused on Phase Four of the EPAA and on fears that, if deployed in sufficient numbers (numbers well beyond those required to counter an Iranian threat, requiring many more basing locations), the SM-3 Block 2B interceptor could pose a risk to Russia's ICBM force. With this system now cancelled, one might expect that Russia's most acute concerns in this regard have been eased. Perhaps so, but publicly Russia's stance changed little in the period following the US decision, and statements by senior officials made clear that Moscow viewed it as neither a concession to Russia nor a resolution of its core concerns.[26] Undoubtedly Moscow believes this decision could easily be reversed at some point in the future, and at least some Russian officials and strategists contend that the SM-3 Block 2A interceptor that will be fielded in Phase Three also poses a significant danger to the effectiveness of Russia's ICBM force.[27] The stated concern here encompasses both the land- and sea-based version of this interceptor, in particular the number of Aegis-equipped ships and their areas of deployment. This could lead Russia to propose numerical and geographical limits on these capabilities despite US protestations that a priori limits of this kind are a nonstarter. A 2012 publication of the Russian Academy of Sciences articulates such restrictions: a limit of two ground bases with no more than twenty-four interceptors at each, and a limit of four to six BMD-equipped ships operating only in the Mediterranean and North Seas (not in the Black, Baltic, White, and Barents seas).[28]

Political Geography

Political geography likely is a factor here, too. Russian military analyses may suggest that Phase Three deployments pose a strategic risk to Russian ICBMs, but the real problem may simply be Moscow's deep unease in seeing the fielding of US BMD assets in Poland, in particular, and Warsaw's elevation to a so-called first-class citizen of NATO and a preferred security partner of the United States. Similarly, Moscow does not wish to see the Baltic States come under a US or NATO missile defense umbrella. These developments would serve to confirm and deepen Russia's loss of influence over this part of Europe.

Reassurance and Cooperation

Writing in 2007, just as the United States had begun to negotiate with NATO allies about hosting US missile defense systems, Henry Kissinger suggested that, in shaping the European program, "what America can and should do is limit the proposed deployment to its objective of overcoming threats from rogue states and find ways to define specific steps that separate the antimissile deployment in Central Europe from a strategy for a hypothetical and highly implausible war against Russia."[29] How to operationalize this strategic imperative remains a challenge today. Russia has not been fully reassured by the US decision to abandon EPAA Phase Four. Nor has Moscow been prepared to accept the findings of operational assessments conducted by the Defense Department and respected American analysts that even Phase Three capabilities do not pose a meaningful threat to Russia's nuclear deterrent under most plausible conditions.[30] Russian proposals to adopt a sectoral approach to European missile defense or a single joint planning and operational capability are unacceptable to the United States and NATO, as are predetermined limits on the size and location of BMD deployments.

Unable, as yet, to influence (i.e., constrain) the contours or operations of the EPAA, Moscow now demands a legally binding assurance that US and

NATO BMD capabilities are not and never will be directed at Russia. Speaking early in 2012, Russian foreign minister Sergei Lavrov stated, "Our principled condition is simple. If the U.S does not want to change anything in its plans, then it should provide reliable guarantees that the missile defense facilities being deployed in Europe will not be targeted against our strategic forces."[31] These guarantees must be "verifiable under mutually approved technical criteria" so that Russia can conduct an objective assessment of risk. According to publicly available Russian Ministry of Defense briefings, these criteria include the number and speed of interceptors, their capabilities at various stages of flight, radar range, command and control capabilities, deployment locations, and operational plans.[32] In essence, this is a demand for a treaty-like document that would codify technical and operational limitations on US and NATO capabilities. US officials have dismissed this demand as unrealistic, not least because such an agreement would require the consent of the US Senate. Russian leaders surely understand this, especially after the 2011 G8 summit, where President Obama chose not to endorse a missile defense agreement drafted by the US Department of State on the grounds that its provisions could be considered a legally binding assurance and a pledge to limit US capabilities.[33]

American officials at all levels have repeatedly expressed a willingness to offer a political assurance that US missile defenses are not directed at Russia, perhaps as part of an agreed statement of principles. NATO has already declared such an assurance at its 2012 and 2014 summits in Chicago and Wales, respectively.[34] In terms of public assurances, a similar statement is all Moscow realistically should expect from the United States. The question then becomes, what other confidence-building measures (CBMs) are possible to address Russia's concerns?

Much of this discussion has centered around a transparency regime based on regular exchanges of information on NATO and Russian missile defense capabilities. NATO's Chicago communiqué proposed to develop such a regime, and a personal letter from Obama to Putin in April 2013 reportedly reiterated the offer. While the letter is widely reported to have referred to this potential agreement as one that would be "legally binding," it is clear from statements by US officials that this referred to an executive agreement that would not be subject to ratification by the US Senate and would not bind a future US administration.[35] Subsequent press accounts indicated that a Russian counteroffer was rejected by Washington in December 2013 because it continued to demand fully binding assurances and limitations.[36] By this time Moscow had in fact asked for a pause in the BMD dialogue, in the continuing belief that its concerns were not adequately being considered. By the time the crisis in Ukraine and Russia's annexation of Crimea led NATO to formally suspend missile defense discussions in April 2014, the process had largely ground to a halt.[37]

If and when political conditions permit a resumption of efforts to bridge the BMD gap, the US position is not likely to have softened, and it is possible that it will have hardened. Accordingly, questions related to transparency likely will remain the focus of any US proposals. What might a transparency regime look like? In considering this, a useful point of departure may be the CBMs offered to Russia by the United States in relation to the third site at the Sochi presidential summit in April 2008. As already noted in this chapter, these ideas received a favorable response from Moscow at the time, and while some undoubtedly were tailored to the Ground-Based Interceptors that were central to the third site concept, others likely were of a more general nature. Given that EPAA continues to feature land-based interceptors and radars, it seems reasonable to assume that some of the Sochi proposals would remain applicable. Other measures and approaches may be possible, as well.

Beyond transparency and CBMs lie the question of actual cooperation on missile defense. Moscow has long been wary of accepting Washington's logic that the surest path to reassurance lies in practical cooperation, which would demonstrate in ways that political declarations cannot that EPAA does not pose a threat to Russia. As Moscow sees it, US plans could change quickly and, with no formal or legal constraints in place, potentially to Russia's disadvantage. Still, one cannot rule out the possibility that at some point Moscow may come to view practical cooperation as a potential means to influence aspects of European BMD and even strengthen its own missile defense capabilities. For its part, Washington and its NATO allies would do well to remain open-minded about Russian ideas if and when political relations improve.[38]

Even then there would be practical limits to cooperation. Given both the firm US position against a system jointly developed, owned, and operated and the widely recognized limitations on Russia's ability to contribute to the most significant technologies, the objectives for any collaboration would be to find useful ways to link two separate missile defense systems and to foster habits of cooperation that could create the foundation for more substantive progress in the future. This suggests an initial focus on the sharing and integration of information that can support early warning through implementation of the long-deferred Joint Data Exchange Centers (JDECs) and possibly the creation of jointly staffed data fusion and planning centers. These data fusion and planning centers, proposed by NATO at its 2012 Chicago summit, would allow US, NATO, and Russian personnel to have simultaneous access to missile launch data from sensors in NATO countries and Russia, and provide them an opportunity to work together to explore concepts and plans for missile defense contingencies.[39] Some Russian specialists have suggested a more deliberate operational integration of US and Russian early warning systems to strengthen launch detection capabilities.[40]

A number of American analysts have suggested additional ideas for cooperative work in BMD, including efforts to improve Russia's capability to track the boost and ascent phases of Iranian missiles; joint development of enhanced Russian early warning radars to fill coverage gaps for Russia, the United States, and NATO; revival of the Russian-American Observation Satellites (RAMOS) project on cooperation in infrared sensors for missile warning; and joint development of airborne boost phase interceptors.[41]

Quo Vadis?

Writing in 2011, when many held out hope for some sort of accommodation—and well before the Ukraine crisis—the American scholar Robert Legvold summed up the dilemma facing Moscow: "As for Russia's [other] demands, its leadership will have to decide whether it gains more by being inside a program whose US component it cannot prevent, rather than standing outside and struggling to fulfill its threat to offset a US-NATO system. And perhaps the better way to assure themselves that the EPAA does not pose a threat to their country is by actively working side-by-side with the United States in NATO and building the system rather than insisting on formal legal guarantees in advance."[42]

Russia's push to resolve this issue on its preferred terms by employing a "rhetoric of crisis" did not yield the desired outcome. Still, the US decision to cancel Phase Four of EPAA might have led Moscow to reassess its stated objectives and the public posture it has adopted in its effort to influence the EPAA. But Russia's position did not change, suggesting that Putin may see the missile defense issue as a useful means to sustain Russia's narrative of grievance and siege and something on which he can make a principled stand in dealing with the United States and NATO. Others argue that even after Ukraine, Putin remains essentially a pragmatist and a transactional, results-oriented politician, suggesting that rather than persist in attempting to dictate unrealistic terms, he will, in the end, negotiate the best outcome he can for Russia's interests.

When that point might arrive is unclear. Even assuming restoration of more normal relations at some point, returning to the BMD status quo ante and simply resuming earlier discussions may prove challenging as the security landscape continues to evolve. Seeking to bolster the confidence of at least its easternmost NATO allies as tensions rose with Moscow, Washington temporarily redeployed a BMD-capable destroyer from Spain to the Black Sea in April 2014. And some NATO governments explicitly linked the emerging missile shield to deterring Russia, despite the fact that there is neither intention nor any plan to alter the configuration of the BMD project to make it responsive to a possible Russian threat. Nonetheless, Moscow predictably pointed to these developments as validating its long-standing assertion that NATO's missile defense project is indeed directed at Russia, suggesting that it would continue to resist US and NATO plans. In this way, the Ukraine crisis may have set in motion a dynamic that deepens mistrust over missile defense and complicates any effort to reach a resolution in the future. Compounding this challenge is Russia's violation of the Intermediate-Range Nuclear Forces (INF) Treaty.

Even as some NATO governments have seized on missile defense as a means to bolster reassurance and deterrence vis-à-vis Russia, others have raised the possibility of scaling back the program if a comprehensive final agreement can be reached with Iran to limit its nuclear weapons potential. While the negotiations did not encompass Tehran's ambitious ballistic missile development efforts, some European officials and some outside observers have suggested that a breakthrough on the nuclear issue inevitably would lead to a reassessment of the Iranian threat that has provided the principal justification for NATO's missile defense program. In pushing back against this idea, US officials have emphasized the global nature of the ballistic missile threat. But given pressures on the US defense budget, some analysts argued that there would be sentiment in the US Congress to seize on a positive outcome with Iran as an opportunity to reduce US investment in the NATO program.[43] Moscow should be expected to look for ways to reinforce any tendency in NATO capitals to rethink the scope of the missile defense project.

Both the Ukraine crisis and the prospect of a resolution of the Iranian nuclear problem pointed to the ways in which new developments in the security environment would continue to shape attitudes about missile defense, with uncertain implications for whether and how the extended standoff between NATO and the Russian Federation could be resolved.

Notes

1. For example, see Anthony H. Cordesman and Abraham Wagner, *The Lessons of Modern War, Volume II, The Iran-Iraq War* (Boulder, CO: Westview Press, 1990), 495–506. The majority of missiles were launched by Iraq, which had a larger and indigenous stockpile.

2. Known as Global Protection Against Limited Strikes (GPALS), this program consisted of smaller-scale application of technologies being developed under the Strategic Defense Initiative program and included ground- and space-based interceptors.

3. US Department of Defense, *Conduct of the Persian Gulf War, Final Report to Congress*, April 1992, 169, www.ndu.edu/library/epubs/cpgw.pdf. In February 1991, an Iraqi Scud hit a US military barracks in Bahrain, killing twenty-eight and wounding ninety-nine.

4. Based on the author's personal communications with experts familiar with Russian thinking at the time, aspects of GPALS as originally conceived by the United States likely would have proven problematic from Moscow's vantage, but it was preferable to SDI and may have led to some US funding for Russia's space industry. For the summit statement, see United States Department of State, *Dispatch* 3, no. 25 (June 22, 1992): 29–30, http://dosfan.lib.uic.edu/ERC/briefing/dispatch/1992/html/Dispatchv3no25.html.

5. Nuclear Threat Initiative, "Treaty on the Limitation of Anti-Ballistic Missile Systems (ABM Treaty)," 13, http://ww.nti.org/treaties-and-regimes/treaty-limitation-anti-ballistic-missile-systems-abm-treaty/.

6. Ibid. See pages 3–12 for details on demarcation issues and negotiations.

7. *Report of the Commission to Assess the Ballistic Missile Threat to the United States*, July 15, 1998, www.fas.org/irp/threat/bm-threat.htm. The commission was chaired by former and future secretary of defense Donald Rumsfeld.

8. National Intelligence Council, *Foreign Missile Developments and the Ballistic Missile Threat Through 2015, Unclassified Summary of National Intelligence Estimate*, September 1999, www.fas.org/irp/threat/missile/nie99msl.htm. Often overlooked in this National Intelligence Estimate (NIE) is the following observation: "Non-missile means for delivering WMD do not provide the same prestige, deterrence, and coercive diplomacy as ICBMs; but they are less expensive, more reliable and accurate, more effective for disseminating biological warfare agents, can be used without attribution, and would avoid missile defenses."

9. The GBIs to be deployed in Poland were slower-moving, two-stage variants of those fielded in the United States. The radar to be deployed on Czech territory was the X-band radar, a highly sophisticated sensor.

10. Peter Baker, "Putin Proposes Broader Cooperation on Missile Defense," *Washington Post*, July 3, 2007.

11. See "U.S.-Russia Strategic Framework Agreement," concluded April 6, 2008, and signed May 6, 2008, http://www.cfr.org/proliferation/us-russia-strategic-framework-declaration/p16193. The declaration states, "The Russian side has made clear that it does not agree with the decision to establish sites in Poland and the Czech Republic and reiterated its proposed alternatives. Yet, it appreciates the measures that the U.S. has proposed and declared that if agreed and implemented such measures will be important and useful in assuaging Russian concerns."

12. Robert M. Gates, *Duty: Memoirs of a Secretary of War* (New York: Alfred A. Knopf, 2014), 160–167. See also Wade Boese, "Bush, Putin Leave Arms Dispute Unsettled," *Arms Control Today*, May 2008, http://www.armscontrol.org/act/2008_5/BushPutin.

13. White House, Office of the Press Secretary, "Fact Sheet on U.S. Missile Defense Policy: A 'Phased, Adaptive Approach' for Missile Defense in Europe," September 17, 2009, http://www.whitehouse.gov/the_press_office/FACT-SHEET-US-Missile-Defense-Policy-A-Phased-Adaptive-Approach-for-Missile-Defense-in-Europe/; "Remarks by the President on Strengthening Missile Defense in Europe," September 17, 2009, http://www.whitehouse.gov/the_press_office/Remarks-by-the-President-on-Strengthening-Missile-Defense-in-Europe/. Former US secretary of defense Robert Gates also emphasizes the political opposition in Poland and the Czech Republic to the Third Site plan, as well other difficulties in negotiating terms with Warsaw and Prague, as reinforcing the move toward EPAA. See Gates, *Duty*, 162, 167, 398–404.

14. White House, Office of the Press Secretary, "Fact Sheet on U.S. Missile Defense Policy," and US Department of Defense, Ballistic Missile Defense Review, February 2010, 24, http://www.defense.gov/bmdr/.

15. See US Department of Defense, "DoD News Briefing on Missile Defense from the Pentagon," March 15, 2013. The US decision restructured the SM-3 Block 2B program and shifted its resources to fund expansion and improvement of the GBI system. This decision reflects the confluence of two developments: technical challenges in developing the SM-3 Block 2B and heightened concern about North Korea's ability to field a long-range missile based on recent tests.

16. Alexei Arbatov, Vladimir Dvorkin, Alexander Pikaev, and Sergey Oznobischev, "Strategic Stability after the Cold War," Institute of World Economy and International Relations, Russia Academy of Sciences (IMEMO RAN), 2010, 27–28.

17. David Deudney and G. John Ikenberry, "The Unravelling of the Cold War Settlement," *Survival* 51, no. 6 (December 2009–January 2010): 41.

18. Ibid., 54.

19. Matthew Rojansky, "Russia and Strategic Stability," in *Strategic Stability: Contending Interpretations*, ed. Elbridge A. Colby and Michael S. Gerson (Carlisle, PA: US Army War College Press, 2013), 297.

20. From Putin's remarks to the 2007 Munich Security Conference, cited in Stephen J. Blank, *Perspectives on Russian Foreign Policy* (Carlisle, PA: US Army War College Strategic Studies Institute, 2012), 129. Putin used similar language in 2009: "The problem is that our American partners are developing missile defenses, and we are not. . . . There could be the danger that having created an umbrella against offensive strike systems, our partners may come to feel completely safe. After the balance is broken, they will do whatever they want and grow more aggressive." See "Putin Says Russia Will Build Weapons to Offset Planned US Missile Defences," *The Guardian*, December 29, 2009, http://guardian.co.uk/world/2009/dec/29/nuclear-weapons-russia. See also "America Suffers from 'Illusion of Invulnerability'—Putin," http://rt.com/politics/putin-us-meeting-media-reset-695.

21. Robert Bridge, "It's Either Common Missile Defense or New Arms Race—Medvedev," www.rt.com/politics/Medvedev-missile-defense-race/. The vocabulary of crisis and transformation appears repeatedly in publications by the most prominent

Russian strategists. As examples, see Arbatov et al., "Strategic Stability," 29–32; Vladimir Dvorkin, "Strategic and Offensive and Defensive Arms," in *Nuclear Reset: Arms Reduction and Nonproliferation*, ed. Alexei Arbatov and Vladimir Dvorkin (Moscow: Carnegie Endowment for International Peace, 2012), 198–203; Arbatov et al., "Strategic Stability," 18–25; and Nuclear Threat Initiative, "Treaty on the Limitation." Additionally, the author has encountered these formulations in Track 1.5 meetings with Russian officials and strategists and in informal "non-papers" associated with these dialogues.

22. See "Russia May Have Conventional Hypersonic Weapons in as Few as Five Years," *Global Security Newswire*, July 1, 2013, http://www.nti.org/gsn/article/russia-eyes-conventional-hypersonic-weapons-few-five-years/.

23. Army General N. E. Markov, First Deputy Minister of Defense of the Russian Federation, "Views of the Ministry of Defense of the Russian Federation on Missile Defense Issues," 2012, http://mil.ru/files/morf/Eng_Views-Of-The-Ministry-Of-Defense-Of-The-Russian-Federation-On-Missile-Defense-Issues.ppt.

24. These Russian proposals have been rejected, including implicitly in the Lisbon Summit Declaration. This statement reaffirms NATO's interest in practical cooperation but rejects Russian proposals to establish a single, jointly operated system or adopt a sector approach, and makes clear NATO's position that BMD cooperation with Russia should emphasize two separate systems linked in appropriate ways. Paragraph 38 states: "We will continue to explore opportunities for missile defence cooperation with Russia in a spirit of reciprocity, maximum transparency and mutual confidence. We reaffirm the Alliance's readiness to invite Russia to explore jointly the potential for linking current and planned missile defence systems at an appropriate time in mutually beneficial ways. NATO missile defence efforts and the United States European Phased Adaptive Approach provide enhanced capabilities to do this."

25. Speaking in January 2012, Russian deputy prime minister Dmitry Rogozin said, "There are no guarantees that after the first, second, and third phases are completed, there will be no fourth, fifth, and sixth. . . . Do you really think they will really halt all their technologies after 2020? That's nonsense! They will go ahead with developing and boosting technical parameters of their interceptor missiles and performance capabilities of their warning systems." See "NATO, U.S. Possess 1,000 Anti-ICBM Interceptors, Russian Official Claims," *Global Security Newswire*, January 20, 2012, http://www.nti.rsvp1.com/gsn/article/russia-claims-nato-us-possess-1000-interceptors-can-counter-icbms/. Concerns are also expressed about potential US development of directed-energy and space-based ballistic missile defense capabilities to supplement land-based interceptors.

26. Speaking to a Russian newspaper, Deputy Foreign Minister Sergei Ryabkov said of the US decision, "That is not a concession to Russia, nor do we regard it as such. All aspects of strategic uncertainty related to the creation of a US and NATO missile defense system remain. Therefore, our objections also remain." See Fred Weir, "US Drops Europe Missile Defense Plan—But Moscow Is Unimpressed," *The Christian Science Monitor*, March 18, 2013, http://www.csmonitor.com/World/Europe/2013/0318/US-drops-Europe-missile-defense-plan-but-Moscow-is-unimpressed.

27. Speaking in May 2012, Deputy Defense Minister Anatoly Antonov stated: "When the Americans begin constructing the third stage of their missile defense plans in Europe and the effectiveness of our strategic nuclear forces is jeopardized, serious issues will arise regarding Russia's appropriate reaction. . . . Such a scenario is likely and we are preparing for it." See "Russia Warns 'Point of No Return' Imminent in US Missile Defense Talks," http://rt.com/politics/russia-us-missile-defense-arms-race-iran-406. Speaking in October 2012, Russian deputy foreign minister Sergei Ryabkov said, "When the implementation of the third and then fourth and subsequent stages of the phased adaptive approach of the [US] global defense system begins, the situation could alter for us." See "Russia Warns U.S. Against Deploying Final Phases of Missile Shield," *Global Security Newswire*, October 1, 2012, http://www.nti.rsvp1.com/gsn/article/russia-warns-us-against-implementing-last-phases-missile-shield/.

28. "10 Years Without The ABM Treaty: The Issue of Missile Defense in Russia-US Relations," Russian International Affairs Council, Institute for US and Canada Studies of the Russian Academy of Sciences, 2012, 25.

29. Henry A. Kissinger, "Don't Rule out Putin's Initiative," *New York Times*, August 9, 2007.

30. See Dean A. Wilkening, "Does Missile Defence in Europe Threaten Russia?," *Survival* 54, no.1 (February–March 2012): 31–53; Stephen J. Cimbala, "Russia and European Missile Defenses: Reflexive Reset?," *Joint Forces Quarterly* 68, First Quarter (January 2013): 10–17; Jaganath Sankaran, "Missile Defense against Iran without Threatening Russia," *Arms Control Today*, (November 2013). Wilkening concludes, "BMD interceptors with speeds below approximately 5.0 km/sec launched from sites in and around Europe cannot intercept Russian ICBMs or SLBMs without violating the laws of physics. In those cases where some missile trajectories might be intercepted, cross-targeting of ICBMs or lofting ICBMs or SLBMs readily negates this capability. Moscow's concern with Phases III and IV of the European Phased Adaptive Approach BMD architecture, therefore, lack technical merit, unless the SM-3 Block IIB interceptor has a maximum speed greater than 5.0 km/sec." US officials publicly maintain that the interceptor, as planned, would have achieved velocity capable of countering only first-generation ICBMs.

31. See "Russia Renews Threat of Military Measures if Antimissile Deal Not Reached," *Global Security Newswire*, March 15, 2012, http://www.nti.rsvp1.com/gsn/article/russia-renews-threat-pursue-security-mesures-if-antimissile-deal-not-reached.

32. Markov, "Views of the Ministry of Defense."

33. In the words of one US official: "Russia has raised the issue of a legal guarantee with a set of 'military-technical criteria' that could, in effect, create limitations on our ability to develop and deploy future missile defense systems. We certainly cannot accept limitations on our ability to defend ourselves, our allies, and our partners, including where we deploy our Aegis ships. These are multi-mission ships that are used for a variety of purposes around the world, not just for missile defense. We also will NOT accept limitations on the capabilities and numbers of our missile defense systems." See US Department of State, "A U.S. State Department Perspective on the Phased Adaptive Approach to Missile Defense," Remarks of Frank A. Rose,

Deputy Assistant Secretary of State, April 12, 2012. On the G8 episode, see Bill Gertz, "Inside the Ring: Obama Rejects Missile Deal," *Washington Times*, June 15, 2001, http://www.washingtontimes.com/news/2011/jun/15/inside-the-ring-380739054.

34. Paragraph 62 of the NATO Chicago Summit Declaration of May 20, 2012 states: "[W]e today reaffirm that the NATO missile defence in Europe will not undermine strategic stability. NATO missile defence is not directed against Russia and will not undermine Russia's strategic deterrence capabilities. . . . While regretting recurrent Russian statements on possible measures directed against NATO's missile defence systems, we welcome Russia's willingness to continue dialogue with the purpose of finding an agreement on the future framework for missile defense," http://www.nato.int/cps/en/natolive/official_texts_87593.htm. See also paragraph 61 of NATO's Wales Summit Declaration, September 5, 2014, http://www.nato.int/cps/en/natohq/official_texts_112964.htm.

35. See Global Security Newswire, "Obama Reportedly Offers Putin Deal on Sharing of Antimissile Data," May 16, 2013; Tom Z. Collina, "Russia, U.S. Trade Missile Defense Offers," *Arms Control Today*, June 2013. The Obama letter has not been publicly released and at the time was handled in a very low key fashion, reflecting low White House expectations that it would help to resolve the US-Russian deadlock.

36. See Bill Gertz, "U.S. Rejects Latest Russian Proposal to Restrict U.S. Missile Defenses," *Washington Free Beacon*, May 1, 2014.

37. See Roberto Zadra, "NATO, Russia, and Missile Defence," *Survival* 56, no. 4 (August–September 2014): 51–52.

38. Steven Pifer, "The Missing Missile Defense Piece at the NATO Summit of Chicago," Brookings Institution, May 15, 2012, http://www.brookings.edu/blogs/up-front/posts/2012/05/15-nato-summit-pifer.

39. Ibid. See also Gates, *Duty*, 531; Zadra, "NATO, Russia, and Missile Defence," 58; Euro-Atlantic Security Initiative, "Missile Defense: Toward a New Paradigm," Carnegie Endowment for International Peace, February 2012, http://carnegieendowment.org/2012/02/03/missile-defense-toward-new-paradigm; US Department of State, "Missile Defense: Road to Cooperation," Remarks of Ellen Tauscher, Special Envoy for Strategic Stability and Missile Defense, May 3, 2012, http://www.state.gov/t/avc/rls/189281.htm. For a Russian perspective on JDEC, see Arbatov et al., "Strategic Stability," 21–24.

40. Dvorkin, "Strategic and Offensive and Defensive Arms," 201. Dvorkin asserts, "Independent U.S. experts estimate that integration of the U.S. and Russian ballistic missile early warning systems would improve missile and booster launch detection effectiveness by between 30 and 70 percent." Based on review of other sources, Dvorkin is referring here principally to the American expert Bruce Blair. See Alexei Arbatov and Vladimir Dvorkin, *Beyond Nuclear Deterrence: Transforming the U.S.-Russian Equation* (Washington, DC: Carnegie Endowment for International Peace, 2006), 153.

41. Author's discussions with US specialists.

42. Robert H. Legvold, "Reconciling Limitations on Non-Strategic Nuclear Weapons, Conventional Arms Control, and Missile Defense Cooperation," in *Reducing Nuclear Risks in Europe: A Framework for Action*, ed. Steve Andreasen and Isabelle Williams (Washington, DC: Nuclear Threat Initiative, 2011), 150–51.

43. See Rachel Oswald, "U.S. Official: 'Not Making Much Progress' with Russia on Missiles, Arms," *Defense One*, November 13, 2013; "Iran Nuclear Deal May Affect Missile Shield: German Envoy," Global Security Newswire, December 4, 2013. On the question of US spending on NATO missile defense, see Rachel Oswald, "U.S. Official Defends Spending on NATO Missile Shield, Under GOP Attack," Global Security Newswire, June 25, 2013.

CONCLUSION

Reconciling Alliance Cohesion with Policy Coherence

Andreas Wenger

Between 2009 and 2012, NATO witnessed its most comprehensive debate about nuclear policy and extended deterrence since the end of the Cold War. The debate involved both extensive consultations behind closed doors and a broader public debate beyond NATO, albeit with varying intensity, at the national level of Alliance member states. Yet while Brussels was focusing on the highly complex political and military role of NATO's nonstrategic nuclear weapons (NSNW) and the related issue of continued allied participation in the Alliance's nuclear-sharing arrangements, the public debate was being driven by the diminishing domestic political appeal of nuclear weapons in many European countries and a simultaneous global vision of a world free of nuclear weapons. The resulting policy debate among allies was marked by strong disagreement about the role of nuclear weapons and a series of notable policy shifts, ultimately forcing NATO's nuclear deterrence policies into the ambiguous and fragile compromise of the Deterrence and Defense Posture Review (DDPR).

In Europe, but also in Asia and elsewhere, the renewed interest in nuclear and deterrence issues had emerged over time as a result of broader changes in the international system. The way various parties felt about the role of nuclear weapons had been shaped by at least three trends, each affecting the allies to varying degrees. First, incentives to develop nuclear weapons had multiplied in the preceding decade, in particular in Asia and the Middle East. The proliferation of nuclear weapons was putting pressure on certain regions, and there was a very real fear that the number of nuclear-armed states was about to increase and that, at some point in the future, nuclear weapons might even fall into the hands of nonstate actors. The United States was particularly concerned because this trend directly affected its deterrence regime vis-à-vis these regions. Second, the normative environment in Western societies' attitudes toward nuclear weapons had changed: The belief that nuclear weapons were militarily useless had strengthened the societal and political base of the nuclear abolishment movement, in particular in key European states such as Germany. Third, whether one looks at bilateral alliances or NATO, or at Alliance members' views on and interests in extended nuclear deterrence, the subject had become more heterogeneous. The enlargement process had added a new set of member states to the Alliance, and their extended deterrence assurances were limited from the outset as a result of negotiations between NATO and Russia.

This book gathers a collection of contributions from academics, policymakers, and think tank researchers to assess how changes in threats, technology, and regional configurations affect extended deterrence arrangements between allies. Each chapter shows how changes at the domestic or international level provoke shifts in how commitments are affirmed by allies and perceived by adversaries. The individual and collective contributions of this book are highlighted in the following sections, with additional points of discussion on the consequences of the ongoing Ukraine crisis for NATO's extended deterrence arrangements.

The Trigger: NATO's Role in Arms Control, Disarmament, and Nonproliferation

In his 2009 Prague Speech, President Obama reintroduced disarmament into international politics. Outlining a long-term vision of a world without nuclear weapons, he reframed the debate about nuclear weapons and initiated a review of the US nuclear posture.[1] This notable policy shift evolved in the context of two factors: the upcoming 2010 review conference on the nuclear Non-Proliferation Treaty (NPT) and growing pressure for nuclear disarmament, on the one hand, and a desire to reset relations with Moscow and engage in bilateral negotiations for a New Strategic Arms Reduction Treaty (START), on the other. Obama's Global Zero agenda resonated throughout the world, and it reshaped NATO's ongoing debate about the future of NSNW in Europe.

In 2009, the newly elected German government decided to seize the opportunity offered by the US policy shift: It began to push publicly for the withdrawal of NSNW from Europe. This commitment to the withdrawal of

US nuclear weapons deployed in Europe reflected growing domestic political pressure for abolition. The German government argued that a gradual change in NATO's nuclear posture would allow the Alliance to play a greater role in supporting global disarmament and nonproliferation efforts. The aim of denuclearizing the Luftwaffe found widespread domestic support, although the German government signaled that it would not act unilaterally but would coordinate policy with its NATO allies. Germany's suggestion of an open-ended debate about NATO's nuclear posture found support in Belgium, Luxembourg, the Netherlands, and Norway. However, it later became obvious that by linking arms control to a reduction of NSNW in Europe, the Alliance had opened up a can of worms with regard to the future role of NATO's extended nuclear deterrence posture. When the allies started to work on a new Strategic Concept (SC) at the NATO summit in Strasbourg/Kehl in 2009, Germany was convinced that there was a real chance that NATO could lead the global arms control, disarmament, and non-proliferation (ADN) process by example. Over time, however, this position was weakened. The idea that the Alliance should move independently on nuclear reductions was fiercely contested. As a consequence, the allies began to shift toward a position in which the withdrawal of NATO's NSNW was linked to reciprocal steps by Russia. Yet as this reciprocity requirement gained currency, further development of NATO's nuclear disarmament policy became blocked.

An Ambiguous Compromise: Alliance Cohesion versus Policy Coherence

The basic tenets of NATO's nuclear policy remained unchanged after the Strategic Concept was approved at the Lisbon summit in 2010 and the Deterrence and Defense Posture Review concluded at the Chicago summit in 2012. The documents, and the process leading up to the public presentation of the policy communiqués, made clear that the allies had settled on an ambiguous compromise that allowed them to uphold Alliance cohesion. However, the price of prioritizing Alliance solidarity and unity was an incoherent policy and a missed opportunity for creating a new and sustainable vision for NATO's nuclear and extended deterrence policies.

The agreement to continue the present arrangements was no small achievement and has to be seen in the context of the Alliance's search for a broader strategic vision, beyond the complexities of extended nuclear deterrence. The SC 2010 provided the transatlantic partners with a chance to overcome the deep disagreements that had troubled NATO since the US-led invasion of Iraq in 2003. Moving toward the SC 2010, the allies successfully rebalanced the functional and geographical scope of NATO's strategic priorities. This is reflected in the three key decisions passed in Lisbon: agreement on a plan for a withdrawal from Afghanistan, agreement on the implementation of a missile defense capability for the entire Alliance, and a complementary agreement on a strategic partnership with Russia.

A closer look at the SC 2010 reveals that the document created an opening for a more thorough discussion of the role of nuclear weapons in NATO's deterrence and defense posture, a task that was subsequently delegated to the DDPR process. The SC 2010 is the first strategic guideline that commits NATO "to the goal of creating the conditions for a world without nuclear weapons" and that acknowledges that the "circumstances in which any use of nuclear weapons might have to be contemplated are extremely remote."[2] Conversely, the document confirms that, "as long as nuclear weapons exist, NATO will remain a nuclear alliance." Thus, deterrence remains a core element of NATO strategy, based on "an appropriate mix of nuclear and conventional capabilities" and supported by missile defense as "a core element of our collective defense."[3] On the more specific issue of the future role of NSNW, the SC 2010 commits the Alliance "to [creating] the conditions for further reductions in the future," but at the same time, it links changes to NATO's nuclear posture in Europe to "Russian agreement to increase transparency on its nuclear weapons in Europe and relocate these weapons away from the territory of NATO members," taking into account the "disparity with the greater Russian stockpiles of short-range nuclear weapons."[4]

The DDPR, by and large, confirmed the compromise formula of the strategic concept. As noted in many chapters in this book, the DDPR was achieved through extensive consultations and despite notable disagreement.[5] It comes as no surprise, therefore, that the final document papered over some major differences of opinion regarding nuclear and deterrence policy. While the document confirms a series of policy shifts already noticeable in the SC 2010, some of its language is contradictory. Although in the DDPR the allies consider the current nuclear force posture to be effective, they also commit the Alliance to creating the conditions "for further reductions of non-strategic nuclear weapons" in Europe.[6] Of particular note is the fact that the document does not contain the earlier standard language about NATO's NSNW, which declared these an essential political and military link between Europe and North America. In the same vein, what NATO means by *disparity* and *reciprocity* remains underspecified. The allies emphasize that NATO "does not consider any country to be its adversary."[7] However, by making further reductions of NSNW in Europe conditional on Russian reciprocity, the Alliance "in effect reinstates Russia as the declared nuclear counterpart for the US nonstrategic arsenal in Europe."[8]

Taking Stock of NATO's Nuclear Policy: Status Quo or Change?

Internal disagreement about nuclear issues will most likely continue to bedevil the Alliance in the future. The authors in this book concur that both the opponents and the proponents of NSNW in Europe will understand the ambiguous language of the two policy documents in favor of their own views. While some observers will interpret the documents as a signal that the status quo can be extended indefinitely, others will read them as an opening for a change to outdated nuclear policies.[9]

At the most fundamental level, the internal disagreements about nuclear deterrence issues reflect differences in the allies' threat perceptions and in the strategies they think are best suited to dealing with these threats. While it was never easy for NATO allies to agree on the intensity of the various threats to the Alliance, the fact that the current threat spectrum is diffuse, complex, and highly dynamic has exacerbated the political problems that inhibit agreement on the likely strategic challenges. Such uncertainty about future threats translates into different threat perceptions among increasingly heterogeneous allies, as highlighted in the Introduction to this book. For example, opponents of NATO's NSNW in Europe are generally more optimistic than those who see them as necessary when judging the situation regarding, for example, Russia and Iran.[10] In other words, varying national geopolitical positions and strategic cultures can lead to very diverse strategic priorities, and these in turn can result in nuclear policy priorities that are difficult to reconcile.

Why Was It So Difficult to Reach a Compromise?

NATO has always struggled to reach agreement on nuclear and extended deterrence issues. It was particularly difficult, for a number of reasons, to reach a compromise in the 2009 to 2012 period, when NATO reprioritized nuclear issues after a period of conspicuous silence in the early post–Cold War years. While new-state and nonstate threats linked to nuclear weapons proliferation had emerged from outside NATO, the normative context inside the Alliance began to shift in favor of nuclear abolition. Although strategic cultures change only slowly, the societal and political context surrounding nuclear weapons is undergoing change at variable speeds and intensities in different member states and societies. Thus, differing views on the political salience of nuclear issues across elites and societies have impeded a quick agreement on a new direction for nuclear policy.

A compromise on nuclear issues has become, over time, more difficult to achieve for several, more specific reasons. Today, more players are shaping NATO's strategic debate, and these have more disparate views on nuclear issues than ever before. First, France has been reintegrated into the Alliance's military structure (excluding the Nuclear Planning Group). While this has increased the role of Paris in NATO's strategic debate, it remains to be seen what effect—inclusive or exclusive—the new bilateral defense cooperation (including nuclear matters) between France and Great Britain will have on defense cooperation in Europe and across the Atlantic. Second, given their historical and geopolitical concerns, the new Central European states (CES) now have a specific interest in the collective defense mission of the Alliance and in a continuing role of the United States in European security. Third, Washington's views on nuclear and extended deterrence issues are being influenced increasingly by developments in the Asia-Pacific region and the Middle East rather than by NATO-internal considerations.

Between 2009 and 2012, Franco-German differences over the role of nuclear weapons in Alliance strategy had been a significant roadblock to a fresh consensus on nuclear issues. During that period, distinct strategic cultures were translated into radically different views on the future of NATO's deterrence posture. Germany pushed for a growing role for NATO in nuclear disarmament and envisioned Alliance-wide missile defense systems to replace US substrategic nuclear forces in Europe in the long term. Conversely, France vehemently opposed changes to NATO's nuclear posture; it believed that nuclear deterrence remained relevant and saw only a very limited role for NATO in arms control. In addition, Paris and Berlin often found themselves at opposite ends of the spectrum in debates about the right mix of military and diplomatic tools in crisis management operations. While Germany emphasized a rule-based approach, in which military operations must be sanctioned by the UN Security Council, France wanted to threaten and/or use force early and, if necessary, without UN authorization in order to uphold regional stability. The two countries' opposite positions in the West's debates about military interventions in Libya, Mali, and Syria left each side frustrated with the other's approach to crisis management.

The opposition of the CES to a change in the Alliance's extended nuclear deterrence posture was a second obstacle to a more fundamental change in NATO's nuclear policies. For some observers, this came as something of a surprise because nuclear weapons had played only a minor role in the public discourse of these countries. However, the debate about the future of NSNW in Europe gave the CES a convenient opportunity to influence NATO's strategic debate and to anchor the United States in regional defense issues.[11] Considering their historical fear of abandonment and their geostrategic position between Russia and Germany, the CES were very keen to keep the United States involved in European security affairs. They understandably displayed a need for reassurance, and there are at least four reasons why this need has grown considerably over the past few years. First, the NATO-Russia founding act ruled out the deployment of nuclear weapons and the permanent stationing of substantial combat forces on CES territories. Second, the more assertive Russian policies for countering Western influence in the post-Soviet space—highlighted by the war in Georgia—confirmed CES suspicions that Russia's foreign policy was primarily revisionist. Third, NATO's focus on out-of-area crisis management missions was seen as weakening its collective defense tasks. Finally, President Obama's rejection of former president Bush's bilateral missile defense deals with Poland and the Czech Republic seemed to signal a reduced role of these states in NATO's strategic deliberations.[12]

In his Prague Speech in 2009, President Obama emphasized that the United States would seriously consider reducing the role of nuclear weapons and the reliance on nuclear deterrence in its security strategy. In line with this statement, Washington publicly signaled that it would support the withdrawal of its NSNW in Europe if the allies so wished and if a withdrawal was possible without damaging the Alliance's cohesion.[13] However, surrounded by growing disagreement among allies regarding nuclear policy, the United States was not willing to push proactively for a policy change. Instead, it decided to keep its options open. Although the United States no longer saw its NSNW in Europe as an essential political and military link between Europe and North America, the Nuclear Posture Review (NPR) 2010 made clear that Washington would retain the capability to deploy nuclear weapons on bombers in forward positions.[14] The decision for a full life-extension program for the B61 bombs signaled that Washington feared that disagreement over nuclear policy could spill over into a disagreement on missile defense.

Once it had become clear that NATO was not prepared to move unilaterally on further NSNW reductions, the only way forward was the prospect that NSNW would be included in the next round of bilateral talks between Moscow and Washington. However, Russia signaled that it was not interested in negotiating on NSNW, pronouncing them as a tool to balance NATO in its new military doctrine. As noted in this book, Moscow preferred to keep stability and deterrence firmly anchored in the nuclear realm, and it feared that the United States was moving toward a form of "high precision deterrence" based on advanced conventional, space, and cyber capabilities.[15] In addition, Russian policymakers perceived US and NATO efforts in missile defense as a catalyst for fixed NATO infrastructures and deployments in Poland, Romania, and the Baltic States. Moscow was worried about the potentially open-ended architecture of NATO's missile defense system, a fear that was feeding into a wider disillusionment with NATO enlargement and the post–Cold War settlement in Central Europe. All this explains why, already some time before the Ukraine crisis in 2014, it seemed unlikely that Moscow and Washington would be able to agree on the next steps toward bilateral reductions. By the end of 2012, it had become clear that NATO would find it difficult to move beyond the ambiguous compromise of the DDPR.

The Stickiness of NSNW in NATO's Deterrence Posture

The quarrel about the 150 to 200 B61 bombs at six airbases in Europe must surprise the casual observer because these weapons represent only a tiny fraction of NATO's total nuclear force.[16] This underlines that NATO's NSNW represent neither the only nor the most important means of extending nuclear deterrence over Alliance members. The future of NATO's NSNW will not define the future of the Alliance. What, then, explains the stickiness of NSNW in NATO's deterrence posture? The evidence in this book points to the political and psychological value of the current nuclear-sharing arrangement as a key factor in shaping the 2009–12 debate about nuclear policy.

The Political and Psychological Value of the Current Nuclear-Sharing Arrangement

The debate about NSNW in Europe is politically sensitive because these weapons have become, over time, the physical and visible symbol of NATO's nuclear-sharing model, a point that is recognized by all authors in this book.[17] While there is widespread agreement that these weapons have no specific military role that other weapons could not take over, many fear that withdrawing NSNW could lead to the withering away of the Nuclear Planning Group (NPG). The decisive point, from a political perspective, is that there would be much less to consult about—a situation that would over time erode the established structures and processes of nuclear consultation and decision making. The NPG has provided the Alliance with a mechanism for collective nuclear learning and has thus been instrumental in establishing a common deterrence culture.[18] On the one hand, it has leveled out the nuclear playing field because even non-nuclear allies have been able to participate in NATO's nuclear planning. On the other hand, it has established a nuclear hierarchy because nuclear sharing has always prioritized a select group of member states: those hosting NSNW on their territory. The NPG has established NATO as a nuclear security community and has signaled the indivisibility of the nuclear and conventional defense of the Alliance. NSNW, as symbols of risk and responsibility sharing in the nuclear field, have been decisive both in reassuring allies and strengthening the Alliance's internal cohesion, and in upholding the credibility of NATO's nuclear deterrence posture in the eyes of its potential adversaries.

NATO's nuclear-sharing arrangements are historically unique, and it is no small irony that Germany—the very country for which the integrative mechanism was initially constructed in the 1960s—has been pushing for a change in nuclear policy.[19] It took the Alliance almost a decade to fine-tune the link between nuclear sharing and nuclear nonproliferation. The key lesson learned was that the shift from a hardware solution to a software solution—from the Multilateral Force (MLF) to the NPG—was essential in order to build the political support for nuclear sharing and for nuclear nonproliferation. The NPG was politically more acceptable to domestic politics in key countries such as Germany. At the same time, the group eased the challenges of Alliance politics, providing NATO with a flexible and adaptable mechanism for striking a balance between political equality and a nuclear hierarchy that was acceptable to all parties. In addition, the shift away from the MLF (i.e., away from an immediate decision to build a new multinational weapons system) was a precondition for Russia's acceptance of an NPT formula that did not rule out a multilateral sharing scheme as long as the allies did not obtain ownership of the warheads.[20]

The final deal on nuclear sharing in the 1960s was hammered out in trilateral talks among the United States, Great Britain, and Germany. It was subsequently introduced into NATO's military structures, a process that was simplified by France's previous withdrawal from those structures. It is noteworthy that Great Britain's and France's nuclear policies were driven by a broad range of political and economic aims, going beyond the strategic logic of extended deterrence.[21] Once the NPG was in place, its primary function was to answer questions about the military role of the thousands of tactical nuclear warheads in Europe and to define a compromise for their employment that would ensure their political function as agents of deterrence and reassurance. Consequently, a look back at the origins of NATO's current nuclear-sharing arrangements shows how it has become more difficult to reach a compromise among more heterogeneous allies, and it illustrates how the complexities of the current mechanisms, and the beliefs about the political functions of the arrangements, are strongly path dependent.

The deconstruction of the nuclear-sharing infrastructure that has survived the end of the Cold War remains politically challenging. For NATO to apply an Asian offshore model, often suggested as a workable alternative, would be a huge challenge because it would require the disbanding of "many Cold War organizational and operational arrangements."[22] The difficulty of moving from an on-the-ground to an offshore extended deterrence posture is highlighted by the political impact that the US withdrawal of tactical nuclear weapons from South Korea has had on Washington's deterrence posture in the Asia-Pacific region. Efforts to compensate for the loss of physical links—as the primary manifestation of US security commitments—in other cases might lead to political disappointment beyond the nation directly affected, a consequence evident in the security relationship between Japan and the United States.[23]

Nuclear Sharing as an Elite Project versus Nuclear Abolishment as a Public Issue

NATO is essentially political: It is based on common norms and values, and its flexible institutions provide transatlantic elites with a forum for shaping transnational and transgovernmental coalitions.[24] This conceptualization of NATO—as a forum for transnational elites to discuss and reflect on the impact of broader social and domestic political trends on the joint provision of security—adds another critical element to our understanding of the highly complex and sometimes obscure debate about the future of NSNW in Europe. While the debate about the appropriateness of the current nuclear-sharing agreement remains essentially an elite project, broader social and domestic political forces are driving the growing call for nuclear abolition. The new direction in the Alliance's nuclear policy has to take these two settings into account.

The NPG is the ultimate tool for negotiation and bargaining at the elite level. Once again, the shift from the MLF to the NPG provides us with the key lesson: The MLF would "draw domestic attention to the unsolvable issues of nuclear crisis decision making," and it would become "the rallying symbol for anti-nuclear protesters and nationalist forces." The NPG, however, was able to "deliver what a hardware solution could not—a clear right to be consulted . . . while at the same time deflecting domestic criticism . . . about the visible symbols of nuclear dependence from the United States."[25] Although the driving forces for NSNW withdrawal have changed fundamentally since the end of the Cold War, the DDPR discussions exhibited the same characteristics as the 1960s discussion. Indeed, the consultations were highly classified and not accessible to the broader public, and when information spilled over into the public realm, all involved prioritized Alliance cohesion over policy coherence.[26] The fact that CES elites have recently leveraged these consultations for their broader national interests shows that they have been successfully socialized into the political procedures of the Alliance.

Already in the 1960s—very much as in the past four years—the elite bargain on nuclear policies was undermined by a growing antinuclear protest movement and serious financial pressure to reduce defense budgets.[27] In the deliberations and consultations leading to the publication of the Harmel Report in 1967, the allies discovered that NATO provided them with a forum for balancing military security against economic prosperity and that the Alliance could be used to manage the disarmament process jointly (as opposed to unilateral troop cuts). Although today's ADN challenges and defense economics are significantly different from those of the 1960s, the mechanisms at work remain the same. The allies know that the changing domestic and social context demands a change in NATO's form and function. Yet strategic considerations need to be balanced with broader political concerns, with regard to both internal NATO cohesion and solidarity, and external deterrence considerations and issues of global and regional order.

The Broader Context of NATO's Nuclear Deterrence Debate

The deep-seated disagreements about the role of nuclear weapons in the Alliance's deterrence and defense posture between 2009 and 2012 highlighted the broader debate about NATO's future in a globalized security environment. The environment surrounding NATO's nuclear deterrence debate had changed fundamentally since the end of the Cold War. During the 1990s, the allies focused on the security challenges of the disbanding of the Warsaw Pact and the Soviet Union, and the disintegration of the former Yugoslavia. After the 9/11 terrorist attacks, the Euro-Atlantic security debate began to shift from the European periphery to the Middle East and East Asia, and to the domain where regional crisis, nuclear proliferation, and the rise of global terrorism intersect. As a consequence, different visions for the Alliance's future emerged among the allies, propelling NATO into a state of strategic drift.

Parallel to the changing focus of the Western security debate, Alliance members began to reconsider the role of extended deterrence in international security affairs. The tenets of deterrence were rethought and adapted to twenty-first-century security challenges. However, this was primarily a debate among North American academics and policymakers.[28] Washington invested a lot of energy into reorganizing the US extended deterrence posture into a global conflict management tool. This broader discussion about the future of deterrence spilled over into the NATO debate on nuclear policy. As a consequence, traditional deterrence concepts and the physical remnants of the Cold War extended deterrence infrastructure in Europe increasingly overlapped with the concepts and policies of post–Cold War deterrence thinking.

What Is NATO's Role in the Twenty-First Century?

NATO is no longer the Cold War defense alliance whose aim is to uphold the territorial and nuclear status quo across the Iron Curtain. Already during the 1990s, the Alliance transformed itself into a more proactive security management institution, strengthened its political role, and radically changed its military structure. In so doing, it had to contend with two fundamental strategic challenges. First, concerned that the power vacuum in Central Europe would reactivate the geopolitical competition between Germany and Russia, the allies decided on an eastern enlargement of NATO.[29] Second, the outbreak of armed conflicts in the Balkans resulted in the decision to employ military force outside Alliance territory for the first time in NATO history. The new role of crisis management and peacemaking rapidly became the Alliance's key military task, and this drove the military transformation process forward.[30]

By the time the allies convened to celebrate NATO's fiftieth anniversary in Washington, the Alliance had reestablished itself as the preeminent security institution in Europe. In the first decade of the twenty-first century, however, deep cracks opened up in NATO's foundation. The terrorist attacks on New York and Washington, and the ensuing reorientation of US foreign policy under former president George W. Bush, triggered a fundamental disagreement about the geographic reach and the functional scope of the Alliance.[31] As a result of the allies' different strategic cultures, threat perceptions, and strategic outlooks, a series of incompatible visions for NATO's future emerged. The United States, with some support from Great Britain, argued for a global NATO open to democracies around the world. The CES remained focused on the evolution of Russian policy and, as a consequence, they favored collective defense. Taking a middle position, countries such as

Germany and France prioritized regional security and crisis management along the European periphery.[32]

The process leading up to the 2010 SC provided the allies with an opportunity for introspection and consolidation. The resulting policy compromise conceptualized NATO as a globally less ambitious and politically more regional alliance. The mission in Afghanistan exposed the Alliance to tensions over strategy, burden sharing, and command and control. The decision to withdraw from this region indicated that NATO would rein in its ambitions in crisis management. The interventions in Libya and Mali seemed to confirm that the Alliance's future focus would be on regional crisis and asymmetric threats emanating from the European periphery. This new orientation, together with the renewed US focus on the Asia-Pacific region, would increase the pressure on European allies to expand their contributions to include crisis management and global stability where such action enhances the security of the Alliance.

NATO's new strategic concept has also redrawn the balance between its own enlargement and its policies on Russia. At the Bucharest summit in 2009, the Bush administration, with the support of the CES, pushed for the extension of the Membership Action Plan to Georgia and Ukraine. Fearing a backlash from Russia, however, Germany and France successfully resisted this proposal. Until the change in US missile defense policy under Obama in 2009, the debate within NATO about US plans to install national missile defense infrastructure in Poland and the Czech Republic had run along the same fault lines. The Obama administration's reconfiguration of its missile defense plans from bilateral agreements to a multilateral setting, including NATO's offer to Russia that it cooperate in the development of the system, allowed the allies to compromise on a new partnership with Russia.

It is remarkable that the allies were able to reach a compromise about the future of the Alliance at all, after coming out of a period of internal turmoil and crisis, which in many respects seems similar to that of the years leading up to the 1967 Harmel Report.[33] The allies successfully rebalanced the three core NATO tasks—collective defense, crisis management, and cooperative security. Yet unlike in the 1960s, the allies realized that modern defense can no longer be limited to territorial defense. In addition, the member states successfully recalibrated the political relationship between the United States and Europe. Also, unlike in the 1960s, the allies realized that the interests of the European partners had become much more disparate. Political compromise had been achieved by 2012, and alliance cohesion had been sustained, at least in the short term, until it once again would be challenged by the Ukraine crisis.

What Is the Nature of Extended (Nuclear) Deterrence in the Twenty-First Century?

During the Cold War, the extension of nuclear guarantees lay at the heart of the Alliance's security policy. Deterrence thinking provided the allies with an overarching framework for defining and implementing their security policies. Western deterrence theory was defined by existential threats to the territorial integrity and sovereignty of states, symmetric conflict interactions among hegemonic alliances, and deterrence signals that emphasized massive punishment through nuclear attacks. Western policymakers and academics alike perceived deterrence as a static concept geared toward upholding the territorial and nuclear status quo in Europe and beyond. Extended nuclear deterrence ensured, on the one hand, crisis stability between the two blocs based on mutual vulnerability (supported by arms control) and, on the other, a nuclear hierarchy within the Alliance based on nuclear guarantees by the hegemon. Nuclear deterrence was complemented by nuclear sharing as a tool to reassure the allies of the credibility of the nuclear guarantee and to limit the further proliferation of sovereign control over nuclear weapons among Alliance members.

Since the end of the Cold War, the nature of extended deterrence has fundamentally changed because of the transformation of the international security system. Nuclear deterrence no longer provides the allies with a framework for defining their security policies. In the twenty-first-century security environment, Western deterrence thinking became increasingly defined by weak threats to a set of broader and increasingly global interests; asymmetric conflict interactions among collective actors beyond states; and deterrence signals that emphasize a mix of denial and punishment tactics including, but not restricted to, the nuclear and military realm. Western policymakers and academics tended to see deterrence as a more dynamic concept designed to protect global norms and uphold a liberal international order.[34] Although no coherent strategic norm had evolved in Western strategic communities by 2012, deterrence was thus increasingly conceptualized as more than just nuclear deterrence; non-nuclear, long-range precision-strike capabilities and multilayered missile defense systems played a growing role. Given the wide range of multilateral security efforts, deterrence was increasingly seen as merely one of many diplomatic and civilian tools that could be used to influence potential adversaries.

Recognizing the growing complexity of international security affairs in the twenty-first century, the scholarly community, in the so-called fourth wave of deterrence literature, had shifted its focus to an exploration of deterrence regimes directed toward states that are keen to develop weapons of mass destruction, to counterterrorism campaigns against nonstate groups that employ terrorist tactics, and to often shady actors who operate in cyberspace.[35] In addition, conventional deterrence had become increasingly interesting to academics and practitioners. This renewed interest was driven by the debate about the revolution in military affairs and the related question about how the proliferation of long-range, precision-strike military technologies might affect the stability of regional military rivalries.[36] Today, NATO member states are confronted with complex deterrence relationships and face a challenge in designing a broader strategy to manage and anticipate regional and global instability.

The Ukraine Crisis and NATO's Nuclear and Deterrence Policy

NATO's 2009–12 debate about nuclear weapons evolved in an international and domestic context that seemed, at least to some allies, favorable for a growing role of the Alliance in ADN and, in parallel, for an open debate about the withdrawal of NSNW from Europe. The DDPR settled the policy debate into an ambiguous and seemingly fragile compromise that papered over fundamental differences of opinion regarding nuclear and deterrence policy. Although, by 2012, it had become clear that there was no political appetite for a renewal of the debate, there remained widespread concern among the expert community—reflected in the chapters of this book—that the DDPR compromise might not be sustainable because broader structural, economic, social, and political changes outside the control of NATO's leaders might push nuclear issues back onto the table.

Yet the Ukraine crisis shifted the attention of policymakers and the broader public away from nuclear disarmament and NATO's nuclear posture to the broader strategic consequences of the deteriorating relationship between Russia and the West. Clearly, the 2009 impulse toward nuclear disarmament has been exhausted. The profound tensions over Ukraine will in effect delay the possibility of bilateral US-Russian talks on nuclear arms reductions and missile defense. A serious debate about different deployment modes of US NSNW in Europe has become politically untenable in the context of the current crisis, and it seems highly unlikely that NATO will change its nuclear posture any time soon.

Conversely, the Ukraine crisis has strategic consequences for European security. The events of the past year have brought the debate about NATO's future role and the nature of the Alliance's overall deterrence strategy into sharp focus. The allies took significant steps to bolster their extended deterrence commitments under Article V toward the CES states. Although the United States deployed a limited number of its strategic bombers to Europe in June 2014, the Alliance is unlikely to reevaluate or shift its nuclear policy during the current crisis. Conversely, the Alliance announced a series of publicly visible changes to its conventional force posture, and these non-nuclear components clearly dominated the Alliance's efforts to bolster deterrence and reassurance. The ongoing crisis deserves a continuing strategic dialogue about the role of deterrence as a core element of the Alliance's overall strategy; about the appropriate mix of nuclear, conventional, and missile defense capabilities as the basis of NATO's posture; and about the relationship between the Alliance's deterrence and defense tasks, its crisis management tasks, and its cooperative security tasks and what this means for the organization of strategic stability underlying the trilateral relationship among Russia, China, and the United States.

A Changing International and Domestic Context: Beyond NSNW and ADN

The lingering concern that broader social changes would put NATO on a slide toward "disarmament by default" reflected two interrelated assumptions.[37] First, fiscal austerity would increase the pressure on authorities to explain why NSNW were needed. The projected costs of modernizing the B61 bombs and the fighter aircraft carrying them are considerable, and this would trigger questions about the relevance of these systems to national and alliance security.[38] As a consequence, the willingness of key allies to sustain the nuclear-sharing mission might decrease over time. Second, electoral change might lead one country to decide unilaterally to withdraw from NATO's current nuclear-sharing arrangements. It seemed no longer unthinkable that electoral choice or a parliamentary vote could lead to the termination of basing arrangements in a key state such as Germany. A unilateral decision by one state would have a negative impact on other members and could potentially unravel the Alliance's nuclear-sharing arrangement in a relatively short time.

As noted in this book, the list of potential changes and alternatives to the deployment pattern and the operational planning assumptions guiding the Alliance's current nuclear arrangements is rather long; they include modernization, a continuation of some form of the status quo, various options for replacing the US NSNW should they be withdrawn, and the termination of NATO's nuclear mission.[39] The future of US NSNW in Europe will remain one of the most contentious issues in NATO's debate about nuclear issues overall. It ties together elements of (so far) nonsubstitutable political utility with highly ambiguous remnants of military utility. A systematic assessment of the benefits and risks of different deployment modes would have constituted a major challenge to the Alliance's committee process in any circumstances. In the context of the current crisis, however, it seems highly unlikely that the allies would want to give serious consideration to moving beyond the maintenance of NATO's existing nuclear posture. NATO's NSNW played no role for deterrence and reassurance in the current crisis, as their opponents were quick to point out, adding that the money required to maintain NATO's NSNW could be better used to bolster NATO's conventional response forces.[40] Conversely, proponents might argue that the time has come to consider moving some of these weapons eastward to the territories of CES states. Clearly, the far more appropriate course for the time being seems to be sticking with the NSNW status quo while concentrating on the broader question of whether NATO's overall deterrence and defense posture remains adequate to the challenge of a more assertive Russia.

The Ukraine crisis has changed the domestic political context in many member states in ways that, at least in the short term, make calls for the elimination of nuclear weapons less attractive. The practicability and desirability of nuclear abolition remains controversial in all member states. Compared to 2009, today there is not much support left for the call that NATO should become a leader in ADN; instead, disagreement about the value of ADN to NATO's overall posture has been increasing. The suspension of all practical cooperation of the NATO-Russia Council delays any serious discussion on confidence-building measures (CBMs) for NSNW. While the Ukraine crisis renders negotiations on arms control with Russia unlikely in the foreseeable future, Alliance members might consider broadening their approach to arms control. As noted in this book, it is indeed questionable if the traditional arms control model that was geared toward strengthening strategic stability and limiting arms competition at an affordable price still fits today's global security environment. Instead, the Alliance should explore reframing its ADN policy along two axes. First, the Alliance should help its three nuclear members reach a common policy in which the key concepts are clearly understood—as a precondition toward disarmament. Second, the ADN committee should be used as a venue to discuss the broader links among ADN, missile defense, and advanced conventional capabilities.

Assessing the Role of Deterrence as One of the Core Elements of NATO's Overall Strategy

Current NATO policy reinforces the role of deterrence as the cornerstone of the Alliance's overall strategy. The SC 2010 and the DDPR 2012 acknowledge that the deterrence and defense tasks of the Alliance are tightly coupled with its crisis management and cooperative security tasks. Given the often geographically distant threats and the strategic logic of a forward-oriented posture, the three tasks—collective defense, crisis management, and cooperative security—in effect mutually reinforce each other.[41] Much needs to be done, however, if the allies want to sustain a common deterrence culture into the twenty-first century. In fact, NATO member states have quite different perceptions of the future role of extended deterrence, and the gaps between their deterrence conceptions has grown in recent years. By contrast, the US deterrence debate among policymakers, think tank members, and academics has been far broader and more coherent than the debate in Europe.

Over the past decade, Washington has reorganized US deterrence policies into a global and more tailored deterrence posture. The 2001 NPR created a new triad of nuclear and non-nuclear offensive strike systems, active and passive defenses, and an integrated defense infrastructure.[42] This implies that the entire US nuclear arsenal will serve the needs of extended deterrence. According to the 2010 NPR, nuclear weapons will continue to strengthen regional deterrence and reassure US allies and partners. However, the role of conventional power-projection capabilities and effective theater ballistic missile defenses in extended deterrence will increase considerably.[43] Taken together, this means that Washington is projecting extended deterrence as a means for keeping threats geographically far away and for managing the global and regional security orders. Thus, NATO is perceived as a collective actor standing force for global security management.[44]

The European members of the Alliance might not appreciate fully how much the reorganization of the US deterrence posture is being driven by the changing dynamics of Washington's extended deterrence regime in Asia. Asia has recently seen considerable nuclear and missile proliferation by state and nonstate actors, and the local and regional nuclear and non-nuclear military balances are changing rapidly. As a consequence, states such as Japan and

South Korea are likely to feel that the credibility of US security guarantees has been eroded, and growing demands for reassurance—along with fears that some allies may move toward a more autonomous defense posture—have pushed Washington toward a more tailored deterrence regime. Although the regional deterrence architectures have always been quite distinct, the changing needs of the Asia-Pacific region and the Middle East have also had repercussions for US deterrence policies in the transatlantic context. Obama's 2012 strategic guidelines are quite clear in this respect. In other words, this rebalancing toward the Asia-Pacific region means that the US posture in Europe will also need to evolve.

European views on deterrence are far less explicit and coherent, which reflects a dearth of deterrence thinking in the policy and academic communities. Among CES members and some smaller Western European states, traditional views of extended deterrence as a tool for protecting territorial integrity and national sovereignty, and for maintaining strategic stability, are still widespread. It remains unclear to what extent European states are buying into the logic of using extended deterrence as a crisis management tool and as an instrument for shaping regional security architectures. The conception of extended deterrence as a kind of insurance policy to protect the existence of member states is one thing; the conception of deterrence as a tool for structuring and supporting the international order is quite another. Using deterrence in the second way is "a politically sensitive topic in Europe."[45] Although there is clearly considerable variance in European deterrence thinking, the important point is that European strategic cultures—with the possible exception of France and Great Britain—tend to perceive deterrence based on military hardware as a generic tool and a weapon of last resort rather than as a dynamic and proactive instrument of diplomacy.

Current NATO policy has expanded the mix of nuclear and conventional capabilities that underpins the Alliance's deterrence and defense posture, adding a ballistic missile defense capacity as an integral part of its defenses.[46] As noted in this book, however, the weighting of the elements in the mix remains open to differing political interpretations. NATO member states must keep investing time and energy in a strategic dialogue on the role of nuclear, conventional, and missile defense capabilities in NATO's evolving deterrence and defense posture. From a military point of view, whether extended deterrence requires forward-based nuclear bombs and/or delivery systems will remain a particularly sensitive question. The modernization of bombs and delivery means will create new military capability.[47] NATO needs to consider if there is a future role for NSNW as a means of escalation control should a strategic threat evolve against exposed allies such as Turkey (by Iran or Syria) or the Baltic States (by Russia).[48] The allies need to be clear about whether they want to keep a joint long-range nuclear option, whether such an option should still be considered nonstrategic, and how that option might be linked to different deployment patterns. When they assess the political-military utility of current and future systems, however, the allies should also assess how their policies might be perceived by third parties and potential adversaries.

The current crisis in Ukraine has highlighted the growing importance of conventional deterrence, including cyber and space components. Resolving the question about how NATO should adapt its deterrence and defense posture in light of hybrid warfare that combines subversion and low-key political violence with external military pressure deserves an in-depth debate. The fact that a strategic response to politicized warfare touches on the realms of politics, policing, and intelligence presents NATO member states with sensitive choices involving democratic principles and, for some CES members, both measures at home as well as abroad. Any tangible strengthening of conventional deterrence involves questions of assurance and forward deployment, which again are linked to the question about how actions in this area might be perceived by Russia and other third parties. The pooling and sharing of new critical conventional capabilities may provide limited alternatives for strengthening the link between allies, especially the CES states. Examples are the limited physical presence of multinational NATO units in Estonia (Cyber Defense Center), Hungary (Heavy Airlift Wing), and Poland (C3 Battalion), or NATO air patrols in the Baltic States.[49]

Assessing the Role of NATO's New Missile Defenses

Current NATO policy has integrated a ballistic missile defense capability into the Alliance's deterrence and defense posture. Missile defense, the DDPR declares, can complement but not substitute for nuclear weapons in deterrence.[50] Adding missile defense to NATO's capabilities was clearly a significant development because it added a denial component to NATO's extended deterrence guarantees, which had been underwritten primarily by offensive means, as noted by two contributors to this volume.[51] The allies perceive missile defense primarily as a tool for protecting forward-deployed forces and exposed allies against regional threats from short-range ballistic missiles (SRBMs) and medium-range ballistic missiles (MRBMs). Because missile defenses provide NATO with a damage limitation option, they are seen as increasing the Alliance's political and military flexibility against assertive regional powers armed with ballistic missiles. A missile defense capability is designed to help NATO protect its population against threats from outside the Euro-Atlantic area and to retain the option of military intervention to reestablish regional order.

Yet the allies will have to come to terms with at least three controversial issues linked to missile defenses as a tool for deterring regional actors such as Iran. First, the act of denying a regional player the coercive power of its ballistic missile and potential weapons of mass destruction (WMD) capabilities will likely need the combined application of defensive and (conventional or nuclear) offensive means, a fact that is probably not appreciated by all European allies. To be credible, such a flexible deterrence strategy would need to combine punishment and denial mechanisms. To link the denial effects of missile defense to regional crisis management operations, the allies will have to reach a strategic consensus about the regional order that is to be upheld or reestablished. Second, missile defenses may have unintended side effects: They might accelerate the proliferation of ballistic missiles, on the one hand, and slow down nuclear disarmament, on the other. Third, in order to build up the technical infrastructure, allies will need to fine-tune the distribution of the benefits (protection) and risks (debris) of the system and design a workable command and control structure.

In their declaratory policy, the allies highlight that NATO's missile defenses are "not oriented against Russia" and do not have the capability "to undermine Russia's strategic deterrent."[52] This raises the question about how NATO can separate its missile defenses from the management of its strategic stability with Russia. Defining a workable way of missile defense collaboration with Russia, while at the same time managing the NATO-internal repercussions of such noncollaboration, would have been problematic in any case. The fact that NATO formally suspended its missile defense cooperation efforts in reaction to Russia's actions in Ukraine confronts the Alliance with an even trickier problem. The need to define the role of missile defense in NATO's deterrence and defense posture in the face of Russian opposition will further complicate the search for a common transatlantic approach to missile defense.

Assessing the Management of Strategic Stability among the United States, Russia, and China

Current NATO policy declares that the Alliance does not consider "any country to be its adversary." More specifically, the Alliance maintains that the planned missile defense system does not "undermine Russia's strategic deterrent."[53] Although the Alliance is not directly involved in the management of strategic stability among the United States, Russia, and China, the evolution of Washington's bilateral and trilateral strategic relationships with Moscow and Beijing will have important repercussions for NATO's deterrence and defense posture. As mentioned in the previous section, Russia's opposition to the Alliance's missile defense plans is a case in point. Growing concern about Washington's high-precision deterrence explains in part both Russia's reluctance to negotiate on NSNW—where it has a definite numerical advantage—and its complaints about the open-ended character of the US and NATO missile defense systems.

The US-China relationship and the trilateral relationship among Russia, China, and the United States have so far received only limited attention within NATO.[54] This is likely to change because Moscow insists that a next phase of US-Russian arms control discussions needs to include China. The lack of Chinese transparency about its nuclear plans and activities has become another stumbling block on the road to zero. As for the bilateral strategic relationship between Washington and Beijing, China is increasingly worried that the evolving US mix of conventional strike capabilities, nuclear capabilities, and missile defense could undermine its own nuclear deterrent. At the same time, the United States is concerned about the destabilizing effects of China's nuclear modernization and its development of robust anti-access area-denial capabilities in the conventional realm. While these developments could lead to a deterioration of the political relationship between the two countries, this need not be the case. In fact, the current political leaders seem reasonably optimistic that they will be able to establish some sort of mutual strategic restraint.[55]

It will be worthwhile for NATO policymakers to study carefully the intense debate about strategic stability underlying the relationship between the United States and China.[56] The US-Chinese relationship is far more complex than the relatively straightforward US-Russian relationship was during the Cold War. The United States and China are not plagued by existential security concerns, and their relationship exhibits far stronger economic dependencies. In such a context, strategic stability can no longer be based on mutual vulnerability only. In the twenty-first century, the requirements of strategic stability must be rethought and must take into account the relationship among nuclear capabilities, broad conventional strike capabilities (including space and cyber components), and multilayered missile defenses. This is all the more true because the way strategic stability is organized at the bilateral level between the United States and China will have important repercussions for Washington's extended deterrence regime in the Asia-Pacific region.[57]

Final Thoughts

The nature of deterrence is changing fundamentally in the twenty-first century. Moving forward, US allies will need to recognize the growing gaps among their individual deterrence conceptions; they will also have to invest more intellectual and political capital into a joint assessment of the requirements of extended deterrence as a core element of overall strategy. Simply recognizing the difficulties involved in crafting a more coherent policy on nuclear and deterrence issues is not enough, as the NATO experience shows. In the long term, ambiguous policy will not be a substitute for a new direction in the Alliance's deterrence policy. In the face of changes in threats, technology, and regional configurations, the allies cannot afford to shy away from tough policy trade-offs.

Consensus building on deterrence and nuclear policy is a precondition for efficient and mutually supportive national investment and deployment decisions. Allies, whether in the NATO context or elsewhere, need to clarify the apparent policy problems through a consistent, ongoing analytical and policy process. For bilateral alliance relationship, this might seem straightforward. For NATO, allies should put pressure on the committee process in Brussels so they are prepared to move toward a more sustainable deterrence and defense posture should the political space for a new compromise emerge. In the context of the Ukraine crisis, the Alliance can no longer afford to let inaction continue to characterize its extended deterrence and defense policies, while deterrence as well as extended deterrence relationships elsewhere in the world are evolving at a different pace.

Notes

1. Barack Obama, "Remarks of President Barack Obama" (hereafter Prague Speech). Prague: Embassy of the United States, April 5, 2009, http://prague.usembassy.gov/obama.html.

2. NATO, "Active Engagement, Modern Defence: Strategic Concept for the Defence and Security of the Members of the North Atlantic Treaty Organisation" (hereafter Strategic Concept 2010), adopted by Heads of State and Government in Lisbon, November 19, 2010, http://www.nato.int/strategic-concept/pdf/Strat_Concept_web_en.pdf.

3. Strategic Concept 2010.

4. Ibid.

5. See chapters 4 and 5 in this book.

6. NATO, "Deterrence and Defence Posture Review" (hereafter DDPR 2012), Chicago, May 20, 2012, http://www.nato.int/cps/en/natolive/official_texts_87597.htm?mode=pressrelease.

7. DDPR 2012.
8. See chapter 5 in this book.
9. See the Introduction and chapters 4 and 5 in this book.
10. See chapter 4 in this book.
11. Liviu Horovitz, "Why Do They Want American Nukes? Central and Eastern European Positions Regarding US Nonstrategic Nuclear Weapons," *European Security* 23, no. 1 (Spring 2014): 73–89.
12. Lukasz Kulesa, "Extended Deterrence and Assurance in Central Europe," in *Perspectives on Extended Deterrence*, Recherches & Documents, No. 3/2010 (Paris: Fondation pour la Recherche Stratégique, 2010), 119–27.
13. Simon Lunn, "The Role and Place of Tactical Nuclear Weapons—a NATO Perspective," in *Tactical Nuclear Weapons and NATO*, ed. Tom Nichols, Douglas Stuart, and Jeffrey D. McCausland (Carlisle, PA: Strategic Studies Institute), 235–56.
14. US Department of Defense, "Nuclear Posture Review Report" (hereafter NPR 2010), Washington, DC, April 5, 2010, http://www.defense.gov/npr/docs/2010%20nuclear%20posture%20review%20report.pdf.
15. See chapter 7 in this book.
16. See chapter 4 in this book.
17. Patrick M. Morgan, "Collective-Actor Deterrence," in *Complex Deterrence: Strategy and the Global Age*, ed. T. V. Paul, Patrick M. Morgan, and James J. Wirtz (Chicago, IL: University of Chicago Press, 2009), 163–64.
18. Andreas Wenger, "NATO's Transformation in the 1960s and the Ensuing Political Order in Europe," in *Transforming NATO in the Cold War: Challenges beyond Deterrence in the 1960s*, ed. Andreas Wenger, Christian Nünlist, and Anna Locher (London: Routledge, 2007), 221–42.
19. David S. Yost, "US Extended Deterrence in NATO and North-East Asia," in *Perspectives on Extended Deterrence*, Recherches & Documents, No. 3/2010 (Paris: Fondation pour la Recherche Stratégique, 2010), p 22.
20. Andreas Wenger, "Crisis and Opportunity: NATO's Transformation and the Multilateralization of Détente, 1966–1968," *Journal of Cold War Studies* 6, no. 1 (Winter 2004): 22–74.
21. See chapter 3 in this book.
22. See chapter 2 in this book.
23. Seok-Soo Lee, "The Future of Extended Deterrence: A South Korean Perspective," in *Perspectives on Extended Deterrence*, Recherches & Documents, No. 3/2010 (Paris: Fondation pour la Recherche Stratégique, 2010), 49–60; Jonathan Trexel, *Deterring the Democratic People's Republic of Korea: The Role of Japan's Ballistic Missile Defense* (Lincoln, NE: University of Nebraska, 2013), http://digitalcommons.unl.edu/cgi/viewcontent.cgi?article=1028&context=poliscitheses.
24. Thomas W. Gijswijt, "Beyond NATO: Transnational Elite Networks and the Atlantic Alliance," in *Transforming NATO in the Cold War: Challenges beyond Deterrence in the 1960s*, ed. Andreas Wenger, Christian Nünlist, and Anna Locher (London: Routledge, 2007), 50–64.
25. Wenger, "NATO's Transformation in the 1960s," 230–31.
26. See chapter 4 in this book.
27. Andreas Wenger and Jeremi Suri, "At the Crossroads of Diplomatic and Social History: The Nuclear Revolution, Dissent, and Détente," *Cold War History* 1, no. 3 (April 2001): 1–42.

28. See chapter 6 in this book.
29. James M. Goldgeier, *Not Whether But When: The U.S. Decision to Enlarge NATO* (Washington, DC: Brookings Institution, 1999).
30. Richard Holbrooke, *To End a War* (New York: Modern Library, 1999).
31. Philip Gordon and Jeremy Shapiro, *Allies at War: America, Europe, and the Crisis over Iraq* (New York: McGraw Hill, 2004).
32. Andreas Wenger, "Europe and NATO and Their Role in the Twenty-first Century," in *Guide to U.S. Foreign Policy: A Diplomatic History*, ed. Robert J. McMahon and Thomas W. Zeiler (New York: CQ Press, 2012), 487–502.
33. Helga Haftendorn, "Entstehung und Bedeutung des Harmel-Berichts der NATO von 1967," *Vierteljahrshefte für Zeitgeschichte* 40, no. 2 (April 1992): 169–220.
34. Patrick M. Morgan, "The State of Deterrence in International Politics Today," *Contemporary Security Policy* 33, no. 1 (April 2012): 85–107.
35. Jeffrey W. Knopf, "The Fourth Wave in Deterrence Research," *Contemporary Security Policy* 31, no. 1 (April 2010): 1–33; James Lebovic, *Deterring International Terrorism and Rogue States: US National Security Policy after 9/11* (London: Routledge, 2007); Andreas Wenger and Alex Wilner, *Deterring Terrorism: Theory and Practice* (Stanford, CA: Stanford University Press, 2012); Martin Libicki, *Cyberdeterrence and Cyberwar* (Santa Monica, CA: RAND, 2009).
36. Michel Fortmann and Stéfanie von Hlatky, "The Revolution in Military Affairs: Impact of Emerging Technologies on Deterrence," in *Complex Deterrence: Strategy in the Global Age*, ed. T. V. Paul, Patrick Morgan, and James Wirtz (Chicago, IL: University of Chicago Press, 2009), 304–21.
37. Malcolm Chalmers, "Not with a Bang but a Whimper: Europe's Pending Denuclearization," *RUSI Analysis*, London, Royal United Services Institute, March 12, 2010; see chapter 5 in this book.
38. See chapter 5 in this book.
39. See chapter 2 in this book.
40. Barry Blechman and Russel Rumbaugh, "Bombs Away," *Foreign Affairs*, 2 (January 2015), http://www.foreignaffairs.com/articles/141484/barry-blechman-and-russell-rumbaugh/bombs-away.
41. Strategic Concept 2010; DDPR 2012.
42. Secretary of Defense Donald H. Rumsfeld, unclassified cover letter for Nuclear Posture Review report to Congress, January 9, 2002, http://www.defense.gov/news/Jan2002/d20020109npr.pdf.
43. NPR 2010.
44. Morgan, "The State of Deterrence," 99.
45. See the Introduction to this book.
46. DDPR 2012.
47. See chapter 5 in this book.
48. See the Introduction to this book.
49. Kulesa, "Extended Deterrence and Assurance," 123–24.
50. DDPR 2012.
51. See chapter 6 in this book.
52. DDPR 2012.
53. Ibid.
54. See the Introduction to this book.

55. Lewis A. Dunn, ed., "Building toward a Stable and Cooperative Long-Term U.S.-China Strategic Relationship: Results of a Track 2 Joint Study by U.S. and Chinese Experts," SAIC, CSIS, CACDA paper, December 31, 2012, http://www.docstoc.com/docs/155706740/Building-Toward-a-Stable-and-Cooperative-Long-Term-US-China.

56. Elbridge A. Colby and Michael S. Gerson, eds., *Strategic Stability: Contending Interpretations* (Carlisle Barracks, PA: US Army War College Press, 2013).

57. Brad Roberts, "Extended Deterrence and Strategic Stability in Northeast Asia," *The National Institute for Defense Studies: Visiting Scholars Paper Series*, no. 1 (August 2013). http://www.nids.go.jp/english/publication/visiting/index.html.

BIBLIOGRAPHY

"10 Years without the ABM Treaty: The Issue of Missile Defense in Russia-U.S. Relations." Russian International Affairs Council, Institute for US and Canada Studies of the Russian Academy of Sciences, 2012.

"America Suffers from 'Illusion of Invulnerability'—Putin." *Russia Today*, March 2, 2012, http://rt.com/politics/putin-us-meeting-media-reset-695.

"Letter by the Foreign Ministers of Belgium, Germany, Luxembourg, the Netherlands and Norway to NATO Secretary-General Anders Fogh Rasmussen," February 26, 2010.

"NATO, U.S. Possess 1,000 Anti-ICBM Interceptors, Russian Official Claims." *Global Security Newswire*, January 20, 2012, http://www.nti.rsvp1.com/gsn/article/russia-claims-nato-us-possess-1000-interceptors-can-counter-icbms/.

"Non-Paper Submitted by Poland, Norway, Germany and the Netherlands on Increasing Transparency and Confidence with Regard to Tactical Nuclear Weapons in Europe." FAS Strategic Security Blog, 2011. http://www.fas.org/programs/ssp/nukes/nuclearweapons/nato-nonpaper041411.pdf.

"Obama Reportedly Offers Putin Deal on Sharing Antimissile Data." *Global Security Newswire*, May 16, 2013. http://www.nti.org/gsn/article/obama-reportedly-offers-putin-legally-binding-deal-sharing-antimissile-data/.

"Putin Says Russia Will Build Weapons to Offset Planned US Missile Defences." *The Guardian*, December 29, 2009. http://guardian.co.uk/world/2009/dec/29/nuclear-weapons-russia.

"Russia May have Conventional Hypersonic Weapons in as Few as Five Years." *Global Security Newswire*, July 1, 2013. http://www.nti.org/gsn/article/russia-eyes-conventional-hypersonic-weapons-few-five-years/.

"Russia Renews Threat of Military Measure if Antimissile Deal Not Reached." *Global Security Newswire*, March 15, 2012. http://www.nti.rsvp1.com/gsn/article/russia-renews-threat-pursue-security-mesures-if-antimissile-deal-not-reached.

"Russia Warns 'Point of No Return' Imminent in US Missile Defense Talks." *Russia Today*, May 2, 2012. http://rt.com/politics/russia-us-missile-defense-arms-race-iran-406.

"Russia Warns U.S. Against Deploying Final Phases of Missile Shield." *Global Security Newswire*, October 1, 2012. http://www.nti.rsvp1.com/gsn/article/russia-warns-us-against-implementing-last-phases-missile-shield/.

"Sustaining U.S. Global Leadership: Priorities for 21st Century Defense." U.S. Department of Defense. January, 2012.

"The Withdrawal of U.S. Nuclear Weapons from South Korea." The Nuclear Information Project, September 2005. http://www.nukestrat.com/korea/withdrawal.htm.

Acton, James. *Low Numbers. A Practical Path to Deep Nuclear Reductions*. Washington, DC: Carnegie Endowment for International Peace, 2011.

Agence France Presse. "Robert Gates: les Etats-Unis n'accepteront jamais une Corée du Nord dotée de l'arme atomique." *Agence France Presse*, October 21, 2009.

———. "Russian Ambassador Warns Denmark Over NATO Missile Shield." *Agence France Presse*, March 22, 2015.

Ailleret, Charles. *L'aventure atomique française*. Paris: Grasset, 1968.

Albright, David, and Mark Hibbs. "Iraq's Bomb: Blueprints and Artifacts." *The Bulletin of the Atomic Scientists* (January/February 1992): 30–40.

Allan, Charles T. "Extended Conventional Deterrence: In From the Cold and Out of the Nuclear Fire?" *The Washington Quarterly* 17, no. 3 (Summer 1994): 203–23.

Apple, R. W., Jr. "Scud Missile Hits a U.S. Barracks, Killing 27." *New York Times*, February 26, 1991. Accessed January 15, 2013. http://www.nytimes.com/1991/02/26/world/war-in-the-gulf-scud-attack-scud-missile-hits-a-us-barracks-killing-27.html.

Arbatov, Alexei. "The Transformation of Russian Military Doctrine: Lessons Learned from Kosovo and Chechnya." *Marshall Centre Occasional Paper*, George C. Marshall European Centre for Security Studies, Garmish Partenkirken, no. 2, 2000.

Arbatov, Alexei, and Vladimir Dvorkin. *Beyond Nuclear Deterrence: Transforming the U.S.-Russian Equation*. Washington, DC: Carnegie Endowment for International Peace, 2006.

Arbatov, Alexei, Vladimir Dvorkin, Alexander Pikaev, and Sergey Oznobischev. "Strategic Stability after the Cold War." Institute of World Economy and International Relations, Russian Academy of Sciences, 2010.

Arms Control Association. "Nuclear Weapons: Who Has What at a Glance." *ACA Press Release*, Washington, DC: Arms Control Association, 2012. http://www.armscontrol.org/factsheets/Nuclearweaponswhohaswhat/.

Arnold, Lorna, and Katherine Pyne. *Britain and the H-Bomb*. London: Palgrave, 2001.

Aron, Raymond. *La République impériale. Les Etats-Unis dans le monde*. Paris: Calmann-Levy, 1973.

Art, Robert J. "The Fungibility of Force." In *The Use of Force: Military Power and International Politics*, 7th ed., edited by Robert J. Art and Kenneth N. Waltz, 3–22. Lanham, MD: Rowman and Littlefield Publishers, 2009.

Australian Defense Department. *Defense White Paper 2013: Defending Australia and its National Interests*. Australian Defense Department, May 2013. http://www.defense.gov.au/whitepaper2013/.

Baehr, Peter. *Caesarism, Charisma and Fate: Historical Sources and Modern Resonances in the Work of Max Weber*. Piscataway, NJ: Transaction Publishers, 2008. Google eBook.

Baker, Peter. "Putin Proposes Broader Cooperation on Missile Defense." *Washington Post*, July 3, 2007.

Bar, Shmuel. "Deterring Non-State Terrorist Groups: The Case of Hizballah." *Comparative Strategy* 26, no. 5 (2007): 469–93.

Baylis, John. *Ambiguity and Deterrence: British Nuclear Strategy, 1945–1964*. Oxford: Clarendon Press, 1995.

———. *Anglo-American Defence Relations, 1939–84: The Special Relationship*. London: Palgrave, 1984.

Baylis, John, and Alan Macmillan. "The British Global Strategy Paper of 1952." *Journal of Strategic Studies* 16, no. 2 (June 1993).

Baylis, John, and Kristan Stoddart. "The British Nuclear Experience: The Role of Ideas and Beliefs (Part I)." *Diplomacy & Statecraft* 23, no. 2 (2012): 331–346.

Bétermier, Jean. "How to Link Deterrence Theory and Strategic Planning." In *NATO and 21st Century Deterrence*, edited by Karl-Heinz Kamp and David S. Yost. Rome: NATO Defense College, Research Division, 2009.

Blank, Stephen J. *Perspectives on Russian Foreign Policy*. Carlisle, PA: US Army War College Strategic Studies Institute, 2012.

Blechman, Barry, and Russel Rumbaugh. "Bombs Away." *Foreign Affairs*, January 2, 2015. http://www.foreignaffairs.com/articles/141484/barry-blechman-and-russell-rumbaugh/bombs-away.

Bleek, Philip. "Why do States Proliferate? Quantitative Analysis of the Exploration, Pursuit, and Acquisition of Nuclear Weapons." In *Forecasting Nuclear Proliferation in the 21st Century. Volume 1: The Role of Theory*, edited by William C. Potter and Guakhar Mukhatzhanova, 159–92. Stanford, CA: Stanford University Press, 2010.

Bobbit, Philip. *The Shield of Achilles. War, Peace and the Course of History*. New York: Anchor Books, 2002.

Boese, Wade. "Bush, Putin Leave Arms Dispute Unsettled." *Arms Control Today*, May 2008. http://www.armscontrol.org/act/2008_5/BushPutin.

Bracken, Paul. *The Bomb Returns for a Second Act*. Philadelphia, PA: Foreign Policy Research Institute, 2011.

———. *The Command and Control of Nuclear Forces*. New Haven, CT: Yale University Press, 1983.

———. *The Second Nuclear Age, Strategy, Danger, and the New Power Politics*. New York: Times Books, 2012.

Bridge, Robert. "It's Either Common Missile Defense or New Arms Race—Medvedev." *Russian Today*, November 30, 2010.

Brodie, Bernard. *War and Politics*. London: Cassell, 1973.

Brown, Andrew. "Historic Barriers to Anglo-American Nuclear Cooperation." In *U.S.-U.K. Nuclear Cooperation after 50 Years*, edited by Jennifer Mackby and Paul Cornish, 36–47. Washington, DC: Center for Strategic and International Studies, 2008.

Buffaloe, David L. "Defining Asymmetric Warfare." *The Institute of Land Warfare*, no. 58 (September, 2006). http://www.ausa.org/SiteCollectionDocuments/ILW%20Web-ExclusivePubs/Land%20Warfare%20Papers/LWP_58.pdf.

Bunn, M. Elaine. "Can Deterrence Be Tailored?" *Strategic Forum*, no. 225 (January 2007): 1–8. http://permanent.access.gpo.gov/lps496/Strforum/sf225/SF225+new.pdf.

Bush, Richard C. "The US Policy of Extended Deterrence in Asia: History, Current Views, and Implications." *Arms Control Series* no. 5, The Brookings Institution, (February 2011).

Byrne, Michael, Douglas Edson, and Andreas Hlosek. "A Nuclear Weapons Free NATO." *American Diplomacy*, 2010.

Cabinet of the Prime Minister. *The National Security Strategy of the United Kingdom: Security in an Interdependent World*. London: Crown, 2008.

Campbell, Kurt, and Brian Andrews. "Explaining the US 'Pivot' to Asia." *Americas 2013/01 Paper*. London: Chatham House, 2013. http://www.chathamhouse.org/sites/files/chathamhouse/public/Research/Americas/0813pp_pivottoasia.pdf.

Carlier, Claude. *L'aéronautique française 1945–1975*. Paris: Charles Lavauzelle, 1983.

Carr, Alan. "How It All Began: The Atomic Bomb and the British Mission." In *U.S.-U.K. Nuclear Cooperation after 50 Years*, edited by Jennifer Mackby and Paul Cornish, 23–47. Washington, DC: Center for Strategic and International Studies, 2008.

Chaban-Delmas, Jacques. *Mémoires pour demain*. Paris: Flammarion, 1997.

Chafetz, Glenn. "The End of the Cold War and the Future of Nuclear Proliferation: An Alternative to the Neorealist Perspective." *Security Studies* 2, no. 3/4 (1993): 125–58.

Chalmers, Hugh, Malcolm Chalmers, and Andrea Berger, eds. "A Problem Deferred? NATO Non-Strategic Nuclear Weapons after Chicago." *Whitehall Report*, London: Royal United Services Institute, 2012, 4–12.

Chalmers, Malcolm. "Words That Matter? NATO Declaratory Policy and the DDPR." In *Reducing Nuclear Risks in Europe*, edited by Steve Andreasen and Isabelle Williams, 52–65. Washington, DC: Nuclear Threat Initiative, 2011.

Chalmers, Malcolm, and Simon Lunn. "NATO's Tactical Nuclear Dilemma." *RUSI Occasional Paper* (2010). Accessed September 25, 2013. http://www.nonukes.nl/media/files/2010-03-rusi-natos-tactical-nuclear-dilemma_0.pdf.

Charles, Daniel. *Nuclear Planning in NATO: Pitfalls of First Use*. Cambridge, MA: Ballinger, 1987.

Chastenet, Patrick, and Philippe Chastenet. *Chaban*. Paris: Seuil, 1991.

Chevallier, Jacques. "La genèse de la force de dissuasion nucléaire française." In *Armement et Vème République. Fin des années 1950–fin des années 1960*, edited by Maurice Vaisse. Paris: CNRS Éditions, 2002.

Chyba, Cristopher F., and J. D. Crouch. "Understanding the U.S. Nuclear Weapons Policy Debate." *The Washington Quarterly* (July 2009): 21–36.

Cimbala, Stephen J. "Anticipatory Attacks: Nuclear Crisis Stability in Future Asia." *Comparative Strategy* 27, no 1 (2008): 113–32.

———. "Chasing Its Tail: Nuclear Deterrence in the Information Age," *Strategic Studies* 19 (2012): 18–34.

———. *Military Persuasion: Deterrence and Provocation in Crisis and War*. University Park: Pennsylvania State University Press, 1994.

———."Russia and European Missile Defenses: Reflexive Reset?" *Joint Forces Quarterly* 68, (January 2013): 10–17.

———. "Russia's Strategic Nuclear Deterrent: Realistic or Uncertain?" *Comparative Strategy* 26, no. 3 (2007): 185–203.

———. *Strategy after Deterrence*. New York: Praeger, 1991.

Cirincione, Joseph. "The Performance of the Patriot Missile in the Gulf War." U.S. House of Representatives, October 1992.

Clark, Ian. *Diplomacy and the Special Relationship: Britain's Deterrent and America, 1957–1962*. Oxford: Clarendon Press, 1994.

Clark, Ian, and Nicholas J. Wheeler. *The British Origins of Nuclear Strategy, 1945–1955*. Oxford: Clarendon Press, 1989.

Cliff, Roger, Mark Burles, Michael S. Chase, Derek Eaton, and Kevin L. Pollpeter. *Entering the Dragon's Lair: The Implications of Chinese Antiaccess Strategies.* Santa Monica, CA: RAND, 2007.

Clinton, Bill. "The Washington Summit: Welcome Letter." 1999.

Clinton, Hillary. "America's Pacific Century." *Foreign Policy* (November 2011): 56–63.

———. "Excerpts from Remarks by U.S. Secretary of State Hillary Rodham Clinton at NATO Working Dinner on Nuclear Issues and Missile Defense." *U.S. Department of Defense*, Tallinn, April 2010.

Cogan, Charles. "American-French Intelligence Relations and the French Nuclear Deterrent." *Journal of Intelligence History* 3, no. 1 (Summer 2003): 55–60.

Cohen, Avner. *The Worst-Kept Secret: Israel's Bargain with the Bomb.* New York: Columbia University Press, 2010.

Colby, Elbridge A., and Michael S. Gerson, eds. *Strategic Stability: Contending Interpretations.* Carlisle, PA: US Army War College Press, 2013.

Collina, Tom Z. "Russia, U.S. Trade Missile Defense Offers." *Arms Control Today* (June 2013).

———. "Turkey to Host NATO Missile Defense Radar." *Arms Control Today* 41 (October 2011). Accessed January 15, 2013. http://www.armscontrol.org/act/2011_10/Turkey_to_Host_NATO_Missile_Defense_Radar.

Commission to Assess the Ballistic Missile Threat to the United States. *Executive Summary of the Report of the Commission to Assess the Ballistic Missile Threat to the United States.* US Congress. July 15, 1998. Accessed January 23, 2013. http://www.fas.org/irp/threat/bm-threat.htm.

Cordesman, Anthony H., and Abraham Wagner. *Defending America: Asymmetric and Terrorist Attacks with Radiological and Nuclear Weapons.* Washington, DC: Center for Strategic and International Studies, 2001.

———. *The Lessons of Modern War, Volume II, The Iran-Iraq War.* Boulder, CO: Westview Press, 1990.

Coutrot, Aline. "La création du commissariat à l'énergie atomique." Revue française de science politique 31, no. 2 (1981): 343–71.

———. "La politique atomique sous le gouvernement de Mendès France." In *Pierre Mendès France et le Mendésisme, l'expérience gouvernementale*, edited by François Bédarida and Jean-Pierre Rioux. Paris: Fayard, 1985.

Crawford, Timothy. "The Endurance of Extended Deterrence: Continuity, Change and Complexity in Theory and Policy." In *Complex Deterrence. Strategy in the Global Age*, edited by T. V. Paul, Patrick Morgan, and James Wirtz, 277–303. Chicago: University of Chicago Press, 2009.

Crouch, J. D. "Special Briefing on the Nuclear Posture Review." United States Department of Defense, January 9, 2002. http://www.defenselink.mil/news/Jan2002/t01092002_t0109npr.html.

Cuau, Yves. "Les forts, les faibles et les fous," *L'Express*, November 11, 1993.

Danchev, Alex. "In the Black Room: Anglo-American Defense Cooperation." In *British Intelligence, Strategy and the Cold War 1945–1951*, edited by Richard Aldrich. London: Routledge, 1992.

Davis, Paul K. "Structuring Analysis to Support Future Decisions about Nuclear Forces and Postures." Rand Corporation (2011). http://www.rand.org/content/dam/rand/pubs/working_papers/2011/RAND_WR878.pdf.

de Gaulle, Charles. *Mémoires d'espoir, suivies d'allocutions et messages sous la IVème et Vème République*. Paris: Plon, 1999.

Delpech, Therese. *Nuclear Deterrence in the 21st Century: Lessons from the Cold War for a New Area of Strategic Piracy*. Washington, DC: Rand Corporation, 2012.

de Roquefeuil, Henry. "Les composantes air de la dissuasion nucléaire aujord'hui et demain." *Défense Nationale* 49 (August/September 1993).

Deudney, Daniel. "Dividing Realism: Structural Realism and Security Materialism on Nuclear Security and Proliferation." *Security Studies* 2, no. 3/4 (1993): 5–36.

Deudney, David, and G. John Ikenberry. "The Unravelling of the Cold War Settlement." *Survival* 51, no. 6 (December 2009–January 2010): 39–62.

Devine, Thomas. "Extended Deterrence and Nuclear Nonproliferation: Lessons from European and East Asian Regimes Applied to the Middle East." *Nuclear Scholars Initiative: Project on Nuclear Issues*. Washington, DC: Center for Strategic and International Studies (December 2011): 33–43.

Dowler, Thomas, and Joseph S. Howard II. "Stability in a Proliferated World." *Strategic Review* 23, no. 2 (Spring 1995): 26–37.

Drogin, Bob, and Patt Morrison. "Iraqi Missile Slams into GIs' Barracks; 27 Killed." *Los Angeles Times*, February 26, 1991. Accessed January 15, 2013. http://articles.latimes.com/1991-02-26/news/mn-1889_1_scud-attack.

Duclert, Vincent. "Pierre Mendès France et la recherche scientifique." In *Le gouvernement de la recherche: Histoire d'un engagement politique, de Pierre Mendès France au Général de Gaulle*, edited by Alain Chatriot and Vincent Duclert. Paris: La Découverte, 2006.

Dunn, Lewis A. ed. "Building toward a Stable and Cooperative Long-Term U.S.-China Strategic Relationship: Results of a Track 2 Joint Study by U.S. and Chinese Experts." SAIC, CSIS, CACDA paper, December 2012. http://www.docstoc.com/docs/155706740/Building-Toward-a-Stable-and-Cooperative-Long-Term-US-China.

Dunn, Lewis A. "Rethinking the Nuclear Equation: The United States and New Nuclear Powers." *The Washington Quarterly* 17, no. 1 (Winter, 1994): 5–25.

Dunn, Simon. "The Role and Place of Tactical Nuclear Weapons—a NATO Perspective." In *Tactical Nuclear Weapons and NATO*, edited by Tom Nichols, Douglas Stuart, and Jeffrey D. McCausland, 235–56. Carlisle, PA: Strategic Studies Institute, 2012.

Duval, Marcel. "Les décisions concernant l'armement nucléaire: pourquoi, comment et quand?" In *Armement et Vème République. Fin des années 1950–fin des années 1960*, edited by Maurice Vaïsse. Paris: CNRS, 2002.

Duval, Marcel, and Dominique Mongin. *Histoire des forces nucléaires françaises*. Paris: PUF, 1993.

Dvorkin, Vladimir. "Strategic and Offensive and Defensive Arms." In *Nuclear Reset: Arms Reduction and Nonproliferation*, edited by Alexei Arbatov and Vladimir Dvorkin, 177–203. Moscow: Carnegie Endowment for International Peace, 2012.

Dylan, Huw. "Britain and the Missile Gap: British Estimates on the Soviet Ballistic Missile Threat, 1957–61." *Intelligence and National Security* 23, no. 6 (December 2008): 777–806.

Eckert, Paul. "Obama's Asian 'Pivot' Advances, but Obstacles Await." *Reuters*, June 15, 2012. Accessed May 3, 2013. http://www.reuters.com/article/2012/06/15/us-usa-pacific-pivot-idUSBRE85E1B420120615.

Edelman, Eric S., Andrew F. Krepinevich, and Evan Braden Montgomery. "The Dangers of a Nuclear Iran. The Limits of Containment." *Foreign Affairs* 90, no. 1 (January/February 2011): 66–81.

Eisenhower, Dwight D. *Foreign Relations of the United States 1955–1957*, vol. XIX. National Security Policy, Document 79, 1990.

Euro-Atlantic Security Initiative. "Missile Defense: Toward a New Paradigm." *EASI Working Group Paper*, Carnegie Endowment for International Peace, February 2012. http://carnegieendowment.org/2012/02/03/missile-defense-toward-new-paradigm.

———. *Toward a Euro-Atlantic Security Community*. Euro-Atlantic Security Initiative Final Report. Washington, DC: Carnegie Endowment for International Peace, 2012.

Evron, Yair. *Israel's Nuclear Dilemma*. Ithaca, NY: Cornell University Press, 1994.

Farmelo, Graham. *Churchill's Bomb: A Hidden History of Science, War and Politics*. London: Faber and Faber, 2013.

Fihn, Beatrice, and Ray Acheson. "Moving towards a Ban on Nuclear Weapons." *Report from the Conference on the Humanitarian Impact of Nuclear Weapons*. Oslo, Norway, 2013. http://www.reachingcriticalwill.org/images/documents/Disarmament-fora/oslo-2013/HINWreport.pdf.

Fitzpatrick, Mark. "North Korean Proliferation Challenges: The Role of the European Union." *Non-Proliferation Papers*, no. 18, EU Non-Proliferation Consortium, June 2012.

Ford, Christopher A. *Playing for Time on the Edge of the Apocalypse: Maximizing Decision Time for Nuclear Leaders*. Washington, DC: Hudson Institute, 2010.

Fortmann, Michel, and Stéfanie von Hlatky. "The Revolution in Military Affairs (RMA) and Deterrence Stability." In *Complex Deterrence: Strategy in the Global Age*, edited by T. V. Paul, Patrick Morgan, and James Wirtz. Chicago: University of Chicago Press, 2009.

Frankel, Benjamin. "An Anxious Decade: Nuclear Proliferation in the 1990s." *Journal of Strategic Studies* 13, no. 3 (September 1990): 1–13.

———. "The Brooding Shadow: Systemic Incentives and Nuclear Weapons Proliferation." In *The Proliferation Puzzle: Why Nuclear Weapons Spread (and What Results)*, edited by Zachary Davis and Benjamin Frankel, 37–78. London: Frank Cass, 1993.

Frear, Thomas, Lukasz Kulesa, and Ian Kearns. "Dangerous Brinkmanship: Close Military Encounters Between Russia and the West in 2014." *European Leadership Network Policy Brief*, November 2014. http://www.europeanleadershipnetwork.org/medialibrary/2014/11/09/6375e3da/Dangerous%20Brinkmanship.pdf.

Freedman, Lawrence. *The Evolution of Nuclear Strategy*, 2nd ed. Basingstoke, UK, Macmillan, 1989.

———. *Deterrence*. Cambridge: Polity Press, 2004.

Friedberg, Aaron L. *Beyond Air-Sea Battle: The Debate over US Military Strategy in Asia*. Abingdon: Routledge for IISS, 2014.

Gabel, Josiane. "The Role of U.S. Nuclear Weapons after September 11." *The Washington Quarterly* 28, no. 1 (2004): 179–95.

Gallois, Pierre-Marie. *Le sablier du siècle*. Lausanne, Switzerland: L'âge d'homme, 1999.

———. *Stratégie de l'âge nucléaire*. Paris: François-Xavier de Guibert, 2009.

Garamone, Jim. "Secretary of State Clinton Meets Japanese Leaders on First Leg of Asian Tour." *Military News*, February 18, 2009. http://www.2010military.com/military-news-story.cfm?textnewsid=2747.

Gates, Robert M. *Duty: Memoirs of a Secretary of War*. New York: Alfred A. Knopf, 2014.

———. "The Security and Defense Agenda (Future of NATO)." Brussels, Belgium: June 10, 2011. http://www.defense.gov/speeches/speech.aspx?speechid=1581.

Gavin, Francis. "Same As It Ever Was: Nuclear Alarmism, Proliferation and the Cold War." *International Security* 34, no. 3 (Winter 2009–2010): 7–37.

George, Alexander. *Forceful Persuasion: Coercive Diplomacy as an Alternative to War*. Washington, DC: United States Institute of Peace Press, 1991.

George, Alexander, and Richard Smoke. *Deterrence in American Foreign Policy: Theory and Practice*. New York: Columbia University Press, 1974.

Gertz, Bill. "Inside the Ring: Obama Rejects Missile Deal." *Washington Times*, June 15, 2001. http://www.washingtontimes.com/news/2011/jun/15/inside-the-ring-380739054.

———. "U.S. Rejects Latest Russian Proposal to Restrict U.S. Missile Defenses." *Washington Free Beacon*, May 1, 2014.

Gijswijt, Thomas W. "Beyond NATO: Transnational Elite Networks and the Atlantic Alliance." In *Transforming NATO in the Cold War: Challenges Beyond Deterrence in the 1960s*, edited by Andreas Wenger, Christian Nünlist, and Anna Locher, 50–64. London: Routledge, 2007.

Gill, David J. *Britain and the Bomb*. Stanford, CA: Stanford University Press, 2014.

Glenn, John, Darryl Howlett, and Stuart Poore, eds. *Neorealism versus Strategic Culture*. Aldershot, UK: Ashgate, 2004.

Goldgeier, James M. *Not Whether but When: The U.S. Decision to Enlarge NATO*. Washington, DC: Brookings Institution, 1999.

Gompert, David C., and Martin Libicki. "Cyber Warfare and Sino-American Instability." *Survival* 56, no. 4 (August–September 2014): 7–21.

Goodman, Michael. *Spying on the Nuclear Bear. Anglo-American Intelligence on the Soviet Bomb*. Stanford, CA: Stanford University Press, 2009.

Gordon, Philip. "Charles de Gaulle and the Nuclear Revolution." In *Cold War Statesmen Confront the Bomb: Nuclear Diplomacy since 1945*, edited by John Gaddis, Philip Gordon, Ernest May, and Jonathan Rosenberg, 216–35. Oxford: Oxford University Press, 1999.

Gordon, Philip, and Jeremy Shapiro. *Allies at War: America, Europe, and the Crisis over Iraq*. New York: McGraw Hill, 2004.

Gowing, Margaret. *Independence and Deterrence: Britain and Atomic Energy 1945–1952, Volume 1: Policy Making*. Basingstoke, UK: St. Martin's Press, 1974.
Guehenno, Jean-Marie. *Défense et sécurité nationale: le livre blanc*. Paris: Odile Jacob, 2008.
Guertner, Gary L., Robert Haffa Jr., and George Quester, eds. *Conventional Forces and the Future of Deterrence*. Carlisle, PA: US Army War College, 1992.
Haftendorn, Helga. "Entstehung und Bedeutung des Harmel-Berichts der NATO von 1967." *Vierteljahrshefte für Zeitgeschichte* 40, no. 2 (April 1992): 169–220.
Hallex, Matthew. "Extended Deterrence in the Gulf." In *Nuclear Scholars Initiative: Project on Nuclear Issues*. Washington, DC: Center for Strategic and International Studies, 2011.
Hassner, Pierre. *Violence and Peace: From the Atomic Bomb to Ethnic Cleansing*. Translated by Jane Brenton. Budapest, Hungary: Central European University Press, 1997.
Hecht, Gabrielle. *The Radiance of France: Nuclear Power and National Identity after World War II*. Cambridge, MA: MIT Press, 1998.
Hennesy, Peter. *Cabinet*. London: Blackwell, 1986.
———. *Cabinets and the Bomb*. Oxford: Oxford University Press, 2007.
Heuser, Beatrice. *Nuclear Mentalities? Strategies and Beliefs in Britain and France and the FRG*. Basingstoke, UK: Macmillan Press, 1998.
Hill, Fiona, and Pamela Jewett. "Back in the USSR: Russia's Intervention in the Internal Affairs of the Former Soviet Republic and the Implications for United States Foreign Policy toward Russia." Occasional Paper, Strengthening Democratic Institutions Project, Belfer Center for Science and International Affairs, Harvard University, John F. Kennedy School of Government, Cambridge, MA, 1994.
von Hlatky, Stéfanie. *American Allies in Times of War: The Great Asymmetry*. Oxford: Oxford University Press, 2013.
Hoffman, David. "Obama's Atomic Choices: Inside the Making of U.S. Nuclear Policy." *Foreign Policy* (April 2010).
Holbrooke, Richard. *To End a War*. New York: Modern Library, 1999.
Holloway, David. "Deterrence and Enforcement in a World Free of Nuclear Weapons." In *Deterrence: Its Past and Future*, edited by George P. Schultz, Sidney D. Drell, and James E. Goodby, 335–72. Stanford, CA: Hoover Institution Press, 2011.
———. "Nuclear Weapons and the Escalation of the Cold War, 1945–1962." In *The Cambridge History of the Cold War. Volume I: Origins*, edited by Melvyn P. Leffler and Odd Arne Westad. Cambridge: Cambridge University Press, 2010.
Horovitz, Liviu. "Why Do They Want American Nukes? Central and Eastern European Positions Regarding US Nonstrategic Nuclear Weapons." *European Security* 23, no. 1 (Spring 2014): 73–89.
Horowitz, Michael C. "Nuclear Proliferation and Militarized Conflict." In *The Nuclear Renaissance and International Security*, edited by Adam Stulberg and Matthew Fuhrmann. Stanford, CA: Stanford University Press, 2013.
Howard, Michael. "Reassurance and Deterrence: Western Defense in the 1980s." *Foreign Affairs* 61, no. 2 (Winter 1982–1983): 309–24.
Hoyle, Ben, and Michael Evans. "Putin Threat of Nuclear Showdown over Baltics." *The Times*, April 2 2015.

Huth, Paul K. "Extended Deterrence and the Outbreak of War." *American Political Science Review* 82, no. 2 (June 1988): 423–43.

———. *Extended Deterrence and the Prevention of War.* New Haven, CT: Yale University Press, 1988.

———. "The Extended Deterrence Value of Nuclear Weapons," *Journal of Conflict Resolution* 34, no. 2 (1990): 270–90.

Hymans, Jacques. *Achieving Nuclear Ambitions: Scientists, Politicians and Proliferation.* Cambridge: Cambridge University Press, 2012.

———. "Britain and Hiroshima." *Journal of Strategic Studies* 32, no. 5 (October 2009): 769–97.

Ichimasa, Sukeyuki. "The Concept of Virtual Nuclear Arsenals and a World without Nuclear Weapons." *NIDS Journal of Defense and Security* 13, no. 3 (December 2012): 23–37.

Ikenberry, G. John. *After Victory: Institutions, Strategic Restraint, and the Rebuilding of International Order after Major Wars.* Princeton, NJ: Princeton University Press, 2001.

———. *Liberal Leviathan: The Origins, Crisis, and Transformation of the American World Order.* Princeton, NJ: Princeton University Press, 2011.

Iklé, Fred. "Can Nuclear Deterrence Last out the Century?" *Foreign Affairs* 51, no. 2 (January 1973): 266–85.

International Commission on Nuclear Non-Proliferation and Disarmament (ICNND). *Eliminating Nuclear Threats: A Practical Agenda for Global Policy Makers.* Canberra, Australia: ICNND, 2009.

International Institute for Strategic Studies (IISS). "Iran Sanctions Halt Long-Range Ballistic-Missile Development." *IISS Strategic* Comments 18, Comment 22, July 2012.

Jacobs, Eli. "Extending Our Umbrella to the Middle East." *Centre for Strategic and International Studies*, November 2011.

Jasper, Ursulla, and Clara Portela. "E.U. Defense Integration and Nuclear Weapons: A Common Deterrent for Europe?" *Security Dialogue* 41, no. 2 (April 2010): 145–68.

Jo, Dong-Joon, and Eric Gartzke. "Determinants of Nuclear Weapons Proliferation." *Journal of Conflict Resolution* 51 no. 1 (2007): 167–94.

Johnson, Dave. "Russia's Approach to Conflict: Implications for NATO's Deterrence and Defence." *NATO Defence College Research Division*, no. 111 (April 2015), http://www.ndc.nato.int/news/current_news.php?icode=797.

Joseph, Robert S., and John E. Reichart. "Deterrence and Defense in a Nuclear, Biological and Chemical Environment." *Comparative Strategy* 15, no. 1 (Spring 1996): 59–80.

Kagan, Robert. *Of Paradise and Power: America and Europe in the New World Order.* New York: Alfred A. Knopf, 2003.

Kamp, Karl-Heinz. "NATO's Nuclear Weapons in Europe: Beyond 'Yes' or 'No.'" *NATO Defense College, Research Division, Research Report* no. 61 (2011). http://www.ndc.nato.int/research/series.php?icode=1.

Kamp, Karl-Heinz, and Robertus C. N. Remkes. "Options for NATO Nuclear Sharing Arrangements." In *Reducing Nuclear Risks in Europe: A Framework for Action*, edited by Steve Andreasen and Isabelle Williams. Washington, DC: Nuclear

Threat Initiative, 2011. http://www.nti.org/analysis/articles/options-nato-nuclear-sharing-arrangements/.

Kampani, Gaurav, Karthika Sasikumar, Jason Stone, and Andrew B. Kennedy. "Correspondence: Debating India's Pathway to Nuclearization." *International Security* 36, no. 2 (Fall 2012): 183–96.

Kartchner, Kerry M. "Missile Defenses and New Approaches to Deterrence." U.S. Department of State, Office of International Information Program, April 2002. Accessed January 20, 2013. http://www.nti.org/media/pdfs/203.pdf?_=1316623847.

Kelleher, Catherine M. "NATO Nuclear Operations." In *Managing Nuclear Operations*, edited by Ashton B. Carter, John D. Steinbruner, and Charles A. Zraker, 445–69. Washington, DC: Brookings Institution, 1987.

Kennedy, Andrew B. "India's Nuclear Odyssey: Implicit Umbrellas, Diplomatic Disappointments and the Bomb." *International Security* 36, no. 2 (Fall 2011): 120–53.

Kilcullen, David. "New Paradigms for 21st Century Conflict: The Need for a Grand Strategy for Combating Terrorism." *E-Journal USA* 12, no. 5 (May 2007): 40–45.

Kimball, Daryl, and Tom Collina. *The Presidential Nuclear Initiatives (PNIs) on Tactical Nuclear Weapons at a Glance*. Washington, DC: Arms Control Association. www.armscontrol.org/factsheets/pniglance.

Kington, Tom. "Training Cuts Could Hurt Italian Readiness." *Defense News*, November 29, 2010.

Kipp, Jacob W. "Russian Doctrine on Tactical Nuclear Weapons: Contexts, Prisms, and Connections." In *Tactical Nuclear Weapons and NATO*, edited by Tom Nichols, Douglas Stuart, and Jeffrey D. McCausland, 116–54. Carlisle, PA: US Strategic Studies Institute, 2012.

Kissinger, Henry A. "Don't Rule Out Putin's Initiative." *New York Times*, August 9, 2007.

Knopf, Jeffrey W. "The Fourth Wave in Deterrence Research." *Contemporary Security Policy* 31, no. 1 (April 2010): 1–33.

———. "Introduction." In *Security Assurances and Nuclear Proliferation*, edited by Jeffrey W. Knopf, 1–12. Stanford, CA: Stanford University Press, 2012.

Kohl, Wilfrid. "Nuclear Sharing in NATO and the Multilateral Force." *Political Science Quarterly* (March 1965): 88–109.

Korchunov, Nikolai. "You say Defense, We Say Threat." *New York Times*, June 6, 2012.

Krause, Joachim. "Emerging Concepts of Deterrence in the 21st Century." In *NATO and 21st Century Deterrence*, edited by Karl-Heinz Kamp and David S. Yost, 143–52. Rome: NATO Defense College, Research Division, 2009.

———. "Multilateralism behind European Views." *The Washington Quarterly* 27, no. 2 (2004): 43–59.

Krause, Joachim, and Charles King Mallory IV. "Strategic Implications of the Iranian Nuclear Programme." In *Iran's Nuclear Programme: Strategic Implications*, edited by Joachim Krause, 11–33. London: Routledge, 2012.

Krause, Joachim, and Benjamin Schreer. "Salvaging Global Zero: Diplomacy in the Second Nuclear Age," *RUSI Journal* 155, no. 3 (June/July 2010): 48–52.

Kristensen, Hans M. "B61 LEP: Increasing NATO Nuclear Capability and Precision Low-Yield Strikes." *FAS Strategic Security Blog*, June 15, 2011. http://www.fas.org/blog/ssp/2011/06/b61-12.php.

———. "B61-12: NNSA's Gold-Plated Nuclear Bomb Project." *FAS Strategic Security Blog.* July 26, 2012. http://blogs.fas.org/security/2012/07/b61-12gold/.

———. "Non-Strategic Nuclear Weapons." Federation of the American Scientists, May 2012. http://www.fas.org/_docs/Non_Strategic_Nuclear_Weapons.pdf.

———. "US Navy Instruction Confirms Retirement of Nuclear Tomahawk Cruise Missiles." *FAS Strategic Security Blog,* March 18, 2013. http://blogs.fas.org/security/2013/03/tomahawk/.

———. "US Nuclear Weapons Withdrawn from the United Kingdom." *FAS Strategic Security Blog,* June 26, 2008. http://www.fas.org/blog/ssp/2008/06/us-nuclear-weapons-withdrawn-from-the-united-kingdom.php.

Kulesa, Lukasz. "Extended Deterrence and Assurance in Central Europe." In *Perspectives on Extended Deterrence,* Recherches & Documents, No. 3/2010, 119–27. Paris: Fondation pour la Recherche Stratégique, 2010.

Lacouture, Jean. *Pierre Mendès France.* Paris: Seuil, 1981.

Lahti, Makreeta. "Security Cooperation as a Way to Stop the Spread of Nuclear Weapons? Nuclear Non-Proliferation Policies of the United States towards the Federal Republic of German and Israel, 1945–1968." PhD diss., University of Potsdam, 2008.

Lanata, Vincent. "Faire face: l'ere des nouveaux defies." *Défense Nationale* 49 (August/September 1993): 12–13.

Landler, Mark. "Obama Says Pact Obliges US to Protect Japan in Islands Fight." *New York Times,* April 24, 2014.

Larrabee, F. Stephen. "NATO Forces Approach Financial Day of Reckoning." *Rand Review* 36, no. 3 (2012/2013): 17–19.

Larrabee, F. Stephen, Stuart E. Johnson, John Gordon IV, Peter A. Wilson, Caroline Baxter, Deborah Lai, and Cali Trekoy-Wermuth. *NATO and the Challenges of Austerity.* Santa Monica, CA: RAND, 2012.

Larsen, Jeffrey A. "The Future of U.S. Non-Strategic Nuclear Weapons and Implications for NATO: Drifting Toward the Foreseeable Future." *Final Report from the 2005–06 Manfred Wörner Fellowship.* Brussels, Belgium: NATO Headquarters, December 2007.

———. "Future Options for NATO Nuclear Policy." *The Atlantic Council Issue Brief,* August 2011. http://www.acus.org/publication/future-options-nato-nuclear-policy.

Lasserre, Isabelle. "Moyen-Orient: la France se donne les moyens de riposte." *Le Figaro,* June 1, 2009.

———. "Les partisans du Global Zero misent sur Obama." *Le Figaro,* December 8, 2008.

Lebovic, James. *Deterring International Terrorism and Rogue States: US National Security Policy after 9/11.* London: Routledge, 2007.

Ledwige, Bernard. *De Gaulle et les Américains. Conversations avec Eisenhower, Kennedy, Rusk, 1958–1964.* Paris: Flammarion, 1984.

Lee, Seok-Soo. "The Future of Extended Deterrence: A South Korean Perspective." In *Perspectives on Extended Deterrence,* Recherches & Documents, No. 3/2012, 49–60. Paris: Fondation pour la Recherche Stratégique, 2012.

le Geulte, Georges. *Les armes nucléaires. Mythes et réalités.* Arles, France: Actes Sud, 2009.

le Mière, Christian. "The Spectre of an Asian Arms Race." *Survival* 56, no. 1 (February–March 2014): 139–56.

Levgold, Robert H. "Reconciling Limitations on Non-Strategic Nuclear Weapons, Conventional Arms Control, and Missile Defense Cooperation." In *Reducing Nuclear Risks in Europe: A Framework for Action*, edited by Steve Andreasen and Isabelle Williams, 134–51. Washington, DC: Nuclear Threat Initiative, 2011.

Levite, Ariel E. "Reflections on Extended Deterrence in the Middle East." *Recherches et Documents* (IFRI) no. 3 (2010).

Lewis, Jeffrey G. "Chinese Nuclear Posture and Modernisation." In *Engaging China and Russia in Nuclear Disarmament*, edited by Christina Hansell and Wiliam Potter, 37–47. Occasional Paper no 15. Monterey, CA: James Martin Center for Nonproliferation Studies, 2009.

———. "From Extended Deterrence to Core Deterrence." *The Interpreter*, February 18, 2011. http://www.lowyinterpreter.org/post/2011/02/18/The-myth-of-the-nuclear-umbrella.aspx.

———. "Minimum Deterrence." *Bulletin of the Atomic Scientists* (July–August 2008). http://www.newamerica.net/publications/articles/2008/minimum_deterrence_7552.

———. *The Minimum Means of Reprisal: China's Search for Security in the Nuclear Age*. Cambridge, MA: MIT Press, 2007.

Libicki, Martin. *Cyberdeterrence and Cyberwar*. Santa Monica, CA: RAND, 2009.

Lieber, Keir A., and Daryl G. Press. "The End of MAD? The Nuclear Dimension of U.S. Primacy." *International Security* 30, no. 4 (Spring 2006): 7–44.

———. "The New Era of Nuclear Weapons, Deterrence, and Conflict." *Strategic Studies Quarterly* 7, no. 1 (Spring 2013): 3–14.

———. "The Rise of U.S. Nuclear Primacy." *Foreign Affairs* 85, no. 2 (March/April 2006): 42–54.

———. "Superiority Complex: Why America's Growing Nuclear Supremacy May Make War with China More Likely." *Atlantic Monthly* 300, no. 1 (July/August 2007): 86–92.

Long, Austin. *Deterrence from Cold War to Long War: Lessons from Six Decades of RAND Research*. Santa Monica, CA: RAND, 2008.

Lunn, Simon. "NATO Nuclear Policy—Reflections on Lisbon and Looking Ahead." Draft chapter for *The NTI Study on Nuclear Weapons and NATO*, forthcoming.

———. "The Role and Place of Tactical Nuclear Weapons—A NATO Perspective." In *Tactical Nuclear Weapons and NATO*, edited by Tom Nichols, Douglas Stuart, and Jeffrey D. MacCausland, 235–56. Carlisle, PA: US Army War College, 2012.

Lunn, Simon, and Ian Kearns. "NATO's Deterrence and Defense Posture Review: A Status Report." *London, European Leadership Network for Multilateral Nuclear Disarmament and Nonproliferation*, February 2011.

———. "NATO's Nuclear Policy after Lisbon: The Summit Documents and the Way Ahead." *ELN Background Brief*, London. European Leadership Network for Multilateral Nuclear Disarmament and Non-Proliferation, 2011.

Maddock, Shane. *Nuclear Apartheid: The American Quest for Nuclear Supremacy from World War II*. Chapel Hill: University of North Carolina Press, 2010.

Maguire, Richard. "'Never a Credible Weapon': Nuclear Cultures in British Government during the Era of the H-Bomb." *British Journal of History of Science* 45, no. 4 (December 2012): 519–33.

Mallard, Grégoire. "L'Europe puissance nucléaire: cet obscur objet du désir." *Critique internationale*, no. 42 (2009).

Mann, William. "U.S. Reaffirms Promise to Defend South Korea." *Associated Press*, October 21, 2006.

Markov, N. E. "Views of the *Ministry of Defense of the Russian Federation* on Missile Defense Issues." 2012. http://mil.ru/files/morf/Eng_Views-Of-The-Ministry-Of-Defense-Of-The-Russian-Federation-On-Missile-Defense-Issues.ppt.

Mazzar, Michael J., ed. *Nuclear Weapons in a Transformed World: The Challenge of Virtual Nuclear Arsenals.* New York: St. Martin's Press, 1997.

———. *Reframing Nuclear De-Alert: Decreasing the Operational Readiness of U.S. and Russian Arsenals.* New York: The East-West Institute, 2009.

McKenzie Jr., Kenneth. *The Revenge of the Melians: Assymetric Threats and the Next QDR.* McNair Paper 62. Washington, DC: National Defense University, 2000.

Mearscheimer, John. "Back to the Future: Instability in Europe after the Cold War." *International Security* 15, no. 1 (Summer 1990): 5–56.

———. "The Case for a Ukrainian Nuclear Deterrent." *Foreign Affairs* 72, no 3 (Summer 1993): 50–66.

Miller, James. *Questions Submitted by Members Post Hearing.* Strategic Forces Subcommittee, House Armed Services Committee, November 2, 2011. http://www.fas.org/irp/congress/2011_hr/nw-qfr.pdf.

Millot, Marc Dean. "Facing the Emerging Reality of Regional Nuclear Adversaries." *The Washington Quarterly* 17, no. 3 (Summer 1994): 41–71.

Ministry of Foreign Affairs of Japan. *Treaty of Mutual Cooperation and Security between Japan and the United States of America.* Ministry of Foreign Affairs, January 1960. http://www.mofa.go.jp/region/n-america/us/q&a/ref/1.html.

Misher, Kimberly. "Why Obama Is Right on Missile Defense—What's Next?" *Carnegie Endowment for International Peace Policy Outlook*, September, 2009. Accessed January 20, 2013. http://www.carnegieendowment.org/files/misher_missile_defense.pdf.

Mongin, Dominique. *La bombe atomique française. 1945–1958.* Brussels, Belgium: Bruylant, 1997.

Montgomery, Evan Braden. "Contested Primary in the Western Pacific: China's Rise and the Future of US Power Projection." *International Security* 38, no. 4. (Spring 2014): 115–49.

Morgan, Patrick M. "Collective-Actor Deterrence." In *Complex Deterrence: Strategy in the Global Age*, edited by T. V. Paul and J. J. Wirtz. Chicago: University of Chicago Press, 2009.

———. *Deterrence: A Conceptual Analysis.* Beverly Hills, CA: Sage Publications, 1977.

———. "Evaluating Tailored Deterrence." In *NATO and 21st Century Deterrence*, edited by Karl-Heinz Kamp and David S. Yost. Rome: NATO Defense College, Research Division, 2009.

———. "The State of Deterrence in International Politics Today," *Contemporary Security Policy* 33, no. 1 (2012): 85–107.

Murdock, Clark, and Jessica Yeats. "Summary of Findings and Recommendations from 3 June 2009 Workshop on Extended Deterrence." Unpublished PPT presentation, Center for Strategic and International Studies, Washington, DC, 2009.

National Intelligence Council. *Foreign Missile Developments and the Ballistic Missile Threat Through 2015, Unclassified Summary of National Intelligence Estimate.* National Intelligence Council, September 1999. http://www.fas.org/irp/threat/missile/nie99msl.htm.

Nitze, Paul. "Atoms, Strategy, and Policy." *Foreign Affairs* 34, no. 2 (1956).

North Atlantic Treaty Organization. "Active Engagement, Modern Defence: Strategic Concept for the Defence and Security of the Members of the North Atlantic Treaty Organization." November 2010.

———. "Active Engagement, Modern Defense. Strategic Concept for the Defense and Security of the Members of the North Atlantic Treaty Organization. Adopted by Heads of State and Government in Lisbon." North Atlantic Treaty Organization, Lisbon, 2010.

———. *The Alliance's Strategic Concept.* North Atlantic Treaty Organization, April 1999.

———. *Chicago Summit Declaration, Issued by the Heads of State and Government Participating in the Meeting of the North Atlantic Council in Chicago.* North Atlantic Treaty Organization, Chicago, 2012.

———. *Deterrence and Defense Posture Review.* North Atlantic Treaty Organization, Chicago, May 20, 2012.

———. *Founding Act on Mutual Relations, Cooperation and Security between NATO and the Russian Federation.* North Atlantic Treaty Organization, Paris, 1997.

———. "Lisbon Summit Declaration. Issued by the Heads of State and Government Participating in the Meeting of the North Atlantic Council in Lisbon." North Atlantic Treaty Organization, Lisbon, 2010.

———. "*NATO's Nuclear Forces.*" North Atlantic Treaty Organization. Last updated October 27, 2010. http://www.nato.int/cps/fr/SID-02093EB1A95A4062/natolive/topics_50068.htm?blnSublanguage=true&selectedLocale=uk&submit=select.

———. "NATO's Nuclear Policy in the New Security Environment." *NATO Issue Brief.* Brussels, Belgium: NATO Headquarters, June 2004.

———. *NATO/OTAN Handbook.* Brussels, Belgium: NATO Office of Information and Press, 2011.

———. "NATO 2020: Assured Security; Dynamic Engagement. Analysis and Recommendations of the Group of Experts on a New Strategic Concept for NATO." NATO Public Affairs Division, Brussels, Belgium, 2010. www.nato.int/strategic-concept/expertsreport.pdf.

———. *Statement by NATO Foreign Ministers.* North Atlantic Treaty Organization, April 2014. Accessed December 14, 2014. http://www.nato.int/cps/en/natolive/news_108501.htm.

———. *Wales Summit Declaration: Issued by the Heads of State and Government participating in the meeting of the North Atlantic Council in Wales.* North Atlantic Treaty Organization, September 2014. http://www.nato.int/cps/ic/natohq/official_texts_112964.htm.

Nuclear Threat Initiative. "Threat on the Limitation of Anti-Ballistic Missile Systems (ABM Treaty)." May 26, 1972. http://ww.nti.org/treaties-and-regimes/treaty-limitation-anti-ballistic-missile-systems-abm-treaty/.

Obama, Barack. "Remarks by President Barack Obama." Hradcany Square, Prague, Czech Republic, April 5, 2009. www.whitehouse.gov/the_press_office/Remarks-By-President-Barack-Obama_In-Prague.

Obama, Barack. "Remarks by the President on Strengthening Missile Defense in Europe." September 17, 2009. Accessed January 23, 2013. http://www.whitehouse.gov/the-press-office/remarks-president-strengthening-missile-defense-europe.

Office of Public Affairs and Office of the Secretary of Defense. "Pentagon Briefing: 2002 Nuclear Posture Review": *Fact Sheet*, (January 2002).

Oswald, Rachel. "Arms Control Groups Accuse NATO of Keeping Nuclear Status Quo." *NTI*, May 22, 2012. http://www.nti.org/gsn/article/nato-failed-change-nuclear-status-quo-experts/.

———. "Iran Nuclear Deal May Affect Missile Shield: German Envoy." *Global Security Newswire*, December 4, 2013.

———. "U.S. Official Defends Spending on NATO Missile Shield, under GOP Attack." *Global Security Newswire*, June 15, 2013.

———. "U.S. Official: 'Not Making Much Progress' with Russia on Missiles, Arms." *Defense One*, November 13, 2013.

Paul, T. V., Patrick M. Morgan, and James J. Wirtz. *Complex Deterrence: Strategy in the Global Age*. Chicago: The University of Chicago Press, 2009.

Payne, Keith B. *The Fallacies of Cold War Deterrence and a New Direction*. Lexington: University of Kentucky Press, 2001.

———. *The Greater American Gamble: Deterrence Theory and Practice from the Cold War to the Twenty-First Century*. Fairfax, VA: National Institute Press, 2008.

———. "Maintaining Flexible and Resilient Capabilities for Nuclear Deterrence." *Strategic Studies Quarterly* (Summer 2011): 13–29.

Pelopidas, Benoit. "French Nuclear Idiosyncrasy: How It Affects French Nuclear Policies towards the United Arab Emirates and Iran." *Cambridge Review of International Affairs* 25, no. 1 (March 2012): 143–69.

———. *Renoncer à l'arme nucleaire: La seduction de l'impossible?* Paris: Presses de Sciences Po, forthcoming.

———. "Renunciation: Restraint, Reversal and Rollback." In *Routledge Handbook of Nuclear Proliferation and Policy*, edited by Joseph Pilat and Nathan Busch. London: Routledge, 2015.

People's Republic of China, Disarmament Commission, United Nations. *Recommendations for Achieving the Objective of Nuclear Disarmament and Nonproliferation of Nuclear Weapons*. United Nations (A.CN.10/2006/WG.I/WP.3.). April 2006.

Perkovich, George, Malcolm Chalmers, Steven Pifer, Paul Schulte, and Jaclyn Tandler. *Looking beyond the Chicago Summit: Nuclear Weapons in Europe and the Future of NATO*. Washington, DC: The Carnegie Endowment for International Peace, 2012.

Perry, William J., and James R. Schlesinger. *America's Strategic Posture: The Final Report of the Congressional Commission on the Strategic Posture of the United States*. Washington, DC: United States Institute of Peace, 2008.

Perry, William, Brent Scowcroft, and Charles Ferguson. *U.S. Nuclear Weapons Policy*. New York: Council on Foreign Relations, 2009.

Peruzzi, Luca. "Italian Force Cuts Hit JSF Numbers." *Jane's Defence Weekly*, February 22, 2012.

Peyrefitte, Alain. *Le mal français*. Paris: Plon, 1976.

Pifer, Steven. "The Missing Missile Defense Piece at the NATO Summit of Chicago." Brookings Institution, May 15, 2012. http://www.brookings.edu/blogs/up-front/posts/2012/05/15-nato-summit-pifer.

———. "NATO, Nuclear Weapons, and Arms Control." *The Brookings Institution Arms Control Series* no. 7, (July 2011).

———. "The United States, NATO's Strategic Concept, and Nuclear Issues: Perspectives and Proposals in the NATO Policy Debate." Arms Control Association and British-American Information Committee, May 2011.

Pifer, Steven, Richard C. Bush, Vanda Felbab-Brown, Martin S. Indyk, Michael O'Hanlon, and Kenneth M. Waltz. "US Nuclear and Extended Deterrence: Considerations and Challenges." *Brookings Arms Control Series* 3 (May 2010).

Pifer, Steven, and Michael O'Hanlon. *The Opportunity: Next Steps in Reducing Nuclear Arms.* Washington, DC: Brookings Institution Press, January 2013.

Pô, Jean-Damien. *Les moyens de la puissance. Les activites militaires du CEA (1945–2000).* Paris: Ellipses, 2000.

Podvig, Pavel, ed. "Instrumental Influences: Russia and the 2010 Nuclear Posture Review." *Nonproliferation Review* 18, no. 1 (March 2011): 39–50.

———. "Soviet and Russian Strategic Nuclear Forces." In *Russian Strategic Nuclear Forces*, 1–31. Boston: MIT Press, 2011.

Polish Institute for International Affairs. "The Warsaw Workshop: Prospects for Information Sharing and Confidence Building on Non-Strategic Nuclear Weapons in Europe." Polish Institute for International Affairs, April 2013. http://www.pism.pl/publications/reports/PISM-Report-The-Warsaw-Workshop-Prospects-for-Information-Sharing-and-Confidence-Building-on-Non-Strategic-Nuclear-Weapons-in-Europe.

Porter, Richard E. "Correlation of Forces: Revolutionary Legacy." *Air University Review* (March/April 1977).

Potter, William. "Back to the Future: Contemporary Relevance of the Nuclear Renunciation Decisions of Ukraine, Belarus, and Kazakhstan." Paper for the Nobel Institute Conference on the Spread of Nuclear Weapons: Past Experience and Future Challenges, Oslo, 2009.

Powell, Robert. *Nuclear Deterrence Theory: The Search for Credibility.* Cambridge: Cambridge University Press, 1990.

Quester, George H., and Victor A. Utgoff. "No First-Use and Nonproliferation: Redefining Extended Deterrence." *The Washington Quarterly* 17, no. 2 (Spring 1994): 103–14.

Reagan, Ronald. "Address to the Nation on Defense and National Security." March 3, 1983. http://www.atomicarchive.com/Docs/Missile/Starwars.shtml.

———. "Star Wars Speech." March 23, 1983. Accessed January 23, 2013. www.pierretristam.com/Bobst/library/wf-241.htm.

Remkes, Robertus C. N. "The Security of NATO Nuclear Weapons: Issues and Implications." In *Reducing Nuclear Risks in Europe: A Framework for Action*, edited by Steve Andreasen and Isabelle Williams, 66–75. Washington, DC: Nuclear Threat Initiative, 2011.

Resnick, Evan N. "Strange Bedfellows: US Bargaining Behavior with Allies of Convenience." *International Security* 35, no 3 (2010–11): 144–84.

Richardson, Philip L. "Proliferation and the Challenge to Deterrence." *Strategic Review* 23 (Spring 1995): 38–48.

Roberts, Brad. *China-US Nuclear Relations: What Relationship Best Serves U.S. Interests?* Alexandria, VA: Institute for Defense Analyses, 2001.

———. "Extended Deterrence and Strategic Stability in Northeast Asia." The National Institute for Defense Studies, Visiting Scholars Paper Series, no. 1 (August 2013).

———. "Great Power Deterrence and Relationships in the Early 21st Century." In *NATO and 21st Century Deterrence*, edited by Karl-Heinz Kamp and David S. Yost, 100–110. Rome: NATO Defense College, Research Division, 2009. http://www.nids.go.jp/english/publication/visiting/index.html.

Roccard, Yves. *Mémoires sans concession*. Paris: Grasset, 1988.

Rohlfing, Joan, Isabelle Williams, and Steve Andreasen. "Reassembling a More Credible NATO Nuclear Policy and Posture." In *Reducing Nuclear Risks in Europe: A Framework for Action*, edited by Steve Andreasen and Isabelle Williams, 1–7. Washington, DC: Nuclear Threat Initiative, 2011.

Rojansky, Matthew. "Russia and Strategic Stability" In *Strategic Stability: Contending Interpretations*, edited by Elbridge A. Colby and Michael S. Gerson, 295–342. Carlisle, PA: US Army War College Press, 2013.

Rose, Frank A. "Challenges in Europe." *Bureau of Verification, Compliance, and Implementation Remarks at the 6th International Conference on Missile Defense*, Lisbon, Portugal, 2010. Accessed January 23, 2013. http://www.state.gov/t/avc/rls/137991.htm.

Rubin, Uzi. "Showcase of Missile Proliferation: Iran's Missile and Space Program." *Arms Control Today* 42 (January/February 2012): 14–20.

Rühle, Michael. "NATO and Extended Deterrence in a Multinuclear World." *Comparative Strategy* 28, no. 1 (February 2009): 10–16.

———. "NATO and Nuclear Weapons." In *Understanding NATO in the 21st Century: Alliance Strategies, Security, and Global Governance*, edited by Graeme P. Herd and John Kriendler. London: Routledge 2013.

Russell, James A. "Extended Deterrence, Security Guarantees and Nuclear Weapons: US Strategic and Policy Conundrums in the Gulf," *Strategic Insights* 3, no. 5 (2009): 16–26.

———. "Nuclear Proliferation and the Middle East's Security Dilemma: The Case of Saudi Arabia." In *Over the Horizon Proliferation Threats*, edited by James J. Wirtz and Peter Lavoy, 47–67. Stanford, CA: Stanford University Press, 2012.

Russell, Richard L. "Military Options for Preventing a Nuclear-Armed Iran." In *Iran's Nuclear Programme: Strategic Implications*, edited by Joachim Krause, 137–58. London: Routledge, 2012.

Rusten, Lynn F. "U.S. Withdrawal from the ABM Treaty." *Center for the Study of Weapons of Mass Destruction*, Case Study 2. Washington, DC: National Defense University Press, 2010. Accessed January 20, 2013. http://www.ndu.edu/press/lib/images/occasionalPapers/cswmd-cs2.pdf.

Ryan, Kevin. "The Elbe Group: Meetings of Military Minds." *InFocus*, Winter 2014.

Rydell, Randy. "The United Nations and a Humanitarian Approach to Nuclear Disarmament." *Nuclear Abolition Forum*, no. 1 (October 2011).

Sagan, Scott D. "Causes of Nuclear Proliferation." *Annual Review of Political Science* 14 (June 2011): 225–44.

———. "Shared Responsibilities for Nuclear Disarmament." *Daedalus* 138, no. 4 (Fall 2009): 157–68.

———. "Why Do States Build Nuclear Weapons? Three Models in Search of a Bomb." *International Security* 21, no. 3 (Winter 1996/1997): 54–86.

Sagan, Scott D., and Kenneth Waltz. *The Spread of Nuclear Weapons. A Debate.* New York: W. W. Norton, 1995.

Sang-Hun, Cheo. "Two Koreas in Doomsday Threats after Vote at U.N." *New York Times*, March 9, 2013.

Sankaran, Jaganath. "Missile Defense against Iran without Threatening Russia." *Arms Control Today*, November 2013.

Sauer, Tom, and Bob van der Zwaan. "US Tactical Nuclear Weapons in Europe after NATO's Lisbon Summit: Why Their Withdrawal Is Desirable and Feasible." *Harvard Kennedy School, Belfer Center Discussion Paper*, no. 2911-05 (May 2011).

Sayler, Kelly. "2011 Nuclear Policy Conferences Summary: Extended Deterrence and the 21st Century." Center for Strategic and International Studies, April 2011. http://csis.org/blog/2011-nuclear-policy-conference-summary-extended-deterrence-and-21st-century.

Schaub Jr., Gary. "When Is Deterrence Necessary? Gauging Adversary Intent." *Strategic Studies Quarterly* 3, no. 4 (Winter 2009): 49–74.

Schelling, Thomas C. *Arms and Influence.* New Haven, CT: Yale University Press, 1966.

———. "A World without Nuclear Weapons?" *Daedalus* 138, no. 4 (Fall 2009): 124–29.

Schneider, Mark. "The Future of the U.S. Nuclear Deterrent." *Comparative Strategy* 27, no. 4 (2008): 345–60.

———. *The Nuclear Forces and Doctrine of the Russian Federation.* Fairfax, VA: National Institute Press, 2006.

———. "Preventing through Strength: Is Nuclear Superiority Enough?" *Comparative Strategy* 28, no. 2 (2009): 116–39.

Schreber, Thomas. "Contemporary Challenges for Extended Deterrence." Unpublished paper for National Institute of Public Policy, Washington, DC, 2009.

Schulte, Paul. "Is NATO's Nuclear Deterrence Policy a Relic of the Cold War?" *Carnegie Endowment for International Peace Policy Outlook* (November 2010).

———. "Tactical Nuclear Weapons in NATO and Beyond: A Historical and Thematic Examination." In *Tactical Nuclear Weapons and NATO*, edited by Tom Nichols, Douglas Stuart, and Jeffrey D. McCausland, 13–74. Carlisle, PA: US Strategic Studies Institute, 2012. http://www.strategicstudiesinstitute.army.mil/pdffiles/PUB1103.pdf.

Schultz, Teri. "Robert Gates Blasts NATO Members in Final Speech." *Global Post*, June 10, 2011.

Segell, Glenn. "Nuclear Delivery Systems Resulting from the MDA." In *U.S.-U.K. Nuclear Cooperation after 50 Years*, edited by Jennifer Mackby and Paul Cornish, 114–125. Washington, DC: Center for Strategic and International Studies, 2008.

Shambaugh, David. *Modernizing China's Military: Progress, Problems and Prospects.* Berkeley: University of California Press, 2002.

Shanker, Thom, and Norimitsu Onishi. "Japan Assures Rice That It Has No Nuclear Intentions," *New York Times*, October 19, 2006.

Shlaim, Avi. "Israel and the Conflict." In *International Perspectives on the Gulf Conflict, 1990–1991*, edited by Alex Danchev and Dan Keohane, 59–79. London: St Martin's Press, 1994. Accessed January 20, 2013. http://users.ox.ac.uk/~ssfc0005/Israel%20and%20the%20Conflict.html.

Shultz, George P., William J. Perry, Henry A. Kissinger, and Sam Nunn. "A World Free of Nuclear Weapons." *Wall Street Journal*, January 4, 2007.

Simon Ball. "Military Nuclear Relations between the United States and Great Britain under the Terms of the MacMahon Act, 1946–1958." *The History Journal* 38, no. 2 (June 1995): 439–54.

Simpson, John. "Options for the United Kingdom's Nuclear Weapons Programme: Deterrence, Disarmament, Non-Proliferation and UK Trident." Discussion Paper for the BASIC Trident Commission 2014. http://www.basicint.org/sites/default/files/basic_tridentcommission_johnsimpsonbrief_mar2013.pdf.

Simpson, John, and Jennifer Mackby. "The Special Nuclear Relationship: A Historical Chronology." In *U.S.-U.K. Nuclear Cooperation after 50 Years*, edited by Jennifer Mackby and Paul Cornish, 3–22. Washington, DC: Center for Strategic and International Studies, 2008.

Singh, Sonali, and Christopher R. Way. "The Correlates of Nuclear Proliferation: A Quantitative Test." *Journal of Conflict Resolution* 48, no. 6 (2004): 859–85.

Snyder, Jack. *The Soviet Strategic Culture: Implications for Limited Nuclear Operations.* Santa Monica, CA: RAND, 1977.

Sokolski, Henry D. *Best of Intentions: America's Campaign against Strategic Weapons Proliferation.* London: Praeger, 2001.

Sokov, Nicolai. "The Evolving Role of Nuclear Weapons in Russia's Security Policy." In *Engaging China and Russia in Nuclear Disarmament*, edited by Cristina Hansell and William Potter, 73–88. Monterey, CA: James Martin Center for Nonproliferation Studies, 2009.

———. "The 'Return' of Nuclear Weapons." *Open Democracy*, November 28, 2014. https://www.opendemocracy.net/od-russia/nikolai-sokov/'return'-of-nuclear-weapons.

———. "The New, 2010 Russian Military Doctrine: The Nuclear Age." James Martin Center for Nonproliferation Studies, February 5, 2010.

Soubrouillard, Régis. "La France, parapluie nucléaire des Emirats Arabes Unis?" *Marianne* 2, June 17, 2009.

Soutou, Georges-Henri. "La politique nucléaire de Pierre Mendès France." *Relations Internationales* 59 (1989): 317–30.

———. "Les accords de 1957 et 1958: vers une communauté stratégique nucléaire entre la France, l'Allemagne et l'Italie?" *Matériaux pour l'histoire de notre temps* 6, no. 31 (1993): 1–12.

Soutou, Georges-Henri, and Leopoldo Nuti. "The F-I-G Story Revisited." *Special Issue of the Journal Storia delle Relazioni Internazionali* 13, no. 1 (1998): 69–100.

Stein, Aaron. "Turkey, Tactical Nuclear Weapons, and Strategic Thinking." *Turkey Wonk Blog*, May 16, 2013. http://turkeywonk.wordpress.com/.

Stocker, Jeremy. "The Strategy of Missile Defense: Defence, Deterrence, and Diplomacy." *RUSI Journal* 156, no. 3 (June/July 2011): 56–62.

Stoddart, Kristan. "British Nuclear Strategy during the Cold War." In *The British Way in Cold Warfare: Intelligence, Diplomacy and the Bomb*, edited by Matthew Grant, 15–31. London: Continuum, 2009.

Tanter, Richard. "Rethinking Extended Nuclear Deterrence in the Defense of Australia." *The Asia Pacific Journal: Japan Focus* (December 2009). http://www.japanfocus.org/-richard-tanter/3269.

Tertrais, Bruno. "Defining the Right Mix of Capabilities: The Irreplaceable Role of NATO Nuclear Arrangements." In *Managing Change: NATO's Partnerships and Deterrence in a Globalised World*, Report from NATO Conference in Bologna, 1–7. June 2011.

———. "Extended Deterrence: Alive and Changing." *Lowy Institute for International Policy, The Interpreter*, February 2011. www.lowyinterpreter.org/post/2011/02/02/Extended-Deterrence-Alive-and-Changing.

———. "Nuclear Proliferation in Europe: Could It Still Happen?" *Nonproliferation Review* 13, no. 3 (November 2006): 569–79.

———. *La France et la dissuasion nucléaire: Concept, moyens, avenir*. Paris: La Documentation Française, 2007.

———. "The Illogic of Zero." *Washington Quarterly* 33, no. 2 (April 2010): 125–38.

The Acronym Institute. "News in Review: Chirac Reasserts French Nuclear Weapons Policy." The Acronym Institute, 2006. http://www.acronym.org.uk/dd/dd82/82chirac.htm.

The Strategic Posture Review Commission. *America's Strategic Posture: The Final Report of the Congressional Commission on the Strategic Posture of the United States*. Washington, DC: United States Institute for Peace, 2009.

The White House. *National Security Strategy*. Washington, DC: May 2010. http://www.whitehouse.gov/sites/default/files/rss_viewer/national_security_strategy.pdf.

Thielmann, Greg. "The National Missile Defense Act of 1999." *Arms Control Today* 39 (July/August 2009). Accessed January 20, 2013. http://www.armscontrol.org/act/2009_07-08/lookingback.

Thomas, Timothy L. "Reflexive Control Theory and the Military," *Journal of Slavic Military Studies* 17 (2004): 237–56.

Thornton, Red. *Asymmetric Warfare. Threat and Response in the 21st Century*. Cambridge: Polity Press, 2007.

Thränert, Oliver. "Europe's Need for a Damage Limitation Option." In *Readings in European Security*, edited by Michael Emerson, 62–77. Bruxelles: Centre for European Policy Studies/London: International Institute for Security Studies/Geneva: Geneva Centre for the Democratic Control of Armed Forces/Geneva: Geneva Centre for Security Policy, 2009.

———. "NATO, Missile Defence and Extended Deterrence." *Survival* 51, no. 6 (December 2009/January 2010): 63–76.

———. "Nuclear Arms and Missile Defense in Transatlantic Security." In *European Security and the Future of Transatlantic Relations*, edited by Riccardo Alcaro and Erik Jones, 69–86. Rome: Instituto Affari Internazionale, 2011.

Till, Geoffrey. *Asia's Naval Expansion: An Arms Race in the Making?* Abingdon: Routledge for IIS, 2012.

Trachtenberg, David J. "U.S. Extended Deterrence: How Much Strategic Force Is Too Little?" *Strategic Studies Quarterly* 6, no. 2 (Summer 2012): 62–92.

Trenin, Dmitri. "Post Imperium—A Eurasian Story." Washington, DC: Carnegie Endowment for International Peace, 2011.

Trexel, Jonathan. *Deterring the Democratic People's Republic of Korea: The Role of Japan's Ballistic Missile Defense.* Lincoln, NE: University of Nebraska, 2013. http://digitalcommons.unl.edu/cgi/viewcontent.cgi?article=1028&context=poliscitheses.

Ülgen, Sinan. "Turkey and the Bomb." *Carnegie Papers.* Washington, DC: Carnegie Endowment for International Peace, 2012.

US Department of Defense. *Ballistic Missile Defense Report.* Washington, DC: US Department of Defense, February 2010. http://www.defense.gov/bmdr/.

———. *Ballistic Missile Defense Review Fact Sheet.* US Department of Defense. March 2013. Accessed January 23, 2013. http://www.defense.gov/bmdr/docs/BMDR%20FACT%20SHEET%20March%202010%20_Final_.pdf.

———. *Conduct of the Persian Gulf War, Final Report to Congress.* April 1992. www.ndu.edu/library/epubs/cpgw.pdf.

———. *Nuclear Posture Review, 2010.* US Department of Defense, 2010. Accessed September 25, 2013. www.defense.gov/npr/docs/2010%20Nuclear%20Posture%20Review%20Report.pdf.

———. *Quadrennial Defense Review Report.* Washington, DC: US Government Printing Office, 2006.

———. *Report of the Secretary of Defense Task Force on DoD Nuclear Weapons Management—Phase II: Review of the DoD Nuclear Mission.* US Department of Defense, December 2008. www.defense.gov/pubs/pdfs/PhaseIIReportFinal.pdf.

US Department of Defense, Office of the Assistant Secretary of Defense, Public Affairs. *Missile Defense Announcement as Delivered by Secretary of Defense Chuck Hagel.* The Pentagon, March 15, 2013.

US Department of Defense, Office of the Secretary of Defense. *Ballistic Missile Defense Review Report.* February 2010.

———. *Nuclear Posture Review Report.* May 2010.

———. *Quadrennial Defense Review Report.* February 2010.

US Department of State. *Dispatch* 3, no. 25 (June 22, 1992). http://dosfan.lib.uic.edu/ERC/briefing/dispatch/1992/html/Dispatchv3no25.html.

———. "Missile Defense: Road to Cooperation." Remarks by Ellen Tauscher, Missile Defense Conference in Russia. Moscow, Russia, May 3, 2012. http://www.state.gov/t/avc/rls/189281.htm.

US Department of State and U.S. Department of Defense. "Proposed U.S. Missile Defense Assets in Europe," June 15, 2007. Accessed January 23, 2013. http://www.fas.org/irp/threat/missile/bmd-europe.pdf.

US Government Accountability Office. *Nuclear Weapons: DOD and NNSA Need to Better Manage Scope and Future of Refurbishments and Risks to Maintaining U.S. Commitments to NATO, GAO-11-387*, May 2011.

United States Information Agency. *Soviet Measures in the "Post-Cold War Era" 1988–1991: A Report Prepared at the Request of the United States House of Representatives Committee on Appropriations by the United States Information Agency.* Washington, DC: United States Information Agency, 1992.

US Secretary of Defense. *Report of the Secretary of Defense Task Force on DoD Nuclear Weapons Management, Phase II: Review of the DoD Nuclear Mission.* Washington, DC: US Government Printing Office, 2008.

United States Government. *DOD and NNSA Need to Better Manage Scope and Future of Refurbishments and Risks to Maintaining U.S. Commitments to NATO.* GAO-11-387, Washington, DC: US Government Printing Office, May 2011.

United States Senate. *Resolution on Advice and Consent to the Ratification of the Treaty between the United States of America and the Russian Federation on Measures for the Further Reduction and Limitation of Strategic Offensive Arms.* Washington, DC: US Senate, 2010.

Vaïsse, Maurice. "Un dialogue de sourds: Les relations nucléaires franco-américaines de 1957 à 1960." *Relations Internationales* 68 (Winter 1991).

———. "Indépendance et solidarité 1958–1963." In *La France et l'OTAN 1949–1996*, edited by Frédéric Bozo, Maurice Vaïsse, and Pierre Mélandri, 219–46. Paris: Éditions Complexes, 1996.

———. "Jacques Chaban-Delmas ministre de la Défense nationale (novembre 1957–mai 1958)." In *Jacques Chaban-Delmas en politique*, edited by Bernard Lachaise, Gilles Le Béguec, and Jean-François Sirinelli. Paris: Presses Universitaires, 2007.

———. "Le choix atomique de la France." Vingtième siècle. *Revue d'histoire* 36 no.1 (1992): 21–30.

———. "Post-Suez France." In *Suez 1956: The Crisis and Its Consequences*, edited by W. M. Roger Louis and Roger Owens, chapter 17. Oxford: Clarendon Press, 1991.

van der Zeijden, Wilbert, Susi Snyder, and Peter Paul Ekker. *Exit Strategies: The Case for Redefining NATO Consensus on US TNW.* Utrecht: IKV Pax Christi, 2012.

———. "NATO Nuclear Weapons and the Defense and Deterrence Posture Review: A Non-Consensual Debate." *Open Security, Reconciliation and Conflict*, 2012. http://www.opendemocracy.net/opensecurity/wilbert-van-der-zeijden/nato-nuclear-weapons-and-defense-and-deterrence-posture-review/.

van Evera, Steven. "Primed for Peace: Europe after the Cold War." *International Security* 15, no. 3 (Winter 1990–1991): 7–57.

Vojtech, Mastny. "Imagining War in Europe." In *War Plans and Alliances in the Cold War: Threat Perceptions in East and West*, edited by Sven G. Hltsmark and Andreas Wenger, 15–45. London: Routledge, 2006.

Walker, William. "Nuclear Order and Disorder." *International Affairs* 76, no. 4 (October 2000): 703–724.

———. "The UK, Threshold Status and Responsible Nuclear Sovereignty." *International Affairs* 86, no. 2 (April 2010): 447–64.

———. *Weapons of Mass Destruction and International Order.* Adelphi Paper no. 370. Oxford: Oxford University Press, 2004.

Waltz, Kenneth. "A Reply." *Security Studies* 4, no. 4 (1995): 802–05.

Weber, Max. "Politics as Vocation." In *The Vocation Lectures*, edited by David Own and Tracy B. Strong. Translated by Rodney Livingstone. Indianapolis, IN: Hackett Publishing Company, 2004.

Weir, Fred. "US Drops European Missile Defense Plan—But Moscow Is Unimpressed." *The Christian Science Monitor*, March 18, 2013. http://www.csmonitor.com/World/Europe/2013/0318/US-drops-Europe-missile-defense-plan-but-Moscow-is-unimpressed.

Wenger, Andreas. "Crisis and Opportunity: NATO's Transformation and the Multilateralization of Détente, 1966–1968." *Journal of Cold War Studies* 6, no. 1 (Winter 2004): 22–74.

———. "NATO's Transformation in the 1960s and the Ensuing Political Order in Europe." In *Transforming NATO in the Cold War: Challenges beyond Deterrence in the 1960s*, edited by Andreas Wenger, Christian Nünlist, and Anna Locher, 221–42. London, Routledge, 2007.

Wenger, Andreas, and Jeremi Suri. "At the Crossroads of Diplomatic and Social History: The Revolution, Dissent, and Détente." *Cold War History* 1, no. 3 (April 2001): 1–42.

Wenger, Andreas, and Alex Wilner. *Deterring Terrorism: Theory and Practice*. Stanford, CA: Stanford University Press, 2012.

Wheeler, Nicholas J. "The Attlee Government's Nuclear Strategy, 1945–1951." In *Britain and the First Cold War*, edited by Anne Deighton. New York: St Martin's Press, 1990.

———. "British Nuclear Weapons and Anglo-American Relations 1945–1954." *International Affairs* 62, no. 1 (Winter 1985–1986).

White House, Office of the Press Secretary. "Fact Sheet on U.S. Missile Defense Policy: A 'Phase, Adaptive Approach' for Missile Defense in Europe." United States Government, September 17, 2009. http://www.whitehouse.gov/the_press_office/FACT-SHEET-US-Missile-Defense-Policy-A-Phased-Adaptive-Approach-for-Missile-Defense-in-Europe/.

———. "Remarks by the President on Strengthening Missile Defense in Europe." United States Government, September 17, 2009. http://www.whitehouse.gov/the_press_office/Remarks-by-the-President-on-Strengthening-Missile-Defense-in-Europe/.

Wikileaks. "Divergences with France on Upcoming Political Issues and Recommendations on Way Forward." 2011. www.wikileaks.ch/cable/2009/12/09PARIS1767.html.

Wilkening, Dean A. "Does Missile Defense in Europe Threaten Russia?" *Survival* 54, no. 1 (February–March 2012): 31–53.

Wilkening, Dean, and Kenneth Watman. *Nuclear Deterrence in a Regional Context*. Santa Monica, CA: RAND, 1994.

Wilson, Ward. *Five Myths about Nuclear Weapons*. Boston, MA: Houghton Mifflin Harcourt, 2013.

Wohlstetter, Albert, and Richard Brody. "Continuing Control as a Requirement for Deterring." In *Managing Nuclear Operations*, edited by Ashton B. Carter, John D. Steinbruner, and Charles A Kraker, 142–96. Washington, DC: Brookings Institution, 1987.

Woolf, Amy F. "Nonstrategic Nuclear Weapons." *CRS Report for Congress*, RL32572. Washington, DC: Congressional Research Service, 2011.

———. "Nonstrategic Nuclear Weapons." *CRS Report for Congress*, February 14, 2012.

———. "Nuclear Weapons in US National Security Policy: Past, Present, and Prospects." *CRS Report for Congress*, RL34226. Washington, DC: Congressional Research Service, December 30, 2008.

———. *US Nuclear Deterrence in the 21st Century: Getting It Right*. Washington, DC: The New Deterrent Work Group, 2009.

———. "US Nuclear Weapons: Changes in Policy and Force Structure." *CRS Report for Congress*, RL31623. Washington, DC: Congressional Research Service, 2006.

Yost, David S. "Assurance and Extended Deterrence in NATO." *International Affairs* 85, no. 4 (July 2009): 755–80.

———. "The Budapest Memorandum and Russia's Intervention in Ukraine." *International Affairs*, vol. 91, no. 3 (2015): forthcoming.

———. "NATO and Tailored Deterrence: Surveying the Challenges." In *NATO and 21st Century Deterrence*, edited by Karl-Heinz Kamp and David S. Yost. Rome: NATO Defense College, Research Division, 2009.

———. *NATO's Deterrence and Defense Posture after the Chicago Summit: A Report on a Workshop in Rome*. Rome: NATO Defense College, 2012. http://www.ndc.nato.int/download/downloads.php?icode=356.

———. "Nuclear Debates in France." *Survival* 36 no. 4 (Winter 1994): 113–39.

———. *The US and Nuclear Deterrence in Europe: Adelphi Paper No. 326*. Oxford: Oxford University Press, 1999.

———. "The US Debate on NATO Nuclear Deterrence." *International Affairs* 87, no. 6 (November 2011): 1401–38.

———. "US Extended Deterrence in NATO and North-East Asia." In *Perspectives on Extended Deterrence*, Recherches & Documents, no. 3/2010, 15–36. Paris: Fondation pour la Recherche Stratégique, 2012.

Zaborski, Jason. "Deterring a Nuclear Iran." *The Washington Quarterly* 28, no. 3 (Summer 2005): 153–67.

Zadra, Roberto. "NATO, Russia, and Missile Defense." *Survival* 56, no. 4 (August–September 2014): 51–61.

CONTRIBUTORS

Paul I. Bernstein is a Senior Research Fellow at the National Defense University Center for the Study of Weapons of Mass Destruction (WMD) Center in Washington, DC. He is engaged in a range of policy support, research, and professional military education activities related to WMD, nuclear policy, deterrence, arms control, and regional security.

Stéfanie von Hlatky is an assistant professor of political studies at Queen's University and the Director of the Queen's Centre for International and Defence Policy (CIDP). She received her PhD in political science from Université de Montréal in 2010, where she was also Executive Director for the Centre for International Peace and Security Studies. She authored the book *American Allies in Times of War: The Great Asymmetry* (Oxford University Press 2013) and has published articles in *European Security*, the *Canadian Journal of Political Science*, *Asian Security*, *the Journal of Transatlantic Studies* and *International Journal*.

Kerry M. Kartchner is currently Senior Advisor for Strategic Communications in the State Department's Bureau of International Security and Nonproliferation. He is also an adjunct professor in Missouri State University's Graduate Department of Defense and Strategic Studies, where he teaches courses on strategic culture as well as on arms control and nonproliferation. He was previously Senior Foreign Policy Advisor to the Director for Resources and Intelligence Integration at the Defense Threat Reduction Agency, part of the US Defense Department. His BA is from Brigham Young University, and his MA and PhD are from the University of Southern California.

Joachim Krause is full professor of political science at the University of Kiel and has held that position since 2001. Before that, he was Deputy Director of the Research Institute of the German Council for Foreign Relations (DGAP) in Berlin and, from 1978 to 1994, he was senior researcher at the SWP Research Institute for International and Strategic Affairs in Ebenhausen,

Germany. He graduated from Hamburg University, received his dissertation degree from the Free University of Berlin, and received his habilitation at the University of Bonn.

Hans M. Kristensen is Director of the Nuclear Information Project at the Federation of American Scientists where he provides the public with analysis and background information about the status of nuclear forces and the role of nuclear weapons. He specializes in using the Freedom of Information Act (FOIA) in his research, and is a frequent consultant to and is widely referenced in the news media on the role and status of nuclear weapons. Kristensen is co-author of the Nuclear Notebook column in the Bulletin of the Atomic Scientists and the World Nuclear Forces overview in the SIPRI Yearbook.

Jeffrey A. Larsen is Director of the Research Division at the NATO Defense College. Prior to this posting Dr. Larsen served sixteen years as a Senior Scientist with Science Applications International Corporation (SAIC) and President of Larsen Consulting Group LLC in Colorado Springs. A retired US Air Force lieutenant colonel, he served for twenty-one years as a command pilot in Strategic Air Command, as associate professor of political science at the Air Force Academy, and as the first Director of the Air Force Institute for National Security Studies (INSS). He holds a Masters degree in national security affairs from the Naval Postgraduate School, and a Masters and PhD in politics from Princeton University.

Benoît Pelopidas is a CISAC affiliate and lecturer in international relations at the School of Sociology, Politics and International Studies (SPAIS), University of Bristol. He was a postdoctoral fellow at CISAC for the 2011–2012 academic year.

Paul Schulte is Senior Visiting Fellow in the Centre for Defence Studies at King's College London. He is also a Non-Resident Senior Associate of the Nuclear Policy Program of the Carnegie Endowment for International Peace in Washington, DC and a Research Fellow in the Disarmament and Globalisation Programme in the Centre for International Studies and Diplomacy and also at the School of Oriental and African Studies (SOAS).

Oliver Thränert is head of the think tank at the Center for Security Studies (CSS). He is also a Non-Resident Senior Fellow at the German Institute for International and Security Affairs (Stiftung Wissenschaft und Politik).

He studied political science, modern history, and sociology and received his doctorate from the Technical University of Braunschweig in Germany in 1986.

Andreas Wenger is professor of International and Swiss Security Policy at ETH Zurich and has been the Director of the Center for Security Studies (CSS) since 2002. He studied history, political science, and German literature at the University of Zurich, where he received his MA in 1991. He holds a PhD from the University of Zurich and was a visiting fellow at the Woodrow Wilson School of Public and International Affairs and the Center of International Studies, Princeton University.

INDEX

The letter *t* following a page number denotes a table; the letter *f* following a page number denotes a figure.